DAVID & CHARLES SOURCES FOR
CONTEMPORARY ISSUES SERIES

TRADE UNIONS
IN GREAT BRITAIN

DAVID & CHARLES SOURCES FOR CONTEMPORARY ISSUES SERIES

TRADE UNIONS

IN GREAT BRITAIN

Compiled and Edited by

John Hughes and Harold Pollins

DAVID & CHARLES : NEWTON ABBOT

0 7153 6001 9

Set in 11 on 13pt Baskerville
and printed in Great Britain
by Latimer Trend & Company Ltd Plymouth
for David & Charles (Holdings) Limited
South Devon House Newton Abbot Devon

Contents

		PAGE
LIST OF ABBREVIATIONS		9
INTRODUCTION		11

PART ONE: THE CASE FOR TRADE UNIONISM 25
1 Trades Union Congress. *The case for trade unionism* 27
2 Association of University Teachers. *The position of the non-member* 31

PART TWO: THE OBJECTIVES OF TRADE UNIONS 34
3 Trades Union Congress. *Trade union objectives* 36
4 Trades Union Congress. *Objects* 46
5 Transport & General Workers' Union. *Objects* 47
6 National Union of Mineworkers. *Objects* 52
7 National Union of Journalists. *Code of professional conduct* 52

PART THREE: TRADE UNION METHODS 1
(A) MEMBERSHIP AND EDUCATION 56
8 Industrial Relations Act, 1971. *Approved closed shop agreements* 58
9 W. E. J. McCarthy. *The continued justifiability of the closed shop* 60
10 Trades Union Congress, Disputes Committee. *Dispute over job control* 65

5

PAGE

11 Post Office Engineering Union. *The Union's Educa-*
    tion scheme   74
12 Trades Union Congress, Education Service. *TUC*
    Training on the Industrial Relations Act   82

    (B) POLITICAL LOBBYING AND CAMPAIGNING   85
13 Trade Union Act, 1913. *Political fund*   87
14 *Constitution of the Labour Party*   90
15 Amalgamated Engineering Union (now Amal-
    gamated Union of Engineering Workers). *The*
    AEU parliamentary group   92
16 Draughtsmen's and Allied Technicians Association
    (now Technical and Supervisory Section of the
    AUEW). *Lobbying Parliament*   95
17 Union of Shop, Distributive and Allied Workers.
    Sunday Trading   96
18 Trades Union Congress. *Prices and Incomes Legislation*   98
19 Trades Union Congress. *Campaign against the Industrial*
    Relations Bill   102
20 Trades Union Congress. *Congress makes policy on the*
    Industrial Relations Act   106

    PART FOUR: TRADE UNION METHODS 2
         (C) COLLECTIVE BARGAINING   109
21 British Leyland Motor Corporation. *Procedural*
    agreement   111
22 Engineering industry. *Procedure—manual workers*   113
23 Transport & General Workers' Union. *Negotiation of*
    comprehensive plant agreements   119
24 *Railway Pay and Efficiency agreement. Footplate staff, 1968* 128
25 *Railway pay and efficiency agreement. Footplate staff, 1969* 134
26 Equity. *Nudity and simulated sex acts—agreement with*
    the Theatres National Committee   144
27 Trades Union Congress. 'TINA LEA' (*This Is Not A*
    Legally Enforceable Agreement)   145

PAGE

PART FIVE: TRADE UNION STRUCTURE 1
(A) INTERNAL

              (A) INTERNAL   149

28 National and Local Government Officers Association.
    NALGO is run by its members   151

29 Post Office Engineering Union. *National Executive
    Council*   152

30 Union of Shop, Distributive and Allied Workers.
    Conference agenda   157

31 Electrical Trades Union (now Electrical Electronic
    Telecommunication Union/Plumbing Trades
    Union). *Proposal for full-time executive*   159

32 J. E. Mortimer. *New categories of technicians*   164

33 Technical and Supervisory Section (of Amalgamated
    Union of Engineering Workers). *Recruiting new
    ranges of worker*   166

34 Transport & General Workers' Union. *The shop
    steward's job*   167

35 National Union of Public Employees. *Facilities for
    trade unions*   169

36 Jack Jones. *Successful Democracy*   172

37 Civil & Public Services Association. *The problem of
    secret group activity*   174

PART SIX: TRADE UNION STRUCTURE 2
    (B) EXTERNAL RELATIONS   177

38 Trades Union Congress. *Principles for the avoidance of
    disputes*   179

39 Trades Union Congress, Disputes Committee.
    Report of a dispute and award   183

40 Associated Society of Locomotive Engineers and
    Firemen. *A union discipline clause*   185

41 Confederation of Shipbuilding and Engineering
    Unions. *Structure and functions*   185

42 Draughtsmen's & Allied Technicians Association
    (now Technical and Supervisory Section) and

Clerical & Administrative Workers Union (now
Association of Professional, Executive, Clerical &
Computer Staff). *Closer working*   196
43 Association of Scientific Workers and Association of
Supervisory Staffs, Executives and Technicians.
*Case for amalgamation to form the Association of Scien-
tific, Technical and Managerial Staffs*   197
44 Will Paynter. *A Guiding Principle for Union Structure?* 202

PART SEVEN: TRADE UNION STRUCTURE 3
                (c) TRADES UNION CONGRESS   205
45 Trades Union Congress. *Rules of the TUC*   206
46 Trades Union Congress. *The 1969 agreement with the
Labour Government*   212
47 *Joint Statement of Intent on Productivity, Prices and
Incomes*   215
48 Trades Union Congress/Confederation of British
Industry. *Conciliation and Arbitration Service (2
August 1972)*   218
49 Trades Union Congress. *Structure and development*   222
50 Trades Union Congress. *Industrial committees*   240
51 Trades Union Congress. *Women trade unionists in
conference*   243

SELECT GUIDE TO FURTHER READING   255

ACKNOWLEDGEMENTS   260

INDEX   261

List of Abbreviations

ADM	Annual Delegate Meeting
AEF	Amalgamated Union of Engineering and Foundry Workers (now AUEW)
AESD	Association of Engineering and Shipbuilding Draughtsmen (now TASS)
AEU	Amalgamated Engineering Union (now AUEW)
APEX	Association of Professional, Executive, Clerical and Computer Staff
AScW	Association of Scientific Workers (now ASTMS)
ASLEF	Associated Society of Locomotive Engineers and Firemen
ASSET	Association of Supervisory Staffs, Executives and Technicians (now ASTMS)
ASTMS	Association of Scientific, Technical and Managerial Staffs
AUEW	Amalgamated Union of Engineering Workers
AUT	Association of University Teachers
CAWU	Clerical and Administrative Workers' Union (now APEX)
CBI	Confederation of British Industry
CIR	Commission on Industrial Relations
CPSA	Civil and Public Services Association
CSCA	Civil Service Clerical Association (now CPSA)
CSEU	Confederation of Shipbuilding and Engineering Unions
CSU	Civil Service Union
DATA	Draughtsmen's and Allied Technicians Association (now TASS)
DHSS	Department of Health and Social Security

9

EDC	Economic Development Committee
EEC	European Economic Community
EETPU	Electrical Electronic Telecommunication and Plumbing Trade Union
ETU	Electrical Trades Union (now EETPU)
FESTUK	Federation of Engineering and Shipbuilding Trades of the United Kingdom (now CSEU)
ITB	Industrial Training Board
JIC	Joint Industrial Council
LDC	Local Departmental Committee
MOD	Ministry of Defence
NALGO	National and Local Government Officers Association
NBPI	National Board for Prices and Incomes
NEC	National Executive Council
NEDO	National Economic Development Office
NHS	National Health Service
NIRC	National Industrial Relations Court
NJC	National Joint Council
NJIC	National Joint Industrial Council
NUAAW	National Union of Agricultural and Allied Workers
NUJ	National Union of Journalists
NUM	National Union of Mineworkers
NUPE	National Union of Public Employees
NUSMWCHDE	National Union of Sheet Metal Workers, Coppersmiths, Heating and Domestic Engineers
NUT	National Union of Teachers
ODD	Organising District Delegate
POEU	Post Office Engineering Union
RSJC	Railway Staff Joint Council
RSNC	Railway Staff National Council
RSNT	Railway Staff National Tribunal
SCWS	Scottish Co-operative Wholesale Society
SICC	Steel Industry Consultative Committee
TASS	Technical and Supervisory Section (of the AUEW)
TGWU	Transport and General Workers' Union
'TINA LEA'	This Is Not A Legally Enforceable Agreement
TUC	Trades Union Congress
USDAW	Union of Shop, Distributive and Allied Workers

Introduction

It is unlikely that trade unions will ever cease to be controversial. The countless volumes of trade union history faithfully reflect one set of attitudes. In them one reads of struggles: attempts to gain recognition from employers, efforts to break the unions, strikes sometimes accompanied by violence. Often these are from the distant past, but not necessarily so. Take, for example, the history of the London County Council Staff Association, published in 1959. The final chapter, entitled 'The Ultimate Threat', starts as follows:

The years 1954 to 1959 saw the final development of the LCC Staff Association from a society into a fully-fledged trade union—and the employers' reaction. It is probably a unique case-study. Briefly, it is the story of an ever-widening gap between prices and wages; increasing exasperation in the ranks; militant public demonstrations; mounting tension in the negotiating committee; compromise settlements angrily received by the membership; the decision to affiliate to the Trades Union Congress; the employers' retort that this created 'a totally new situation'; their abrogation of the negotiating committee; and a long march through 'a darkling plain swept with confused alarms of struggle and flight'. As yet no light breaks over the sombre horizon.*

More recently, the Industrial Relations Act of 1971 is seen as

* Andrews, C. D. and Burger, G. C. *Progress Report 1909–1959: The First Fifty Years in the History of the London County Council Staff Association* (1959).

a political attack on the effectiveness, indeed on the very existence, of trade unionism, despite the fact that the Act, along
with much other labour law, does provide certain rights for
workers. One way of understanding the bitter opposition to
the Act is to pay regard to history. Part arises from the fact that
there has been much less legal regulation of unions and of
industrial relations in Britain than in most other countries.
Equally, trade unionists are quick to recall those occasions
when the law has attacked them. The case of the Tolpuddle
Martyrs of the 1830s, whose conviction was one of the causes of
the collapse of Robert Owen's Grand National Consolidated
Trades Union, or that of the Taff Vale Railway in the 1900s,
where after a strike the company obtained an injunction which
enabled them to obtain damages from the union, are events
which, although far distant, remain significant conditioners of
union attitudes.

A completely different view regards unions not as valiant
fighters against despotism but as sources of dislocation. Unions
call strikes which interfere with production, and they demand
improvements for their members irrespective of the cost to
industry and to society. Moreover, and this is the essence of
much recent discussion, they cannot control their members;
most strikes are unofficial, and shop stewards seem to operate
outside the official institutions, ignoring their union officers as
much as the employers.

No one studying trade unions can pretend to be neutral about
them and a collection of documents, intended to illustrate their
work and particularly recent developments, is inevitably highly
selective. We have concentrated on material from union sources
on the grounds that the obvious basis for the understanding of
an institution is the verbal output of the institution itself. The
reader interprets this material as he wishes. Our own interpretation is given in this general introduction and in the briefer
introductions to the various sections and sub-sections. Here we
try to set the scene, sketching the changing context in which
unions operate.

We discuss fairly recent changes, but it is important to reiterate that union behaviour can be affected by history. There can be no doubt at all, for example, that the General Strike of 1926—which the unions lost—conditioned the minds of union leaders and members for the next four decades. There was no question during that period that the unions would attempt another political strike. It was not until the summer of 1972, in the special circumstances of the emotion aroused by the operation of the Industrial Relations Act and especially of the imprisonment of five dockers for contempt of court, which evoked memories of Tolpuddle, that the TUC was able to throw off its inhibitions and recommend to its affiliated unions that they should strike in concert. But we must not give the impression that the only important changes affecting trade unions are those emanating from the law. The context of change is much wider than the Industrial Relations Act, with its novelties and the anxieties it has produced.*

Over a wide range of their work, trade unions are driven to respond defensively to changes in the economic and social environment within which they operate. Many of these changes are not of their own creation. Unions are largely at the receiving end of the economic system and of the shocks that accompany its development. Most of the time they are coping with the effects of other people's decisions, the decisions of those groups which have positive economic power and command over resources—not least the state and those who direct the large-scale enterprises that dominate our economy.

The consequences of those decisions can be seen, to some extent, in the changing composition of union membership. During the 1960s a number of industries that were fully unionised, such as mining, experienced a rapid decline in employment. The occupational balance of the labour force was shifting from the more unionised manual occupations to an increasing propor-

---

* We have ignored the fact that under the Act 'trade union' has the restricted meaning of 'organisation of workers registered under the Act' and have retained the title 'trade union' for all such bodies whether registered or not.

tion of the less unionised non-manual ones. Yet this apparently
adverse environment for union growth did not produce stagna-
tion; on the contrary. By 1970 there were nearly 10·7 million
trade union members in Great Britain; including Northern
Ireland, nearly 11 million. These figures represented an increase
of over a million in the decade from 1960. This apparently
modest growth was in fact more important than it might
seem.

During a decade in which the number of male employees in
the economy did not rise at all, there was a 5 per cent increase
in male membership of trade unions to over 8 million, and the
proportion of all male employees who were union members rose
from about 53 per cent in 1960 to over 56 per cent in 1970.
Female membership of trade unions rose even more strongly, by
nearly 40 per cent during the decade, to 2·7 million, just over
30 per cent of the total number of all female employees. This
achievement was the more striking since female employment
had only risen 10 per cent during the decade, and there
were major declines in industries, such as textiles, which
had earlier established a high level of unionisation among
women.

Even this presentation of the facts understates how unionised
is the adult British labour force, for the total numbers of employees include several million part-time workers and juveniles
with relatively low levels of union membership. Part of the research work for the Royal Commission on Trade Unions and
Employers' Associations (henceforth the Donovan Commission
after the name of its chairman) included a survey of trade union
membership among full-time adults—the definition then being
twenty-one years or older. Since this survey was carried out, in
1967, trade union membership has risen nearly 10 per cent,
while the number of employees has fallen slightly. The Donovan
Commission's researchers found that over 54 per cent of full-
time adult workers were in trade unions and that, of those who
were non-unionists when interviewed, nearly half had been
trade unionists at some time in the past. Most of the lapsed

members had left because they changed their jobs; only one in six expressed dissatisfaction as a reason for having left a trade union. Thus, it turned out that three-quarters of the entire adult labour force was either in a trade union or had been in one. That proportion has certainly risen since the 1967 survey.

As a reflection of such developments it now occasions no surprise to find that white-collar people—even managers and executives—are in trade unions and not averse to strike action if necessary. Teachers, bank clerks, local government officers, draughtsmen—especially—have used this method. Indeed it is right and proper to note that in general the dividing line between trade unions and professional associations is by no means definite. It has become blurred as professional people look to industrial action to achieve their demands—doctors have threatened to leave the National Health Service, for example. More important, their range and effective management of restrictive practices make most unions, by comparison, look weak and powerless.

The effect of economic changes, whether expected or not, on trade union membership is only one important factor in working people's lives. Alterations in the industrial balance and occupational composition of the labour force, for example, signal more profound changes in jobs and labour markets. Thus, in some industries, such as coal mining, the traditional expectations as to the life cycle of work within them have been disrupted. The progression from day-wage jobs as a youth to the arduous work at the coal face, and in later working life the return to day-wage elsewhere in the pit, has been broken into by a hectic rate of internal technological change and external shocks administered by market forces. Elsewhere the labour market has been changing in ways which alter the whole pattern of trade union behaviour. Some areas of casual employment have been transformed, as in electrical contracting and in some ports. But in others casual employment patterns have extended; in construction, the process has been aided by the greater mobility of many workers and the extension of 'contract' instead of employer-employee relationships in the use of labour. In clerical work in the big towns, specialist employment agencies have sharply influenced the operation of the labour market, not only by stimulating labour turnover in pursuit of higher pay but also by developing systems of temporary labour. This is in contrast to much trade union effort, which typically aims to improve pay and conditions within an enterprise rather than generate pressure by encouraging mobility, and to develop job security and continuity of employment rather than casualise employment.

The structure of industrial organisation has been at the same time subject to major abrupt and largely unpredictable changes. The merger movement in the company sector leapt into importance in Britain from the beginning of the 1960s, but accelerated further by the middle of the decade and even more dramatically by the end. The Monopolies Commission's study of the results of mergers in manufacturing industry up to 1968 showed that between 1961 and 1968 the population of large manufacturing companies fell from 1,312 to 908, or by over 30 per cent, and that the assets taken over by acquiring companies were equivalent to about a fifth of the total assets of the big manufacturing companies in their survey.

In the public sector as well there were repeated reorganisations of enterprises and services, quite apart from the grouping into one public corporation of the fourteen largest iron and steel companies. Thus concentration of employment into giant firms—whether companies in the private sector or public corporations—has proceeded apace. The report of the Donovan Commission quoted preliminary figures from the 1963 Census of Production covering 8·5 million employees in the private sector of mining, manufacturing and construction. Nearly 40 per cent—some 3·5 million—worked for companies employing 5,000 or more people. In 1935, the pre-war Census year, fewer than a million people worked for firms of that size. Towards the end of the 1960s, according to the Monopolies Commission, a mere twenty-eight firms in manufacturing accounted for about 40 per cent of all manufacturing assets in the private sector.

The growth of large-scale enterprise is highly significant for trade unions. The social survey carried out for the Donovan Commission produced some telling figures as to the importance of the size of establishment, that is, plant or unit of production. From their sample one can arrive at the following picture: of 18 million adults employed full-time in Britain, half work in establishments with a hundred or more workers; these establishments account for 6 million trade union members and only 3 million non-unionists. By contrast, in establishments with under a hundred workers, over 5 million full-time adult workers were not in trade unions, and only about 3·5 million were trade unionists. Managements of the large firms are more likely to need to elaborate a consistent industrial relations approach and to identify and deal with representatives of their employees. Established workplace organisation emerges more readily in the larger units; thus, nearly four-fifths of all shop stewards are to be found in the establishments with a hundred or more workers. Within the multi-plant combine, the trade union can open up more points of contact and comparison with workers in different plants. For large firms, mergers mean that both the insecurity engendered and the complexities of reorganisation enhance the defensive, protective role of trade unions. But, beyond this, the enormous power of the massed capital resources of giant firms, and the social and economic impact of decisions taken by such firms—whether of investment or plant closure—involve the trade unions in a wider political and policy response. Trade unions cannot take the power and initiative of giant firms as given or unalterable, and do the best they can in bargaining with them. They are driven to develop programmes involving social control, as well as demands for their own direct access to the decision making of industrial management. A period such as the 1960s, with its shift of industrial organisation towards increased dominance of giant firms, is therefore likely to stimulate the trade unions to a much wider view of their functions and objectives than that implied by the Donovan Commission's emphasis on orderly bargaining within the system of industrial power we now have.

Possibly the changes which attracted most public attention have been in the public sector and in the economic role played by the state. These have shattered the state's traditional attitude of a disinterested and non-interventionist encourager of voluntary collective bargaining. As employers, public agencies have been favourable to the development of a high degree of unionisation: large units; full recognition of trade unions as representatives of employees; formal, bureaucratic modes of organisation —all these have been a stimulus. Yet it is highly significant that since 1964 the two largest public sector trade unions that had stood aside from the rest of the trade unions—the National and Local Government Officers (NALGO), and the National Union of Teachers (NUT)—have affiliated to the TUC. The reason must be sought in the new economic role of the state. Both in the public sector, where it can lean heavily on employers' representatives in the bargaining process, and throughout the economy, the state has intervened more and more extensively in the determination of pay and conditions. Managing the economy has implied intervening in industrial relations, and the state's approach has shifted from the traditional conciliation role to a much more critical and restrictive one. From spasmodic and arbitrary intervention, such as the public sector pay freeze of 1961, there has been a progression to a more pervasive and comprehensive intervention. This has spread from challenging the outcome of pay determination, through all the agencies and devices of incomes policy, to turning more critically to the forced reform of the underlying system of industrial relations, and to a more repressive approach to disputes involving industrial action.

It is the kind of situation where if trade unions do not hang together they are likely to hang separately. In consequence the 1960s have witnessed a tremendous strengthening of the co-

ordination and self-discipline of the trade unions. The TUC
and its General Council, for example, have come nearer in
recent years to fulfilling the strategic role envisaged when the
organisation was refurbished in the 1920s than would have been
thought possible a few years ago. Once again, the response to
change goes well beyond the notion of a restricted collective-
bargaining role, and some of the developments point to extended bargaining on the part of the TUC, directly with the
government. Partly, they involve a new emphasis on the co-
ordination of the organisational and bargaining efforts of
member trade unions of the TUC. Partly, they raise anew the
question of the wider political interests of the trade unions in
influencing the parameters of state action.

Besides, this growing complexity of relationships with an in-
trusive state power has not gone along with any evident success
in national economic management as a result of state intervention—not, at least, over a wide range of labour conditions of
direct concern to the trade unions. The background of economic
crises and the awkward handling of national economic development have propelled the trade unions into a much more systematic concern with economic policy—both critical and constructive—than in the past. In recent years, the General Council
of the TUC has become the main source of an alternative
economic analysis, and of a strategy for growth and economic
management, to those being pursued by the government of the
day. To develop such a view is an understandable extension of
trade union action designed to improve the pay, conditions,
security and prospects of the labour force. But it goes beyond
the description of 'permanent opposition', which is sometimes
applied to unions. In a variety of ways—from arguing and bargaining with the government of the day to extending their
political initiative in developing and shaping the economic and
social policies and objectives of the Labour Party—the trade
unions try to break out from a role outside and in opposition to
the main decision making that shapes economic development.
But this search for a new degree of influence, of participation in

economic control, involves new kinds of commitment and responsibility for the trade unions, collectively and individually, at every step at which they really assert their power.

Take, for example, the range of methods involved in political affiliation and political lobbying, and the associated concern with legislative protection and scrutiny of the actual operation of protective statutes. This political process may increasingly encompass wide social issues, such as educational opportunity and equality, as well as narrowly defined specialist concern with specific industrial training needs. It may raise the question of social accountability and protection of worker interests in giant multi-national enterprises, as well as the traditional statutory surveillance of physical conditions in the workplace. It may be concerned with the distribution of income and wealth through particular fiscal strategies, as well as the minutiae of enforcement of minimum pay standards in Wages Council trades. Other methods are merging which are much more obviously positive. In a number of directions there are now joint (trade union and employer) or tripartite (with the state also involved) bodies with administrative, executive and supervisory functions, as well as a whole panoply of consultative agencies. Some of these bodies emerge from new features of the collective bargaining process, some from a statutory basis. Moreover, we find trade unions joining together, not only through the TUC, in analysis and policy formulation over a wide field. The *cumulative* significance of such methods of work may on particular subjects count for more than the role accorded to collective bargaining. This is almost certainly true of labour market policies; probably true of the accountability to workers and the community of giant firms (during or after merger movements), and possibly true of the rate of growth of real wages.

Collective bargaining itself is in turmoil. This is at one level a matter of economics and the structure of product markets. The ostensible redistribution between capital and labour is largely side-stepped by administered prices and an inflationary process. In addition, the state reaches out, however incoherently, to try to relate bargaining, inflation and the utilisation of capital and labour within some kind of growth strategy. But whether or not any particular incomes policy is declared to be in action, the context of trade union collective-bargaining strategy now has to include the whole complex of interventionist state management of the economy, and the two-fold implications it has for real pay through redistribution of incomes and through economic expansion. Perhaps the most crucial discussion and argument has been precisely how, or if at all, the state—or the national economy or the public interest—can be or should be a third party in collective bargaining. The difficulty of trying to make changes can be seen from a consideration of the discussions of the 1960s. There the emphasis was on reform of industrial relations through an emphasis on local bargaining; the older, formal system of national, industry-wide agreements was under attack. Yet from 1970 onwards Britain experienced industry-wide pay settlements of unprecedentedly large amounts and industry-wide strikes. No doubt these can be explained, with hindsight. They were not predicted.

All these elements of ferment and change have had a reflection not merely in trade union organisation, but in many cases have led to major reconstruction of British unionism. Amalgamations of trade unions have been quite as important in transforming the structure and balance of power of the trade union movement as have mergers in transforming market relations and industrial organisation in the commercial world. Over and above the complex of relations in which the trade unions have been caught up, as they dealt with employers, federations of employers and the state, have been major developments in the pattern of representation within the ranks of their own membership. The larger unions in particular have developed considerably in recent years their ability to handle within the framework of one union a multiplicity of forms of representation.

This has to be attempted in a social and economic context where the near balance and harmony, which are perhaps achievable with a slow rate of development, and with stable

patterns of organisation and labour requirements, are over-
turned by accelerated and qualitative change. Each partial
attempt, whether by giant firms through mergers or the state in
its efforts at economic management, to stabilise or to dominate
this process of development simply produces new areas of imbalance and of tension. Meanwhile, in a number of industries
the technology and market pattern has changed more in a decade or so than in the previous eighty or hundred years. Thus,
from all directions, dynamic imbalance has been thrust upon
the labour force and upon the trade unions. With regard to the
labour force, for many their working life looks more like a
game of snakes and ladders than an orderly progression; recent
official guesstimates were that, whereas a mere 50,000 to
100,000 workers were dismissed each year because of involun-
tary retirement, between 750,000 and a million a year were
dismissed as redundant. As for the trade unions, they have been
called upon to react in both organisation and policy in a quite
unprecedented range of subjects and at various levels from the
parochial to the national. As the system has been under stress,
the arguments within the trade unions as to policy and the
future direction of effort mount in intensity.

Even with two or three times the space at our disposal, we
could not have illustrated all these various developments.
Moreover, the pace of change is rapid, not least regarding the
various judgements under the Industrial Relations Act. What,
for example, will be the effect of the decision of the House of
Lords on 26 July 1972 that a trade union is responsible for the
actions of its shop stewards? Nor have we the space to show the
differences which exist between unions. Each has its own history
and peculiarities, and we have adopted the criterion of choosing
documents which pinpoint a feature of general interest.

Not that documents tell the whole story. One of the major
features of British trade unionism since the war has been the up-
surge of activity at the workplace associated with shop stewards.
In most cases none of this is written down and it was not really
until the 1960s that the significance or extent of it was appre-

ciated.* For these reasons we put forward in each section a brief explanatory analysis as well as notes on the documents themselves.

* Much more is now known about shop steward activity from such general surveys as that produced for the Royal Commission on Trade Unions and Employers' Associations (1965–8), published as Research Papers Nos 1 and 10, and also Government Social Survey. *Workplace Industrial Relations* (1968). There is an interesting personal account by a full-time convenor of shop stewards in a Coventry engineering factory: Higgs, Philip. 'The Convenor', in Fraser, Ronald (ed), *Work* 2 (1969), 109–29.

PART ONE

The Case for Trade Unionism

We start with obvious, yet fundamental questions: why do we have trade unions at all? Why do employees join together in order to act collectively in their relations with employers?

One answer is in terms of the benefits that members can get. These can be material, such as higher earnings negotiated by their union; legal assistance; friendly benefits of one kind or another; or the representation of members' views to outside bodies, such as the government, which are likely to take decisions affecting them. Such inducements are often stressed in union appeals to non-members, as exemplified by the Association of University Teachers' notice in its Bulletin.

All this is valid but tells only part of the story. The TUC evidence explains rather more fully the reasons for the existence of unions. What it says boils down to two propositions. The first is a question of power relationships. The individual employee is weak as compared with the employer; he needs a collectivity to help to counteract the imbalance of power. Even so, the employer still retains the greater power—the power of initiating change. He can, in the last resort, reduce employment or even close the enterprise, and it is very difficult indeed for workers or unions to influence that kind of decision. This first approach is basically negative. A more positive reason is that employees have interests which are different from those of employers, as the notion of a 'pluralistic frame of reference' denotes. An enterprise, it is argued, is composed of various

25

groups whose interests are different and likely to be in conflict. The managers emphasise production and profits as the objectives of the organisation; workers stress their incomes from work and the various topics included under the heading of 'conditions'. The conflict is most obvious over wages and salaries. To management they are costs and, other things remaining unchanged, an increase may result in higher prices. To workers they are their standard of living and the pressure to raise them is never-ending. The conflict goes beyond the distribution of the enterprise's revenue and embraces questions of status and power. Unions are not concerned solely with economic matters. They are political institutions in the sense that they are involved in power relationships in employment. Thus they may be party to differences over such non-economic matters as tea-breaks: for example, the attempt by management to reduce or abolish them; or promotion: does the management have the right unilaterally to decide who is to be promoted?

Thus the aim of the unions is to influence the decisions which affect their members. They place constraints on the management's ability to take unilateral action; they try to reduce managerial prerogatives.

We can go a little further by arguing that we are really talking about democracy in industry. In general, this means that workers ought to have rights in employment, particularly the right to participate in some way in the making of decisions that affect them. 'The presence of the union', say Chamberlain and Kuhn, 'allows the workers, through their union representatives, to participate in the determination of policies which guide and rule their work lives.' This means that in the process of job regulation—the making of rules which determine the behaviour of people at work—the workers can and do have some influence. Workers are thus involved, normally through trade unions, in the governmental aspects of industry.† While it is true that the interests of workpeople could be enhanced by state intervention or by benevolent employers, 'trade unions', as the TUC puts it, 'are the unique means whereby men and women in employment can themselves decide how their interests can best be furthered'. These matters will be treated more fully in Parts Three and Four;*

---

* Chamberlain, N. W. and Kuhn, J. W. *Collective Bargaining* (2nd ed, 1965), 130.
† Of course, they may be so involved through informal work groups; indeed, these may be of great significance to them in the determination of behaviour.

suffice to say here that the notion of employees having rights to some kind of involvement in the decisions that affect them is, of course, comparable to the rights enjoyed by citizens under political democracy.

Yet such approaches are really too narrow; trade unions do not confine themselves to the workplace:

Not only are they vocational associations, factors in wage determination or parties in industrial relations; they are also vehicles of social protest, a brotherhood, 'a sword of justice' . . . Momentary concentration on short-term objectives, immersion in administrative and organisational routine, or the occasional pursuit of purely sectional interests may, from time to time, obscure this aspect of British trade unionism, but without an appreciation of its continuing reality, no adequate assessment of the movement is possible.*

* Bell, J. D. M. 'Trade Unions' in Flanders, A. and Clegg, H. A. (eds). *The System of Industrial Relations in Great Britain* (1954), 130. The phrase 'sword of justice' is taken from Roper, J. I. *Trade Unions and the New Society* (1942).

1 TRADES UNION CONGRESS: THE CASE FOR TRADE UNIONISM

82 The status of the employed person in an industrial economy is one of dependence on earnings with little or no individual power of direct decision. The individual contract between an employee and an employer does not reflect a position of equal strength on the two sides. Equality before the law is only relevant to the observance of the contract and not to its terms or to the procedure by which it is made. In these circumstances the economic freedom of the individual employee is very small. This must be the starting point of any objective examination of the rights and needs of employed persons.

The rights of employed persons
83 These fundamental rights and needs deriving from the nature of the employment relationship are in essence permanent and enduring, though they lead to changes in substantive terms, for example in the level of wages, as the years go by.

84   It would be generally recognised that employed persons can justly claim the right to have their interests taken into account. In order to be assured that these interests are taken into account, the needs and experience of workpeople must be known to the employer. Given that condition, a benevolent employer, or a benevolent state, might well provide adequate substantive standards, though benevolence is not a universal characteristic. However that might be, workpeople assert that they themselves have the right to ensure that their interests in the widest sense are fully safeguarded. Trade unions are the unique means whereby men and women in employment can themselves decide how their interests can best be furthered. Workpeople have the right to combine to form their own organisations and through this means to advance and protect their interests.

The essence of trade unionism
85   Thus the essential characteristic of free trade unions is that they are responsible to the workpeople themselves who comprise their membership and cannot be directed by any outside agency. Being the free and spontaneous choice of working people, their purposes and practices are continually subject to the wishes of the membership, through a process of democratic choice. Neither a benevolent state nor a benevolent employer can provide this means whereby the great variety of circumstances and individual preferences represented in a trade union can be reflected in a collective choice. Likewise, on a wider plane, there is within the trade union Movement as a whole the inherent capacity, through a similar process of choice, to provide a means for reconciling the interests of the vast majority of employed persons.
86   Recognition of the fact that the interests and preferences of individuals and groups are different, according to the perspective of each of them, is embodied in the structure of individual trade unions and in the trade union Movement as a whole. Recognition of the legitimacy of distinct and often diverging interests is also the basis of bargaining between trade unions and

employers. Bargaining depends on each side recognising the legitimacy and representative capacity of the other. A bargain is a method of reconciling differences in the interests of both sides. Just as trade unions, whilst being responsible to their membership, recognise that other people have their own interests, they expect that their interests, too, should be recognised and respected by other people.

87   These rights which employed people claim cannot be recognised and conceded on a theoretical or abstract plane and then not be recognised and not be conceded when they are translated into trade union function and trade union practice. That they are recognised in this country is not due to the intellectual or moral force of the arguments advanced above but to the efforts of working people in asserting them and exercising them.

Why workpeople combine

88   Arising out of their status as employed persons, dependent on earnings, dependent on securing and retaining employment, workpeople know that to exercise their rights they must find a means to redress the balance of unequal strength vis-a-vis their employers. Whilst the position of the individual employee, both in law and in practice, is one of subordination, individual employees together recognise that it is through combination that they can develop a means, the essential means which they possess, to harness their own potential strength. It is in the nature of the employment situation that working people readily identify themselves with their fellows in groups. This feeling of collective identity enhances the economic freedom of the individual, a freedom which rests on the knowledge that unity is strength.

89   Just as the bargaining strength of the individual is enhanced when he combines with his fellow workers in a group at a place of employment, so on a wider plane, trade unions grow in size and extent to become whatever may be the most effective combination of workpeople to advance and protect those interests, arising from their employment, which they have in common.

Thus the structure of the trade union Movement reflects whatever may at any point in time appear to be the most effective for these purposes.

Residuary role of the state

90   This is not the place to consider trade union function in its full range and detail... Sufficient here to say that trade unions have developed their competence in pursuing these purposes and in exercising these rights. It is where trade unions are not competent, where they have not exercised or cannot exercise this function in safeguarding the interests of working people, that the Government through Parliament rightly plays a part in establishing statutory machinery whereby minimum substantive standards are laid down, and enforced by the state. Such a role is recognised in this country as the second best alternative to the development by employed people themselves of the organisation, the competence, the representative capacity to bargain and to achieve for themselves satisfactory terms and conditions of employment. In some fields, trade union strength and organisation is sufficient to make a satisfactory bargain but insufficient to see that it is enforced, e.g. some Wages Councils, though it should be noted that in many cases it is the lack of organisation among employers which makes this so. In other fields, both kinds of competence may be lacking. In general, however, this competence exists and Government stands aside. Its attitude is one of abstention, of formal indifference. In other words, it recognises that these jobs are being done by trade unions, by free collective bargaining. Recognition of trade union competence and trade union function has certain implications. As the instruments which workpeople use to safeguard their interests, the means and methods adopted in practice to exercise these functions must likewise be left to the free choice of working people.

Trade union objectives and achievements

91   The actual choice which workpeople make through trade

unions among the alternative courses of action open to them will depend on which of these they see as being the most effective to achieve the object in view. Likewise, the objects themselves are identified in the light of the interests which the trade union membership have in common. An individual trade union comprises membership in many different plants, and safeguards the interests of members in a particular plant the more effectively because of this. The objectives which may be pursued are wider than those which can be met by bargaining with employers. There can be no theoretical limit to the scope of advancing and protecting the interests of employed people, and trade union objectives will extend into any field which is of common concern to their members. In this way, in extending their fields of interest to take account of the increasing complexity of the economy, trade unions reflect society, at the same time as playing a part in changing it.

92　This fact stands to the credit of trade unions; their role in enhancing the dignity of working people and in bringing about greater social justice is one of which trade unionists are proud. They would not wish to deny therefore that the community as a whole has an interest in the results of their activities. This interest is one which they welcome. . .

Source: *Trade Unionism*. The Evidence of the Trades Union Congress to the Royal Commission on Trade Unions and Employers' Associations (1966), 29–32

2 ASSOCIATION OF UNIVERSITY TEACHERS
THE POSITION OF THE NON-MEMBER

When this Bulletin appears most Universities will be preparing to pay out the 10% salary increase negotiated by the Association through the Universities' Negotiating Machinery.

Together with the increase, staff will be paid a lump sum in respect of back pay, since the new scales attract a retrospective date (October 1st, 1970).

Who pays?

Members of the Association by their subscription have paid towards achieving these increases since one cannot conduct national negotiations on thin air.

It will, therefore, be a source of annoyance to reasonable people that the five thousand non-members of the Association who are serving as university teachers, administrators, librarians and research staff will pocket these increases and back pay without contributing towards them.

One hears a great deal about those who on conscientious grounds will not join their fellows in an organisation responsible for negotiations on conditions of employment.

One hears very little about a lack of conscience on the part of those who take without contributing.

Not only salaries

Reference is made elsewhere in this Bulletin to other matters where our twenty thousand strong Association is trying to protect and improve the conditions of university academic staff.

Representations are continually being made to the Government, University Grants Committee, the Committee of Vice-Chancellors and Principals, individual universities and other bodies to look after not only the interests of university staff but also to protect and improve the whole position of higher education.

The weak link

Every non-member of the Association is a weak link in the chain of this effort being put in on behalf of all university staff. We are aware that apart from a handful of staff most persons who are not members of the Association would willingly join if it was pointed out how necessary it was for them:—

(a) To contribute towards the improvement of their own and their colleagues' conditions.

(b) To pay a fair share towards this.

(*c*) To recognise, by joining, that university staff are fundamentally affected by matters with which only a national association can deal.

To the converted who are members, we appreciate this fact and we ask them to do all they can to ask their colleagues who are not members to join.

To the non-member who happens to read this Bulletin (intended for members who pay the cost by their subscription) we ask them to join the Association as a matter of principle and personal conscience.

SOURCE: AUT. *Bulletin*, 36 (January 1971), 13

PART TWO

The Objectives of Trade Unions

The objectives of British trade unions cannot simply be set down in a phrase. It is not just that the classic definition offered by the Webbs, 'a continuous association of wage-earners for the purpose of maintaining or improving the conditions of their working lives', is too narrow.* Of course, one now has to add that wage-earners must be extended to embrace employees of all kinds, and that the increased unionisation of non-manual employees is an important feature of modern trade unionism. Trade union interests in the rights and opportunities of their members, or of working people in general, extend well beyond their working lives. As the TUC argued in its evidence to the Donovan Commission, 'there can be no theoretical limit' to the scope of trade union objectives since the economic, political and social relationships that affect real pay, security and opportunities ramify from the workshop to the national economy and beyond, since increasingly the trade unions are confronting multinational combines.

The functional inadequacy of the definition offered by the Webbs in the History of Trade Unionism *was made clear by Beatrice Webb herself. As she wrote later: 'When we had actually completed and published our* History of Trade Unionism . . . *we found . . . that we had no systematic and definite theory or vision of how Trade Unionism operated, or what it effected.'† That theory only emerged in their book*

---

* Webb, S. and B. *History of Trade Unionism* (1920 ed), 1.

† Webb, B. *My Apprenticeship* (1929 ed), 433.

34

Industrial Democracy *after further analysis in which they examined the evolution of trade union government and the means that trade unions had used to achieve their objectives. Thus, what we require as a framework of reference in exploring these objectives is some sense of this continuing evolution and development of trade union government, policies and methods of work; all of which are likely to be in process of transformation in the course of time. Consequently, any definition of trade union purposes is likely to be historically conditioned, to reflect the perspective and limitations of particular periods and situations.*

*The TUC in its evidence to the Donovan Commission nevertheless attempted to set down 'permanent' or 'continuing' objectives, although, as they said, 'their precise connotation will alter as the years go by'. We may leave the extracts from that evidence to speak for themselves. But there are two aspects of trade union objectives which do not emerge clearly from the TUC extract and which are worthy of further comment. One is the relation of trade union organisation and government to trade union 'purposes'. It is too easy to say that membership and democratic government are simply means to the attainment of the broad economic and social ends of trade unionism. This is to place material objectives as in some sense superior to the achievement of representative organisation by various groups of workers. But the democratisation of industrial and social life provides a persistent element in trade union ideas, and their representative capacity is a pre-condition of effective pressure in the attainment of other objectives. Thus not merely the attraction of workers into membership, but their active participation in processes of democratic self-government, should appear as a persistent objective of trade unionism.**

Secondly, there may be a continuing element of unresolved tension in the stated objectives of trade unionism. At one level, it is a matter of whether trade unions in practice pursue their functions within the framework of the existing industrial system, or whether they radically challenge and seek to change the power and property relations of society—or of the particular sector that most concerns a particular union. At another level, there are different views from union to union, and from one period to

---

* On the significance of membership participation in trade union government, see Hughes, J. *Trade Union Structure and Government* (Royal Commission on Trade Unions and Employers' Associations Research Paper No 5), Part 2, 5–6.

another, about the acceptance of the 'wages system', with its employee-employer relationship (of course, modified by collective bargaining), or as an alternative the pursuit of workers' control, and the self-government by various combinations of workers and work groups of an increasing range of industrial decisions.

Trade union rule books, in their formal statement of the objects of the union, often reveal distinct traces of these more challenging objectives. One reason for this is that the amalgamations that produced many powerful trade unions took place in periods of a ferment of ideas, and represented new organisational forms designed to achieve more ambitious aims. A good example of a rule book that offers an extended statement of objectives of this kind is that of the Transport and General Workers' Union, which is reproduced in this section. Similar aspirations are to be found in many other rule books, though often related much more specifically to the context of a particular industry. Thus the objectives of the National Union of Mineworkers concentrate primarily on the affairs of the coal industry; but as so often in trade unionism the wider millennial aspirations appear in clauses otherwise full of prosaic detail. One feature of unions of skilled occupations is their emphasis, as a persistent objective, on the maintenance of high professional standards. The extract from the Rules of the National Union of Journalists is one example.

3 TUC: TRADE UNION OBJECTIVES

93 Because they are adaptable to changing external circumstances, trade union objectives are always changing, yet in another sense they always remain the same. There are in fact many different senses in which the phrase 'trade union objectives' can be used. There are objectives which are capable of achievement once and for all; those which can be met but which are immediately replaced by new ones, and there are those which are of such a nature that they can be termed permanent objectives, though their precise connotation will alter as the years go by. It is in terms of this third usage that trade union objectives are enumerated and discussed in this chapter.

94 Several kinds of continuing objectives can be distinguished. These are to some extent complementary and there is always a choice to be made as to which broad objective is to be given the greatest emphasis at any given time. This problem of priorities is inseparable from one of the most important facets of trade union function, that of providing a means whereby working people can discuss and decide which objective corresponds to the greatest degree of common interest among them at a given time.

95 The trade union Movement, comprising a whole spectrum of occupations from musicians to doctors, miners to shop-workers, obviously cannot formulate even a general list of objectives which are equally relevant to the competence of all its constituent unions or to the needs of all their members.

96 To attempt to set out the objectives of trade unions as a whole is to describe these objectives in a way which no individual union and no individual trade unionist might find entirely adequate or satisfactory. It is perhaps for this reason that the Webbs, when writing the definitive work of their time, did not describe trade union objectives at all explicitly but stated simply that a trade union was 'a continuous association of wage earners for the purpose of improving the conditions of their working lives'. This remains a valid statement of trade unions' central purpose and it is to elaborate on the several facets of this central purpose which is the aim of this section of the evidence.

97 These objectives can be distinguished as follows:
    (i) improved terms of employment
   (ii) improved physical environment at work
  (iii) full employment and national prosperity
   (iv) security of employment and income
    (v) improved social security
   (vi) fair shares in national income and wealth
  (vii) industrial democracy
 (viii) a voice in government
   (ix) improved public and social services

(x) public control and planning of industry.

98　It will be seen that these objectives are of many different kinds. Some do not concern employment as such but are nevertheless common objectives of employed persons. Again, some may be termed substantive in nature and others more concerned with the way in which things are done. There can be no absolute distinction however between methods and objectives. All these objectives are seen as the means to the good life, which is the ultimate objective in all of them.

Improved terms of employment

99　The order in which the objectives are listed is not intended to imply a precise rating of their order of importance. However, there can be little doubt that improved wages and terms of employment stand at the top of the list. Nevertheless, because there are different objectives means that this is always a question of priorities and in many circumstances, higher wages may not be the most important immediate objective of a trade union; this is also true of the trade union Movement as a whole. While there are wider questions of trade union economic policy (discussed in detail in chapter eight) trade unions see higher wages as being a most effective means of enhancing the economic welfare of their members: they also regard their capacity to win higher wages through collective bargaining as one of their most effective methods of attracting membership. The emphasis at any given time may be on shorter hours or increased holidays and this choice of emphasis must reflect the members' wishes. Again the terms of employment represent a bargain about payment and work. The negotiations leading to the bargain always give close attention to payment, whereas the work to be performed may be defined with varying degrees of precision. In some cases the work to be performed is specified in detail, stipulating that it shall be done in a particular way and within a particular time. In other cases much may be left to the worker's skill and discretion to achieve an objective which itself may be stated only in general terms. However, in all cases the work to be performed is as important a part of the bargain as the payment: what has to be done is a vital factor in determining the adequacy of the reward.

Improved physical environment at work

100   The pace of work and the content of a job are important elements in its general attractiveness and so is the physical environment in which it is to be done. Pressure for improved standards of safety and health, as well as other aspects of physical working conditions has always been an important part of trade union function. It is increasingly recognised that it is only as part of a general improvement in the working environment that there can be fully effective measures to deal with the hazards to life and health which many jobs have involved for too long. Many of these improvements can best be brought about by the Government laying down minimum standards. If they are not achieved through collective bargaining, this does not therefore indicate that these matters are low on the list of trade union priorities. If they can best be dealt with by statutory regulation, trade unions will pursue the method of pressure on Government to achieve their objectives in this field. Choice of method must always be related to the particular objective ...

Full employment and national prosperity

101   A policy of full employment involves the Government accepting a responsibility for creating conditions in which a wide range of suitable employment opportunities are available for people to choose from. Trade unionists see full employment as an end in itself, but also as a necessary means to achieving consistently rising national prosperity. To trade unionists, full employment is the pre-condition for rising output and thus for rising real incomes. For many reasons therefore it is impossible to over-emphasise the importance of full employment. Policies for full employment took shape before and during the last war and the TUC played a major part in their formulation. Right through the inter-war period trade unions consistently proposed

a set of alternative policies to those of retrenchment and the gold standard. By 1944 the necessary revolution in Government thinking had taken place and it was in the same year that the TUC produced its detailed plan for Post-War Reconstruction. The TUC has always recognised that the characteristics of a full employment economy are quite different to those of an economy with a wildly fluctuating level of employment. The TUC pointed out more than twenty years ago what many of the implications of full employment were. Those affecting trade union practice are considered in subsequent sections of this evidence. It must however be emphasised that it is in the light of the enormous benefits which full employment brings that these problems have to be examined.

Security of employment and income

102   Trade unions exist to safeguard the interests of their members. To safeguard means to advance and protect, and both aspects are important. Trade union purposes and practices are often misunderstood when they involve protecting the interests of their members. Job security and redundancy provide the best example of this. Observers whose perspective is different to that of most workpeople cite the national interest and argue that this implies or demands certain actions on the part of groups and individuals. Yet there can be no national interest divorced from individual interests. People in employment, whose status was described at the beginning of this part of the evidence, comprise a large part of the nation. Therefore, when workpeople demand certain safeguards or otherwise refuse to do this or that, the argument that they are acting against the national interest often begs important questions. No-one would deny in the abstract that progress involves change, and that changing jobs is an important element in this change. Yet if the change produces a benefit for the nation as a whole trade unionists ask why it should involve a loss to those directly involved. If there is an overall gain, it is not true that someone's gain is automatically someone else's loss. If, on the other hand,

there is no overall benefit, then the change should not take place. The trade union objective of security of employment and security of income should therefore be seen as consistent with the process of change from which working people as a whole stand to benefit. The precise terms on which trade unions will accept change cannot by their nature be generalised. Yet it is clear enough that uncertainty about employment and uncertainty about income are not acceptable conditions for change.

Improved social security

103   The needs covered by social security in its widest sense comprise not only full employment and economic security, but health, education, housing and much else. In other words it is concerned with provision for needs shared by all members of the community in a common basis of citizenship, as well as with needs arising out of employment. These two divisions of social security are complementary. The frontiers between them are not static. The broad tendency has been for improved standards of occupational security to stimulate and promote improved general standards. This, however, has not been invariably so. Occupational health standards, for example, have lagged behind improvements in the general health services. While trade unions are vitally concerned with all aspects of social security, they have special responsibilities for promoting those needs of their members which arise out of employment, namely, adequate income maintenance when earnings are interrupted by sickness, accident, unemployment, old age and the other contingencies covered by national insurance; adequate standards of safety and health at work, including prevention, rehabilitation, compensation and research.

Fair shares in national income and wealth

104   The demand for fair shares is a continuing trade union objective and in common with other objectives it is not likely to be achieved once and for all time. One of the main characteristics of a laissez-faire free market economy is gross inequality of

income and wealth and social injustice. While taxation has made a significant change in the underlying pattern, the concentration of power and privilege persist, and the equality of opportunity which is continually in prospect is still in the future. Grossly unequal rewards are not consistent with equality of respect, which is the meaning of equality in everyday life. The object of greater equality is not one which requires a precise or final interpretation, and, at a time when 10 per cent of the people own 90 per cent of the wealth, trade unionists assert that redistribution has still got a long way to go.

105   The major scope for further redistribution is in the ownership of capital. However, important questions for the trade union Movement arise from the degree of inequality in the incomes of employed persons themselves. Agreement on the need for redistribution in this field implies that some people would be willing to forgo part of what they could earn to assist those in a weaker position. Although self-interest may well be the main motive among workpeople both in joining a trade union and in subsequently deciding what its policy should be, it would be mistaken to think that phrases such as brotherhood and social justice are only rhetoric. Trade unionists have a strong sense of community and it would be wrong to assume that any apparently disinterested act can only be explained in terms of long term self-interest. They have supported an expanded programme of economic assistance to the two-thirds of the world where living standards and opportunities are well below those which obtained in Britain a hundred years ago, while insisting that the cost of such a programme must be equitably shared.

Industrial democracy
106   Workpeople form trade unions to assert their right to have a say in matters which are of close concern to them. As has already been pointed out, even the most limited definition of what constitutes the terms of employment covers the content of the job as well as the wages to be paid for doing it. However,

workpeople do not just have views on this limited, though important, subject. They have a continuing interest and experience in all matters affecting their employment and together have potentially the competence to make an essential contribution to decisions affecting the enterprise in which they work. The extent of this contribution has hitherto been limited by the nature of the master and servant relationship. Workpeople, through their trade unions, can play no responsible role in such circumstances as there is nothing that they can be responsible for. If all decisions affecting the running of an enterprise are made unilaterally by the employer there can be no basis of mutual respect. Workpeople seek to enhance their status in industry and to make a real contribution to the advancement of their own interests which over a wide range of matters are the common interest of all those concerned with the enterprise in which they work. There are many unsolved problems associated with the objective of furthering industrial democracy. Not least, there are problems of trade union function and trade union organisation. There exists, however, within the trade union Movement a growing determination to tackle these problems.

Voice in government

107 Decisions affecting the interests of workpeople are made at a multitude of levels and in a multitude of ways. Workpeople's right to a view on matters which affect their interests applies therefore at the level of Government as well as at the level of firm or industry. The trade union claim to a voice in Government rests on the wide-ranging scope of modern Government. If trade unions are at arms length from Government, there is a lack of influence in both directions: trade unions are in a poor position to state their views and Government also does not have the facility to take account of trade union experience or to prepare the ground for new policies which will affect the interests of working people. There has, therefore, developed a relationship which trade unions wish to strengthen,

a relationship which, at the same time, keeps quite distinct the respective responsibilities of trade unions and Government but minimises the dangers of misunderstanding and in fact takes advantage of the contribution which each can make to the functions and purposes of the other. The relationship is therefore an exceedingly complex one. . .

Improved social and public services

108   Although the two broad divisions of social security are interrelated and complementary, it is necessary to explain the close interest which trade unions take in the provision of services which are shared by all members of the community, services which do not arise exclusively from needs based on employment. It is of course a national tradition that general health services, educational services, housing, transport and other services are not in this country to any significant extent provided by employers, but on the basis of common provision for all citizens. Nor is there any general desire for this situation to be changed. Trade unionists appreciate that the quality of life and general standard of living in any civilised community depends for the majority not only upon the level of individual incomes, but also upon the scale and quality of public services. Working people therefore have a common interest in the improvement of these services and to a greater extent than other groups in the community are very dependent on a proper share of increasing national resources being allocated into those fields, into services which are widening in scope and for which, by their nature, there cannot be adequate provision on the basis of separate purchase by each individual. Public authorities must, therefore, provide for a growing range of such needs. They deserve to be given higher priority so that they become a manifest yardstick of national prosperity.

Public control and planning of industry

109   In the 1944 Report on Post-War Reconstruction, and again in the Report adopted in 1950 on the Public Control of

Industry, the TUC outlined the objectives and methods of public control and showed that the other objectives of the trade union Movement could not be achieved without a great measure of public control and planning of industry. This objective is therefore a means as much as an end, but on that count of course it is not unique. It needs to be distinguished from the objective of industrial democracy on the one hand and the objective of a voice in Government on the other. As the term implies, the public control and planning of industry is concerned with the performance of industries rather than with the details of the management of particular firms. In calling for greater public control and planning of industry, trade unionists are not simply saying that they want their view to be heard. In other words, they are not concerned solely with the circumstances in which decisions are taken in the individual firm or in Government, but with ensuring that the great industries of the country are making the best use of their resources and that their policies with regard to prices, investment and exports, for example, reflect the needs of the community as a whole. The public ownership of certain industries, advocated by the TUC in 1944, was one means, and trade unionists would argue a successful one, of redressing the balance of private power and of improving the structure of these industries and their economic performance. In other industries, however, other means of public control and planning may be more appropriate, and the current policy of establishing Economic Development Committees which played a big part in the preparation of the National Plan may prove to be equally successful in its own way. Between these two alternatives there are a wide range of other methods of public control and the TUC has over the years made proposals for a variety of new types of machinery to further this general objective.

SOURCE: *Trade Unionism*. The Evidence of the Trades Union Congress to the Royal Commission on Trade Unions and Employers' Associations (1966), 32–9

4 TUC: OBJECTS

(*a*) The objects of the Congress shall be:

To do anything to promote the interests of all or any of its affiliated organisations or anything beneficial to the interests of past and present individual members of such organisations.

Generally to improve the economic or social conditions of workers in all parts of the world and to render them assistance whether or not such workers are employed or have ceased to be employed.

To affiliate to or subscribe to or to assist any other organisation having objects similar to those of the Congress.

To assist in the complete organisation of all workers eligible for membership of its affiliated organisations and subject as hereinafter set forth in these Rules to settle disputes between the members of such organisations and their employers or between such organisations and their members or between the organisations themselves.

In pursuance of such objects the Congress may do or authorise to be done all such acts and things as it considers necessary for the furtherance of those objects and in particular shall endeavour to establish the following measures and such others as any Annual Congress may approve:

Public Ownership and control of natural resources and of services—

> Nationalisation of land, mines, and minerals.
>
> Nationalisation of railways.
>
> The extension of State and municipal enterprise for the provision of social necessities and services.
>
> Proper provision for the adequate participation of the workers in the control and management of public services and industries.

Wages and hours of labour—

> A legal maximum working week of 40 hours.
>
> A legal minimum wage for each industry or occupation.

Unemployment—
Suitable provision in relation to unemployment, with adequate maintenance of the unemployed.

Establishment of training centres for unemployed juveniles.

Extension of training facilities for adults during periods of industrial depression.

Housing—
Provision for proper and adequate housing accommodation.

Education—
To raise the school leaving age to 16 and to ensure that full educational facilities are provided by the State from the elementary schools to the universities.

Occupational accidents and diseases—
Adequate maintenance and compensation in respect of all forms of industrial accidents and diseases.

The promotion of legal standards of health, hygiene and welfare in all places of employment.

Pensions—
Adequate State pensions for all at the age of 60.

Adequate State pensions for widowed mothers and dependent children and mothers whose family breadwinner is incapacitated.

(*b*) In the interpretation of the above objects the General Council shall have complete discretion subject only to the power of the Annual Congress to revise its decisions.

SOURCE: TUC. *Rules* (revised 1971), rule 2

5 TRANSPORT AND GENERAL WORKERS' UNION: OBJECTS

1.—The principal objects of the Union are the regulation of the relations between workmen and employers, and between workmen and workmen, and also the provision of benefits to members.

2.—The objects of the Union shall further include:

(*a*) The organisation of all members and other persons qualified for membership, being seafarers and employees in port, harbour, dock, warehouse, waterside, waterway, road, aerial, and other transport services, general workers, and such other workers as may be deemed eligible by the General Executive Council of the Union, and the obtaining and maintaining of just and proper hours of work, rates of wages, and to endeavour by all means in their power to control the industries in which the members are engaged.

(*b*) The settling and negotiating of differences and disputes between the members of the Union and employers, and other Trade Unions and persons, by collective bargaining or agreement, withdrawal of labour, or otherwise.

(*c*) Generally, the power to promote the welfare of the members of the Union in such manner as the General Executive Council from time to time shall deem expedient.

(*d*) The provision of benefits to members as follows:

    (i) Assistance to members, or particular classes of members, (1) when out of employment or in distressed circumstances; (2) in cases of sickness, accident and disablement; (3) in old age; (4) in trade disputes; (5) for funeral expenses; and such other forms of assistance as may from time to time be decided by the Union, or the General Executive Council provided that it shall not assure to any member a sum exceeding five hundred pounds by way of gross sum or one hundred and four pounds by way of annuity.

    (ii) Legal advice and legal assistance to the Union or its members where, in the opinion of the General Executive Council, it is necessary or expedient.

    (iii) Grants and endowments, including scholarships, to members and to the colleges or institutions having among their objects the education of trade unionists.

(*e*) The furtherance of political objects of any kind.

(*f*) The transaction of insurance business.

(g) The extension of co-operative production and distribution.

(h) The establishment or carrying on, or participation, financial or otherwise, directly or indirectly, in the business of printing or publishing of a general newspaper or newspapers, or of books, pamphlets, or publications, or of any other kind of undertaking industrial or otherwise in the interest of and with the main purpose of furthering the interests of the Union or of trade unionism generally, together with such subsidiary action and purposes as may be calculated to enhance the prosperity of the publications or the business generally, after submission to the Biennial Delegate Conference or ballot of members.

(i) The furtherance of, or participation, financial or otherwise, directly or indirectly, in the work or purpose of any association or federal body, having for its objects the furthering of the interests of labour, trade unionism, or trade unionists, including the securing of a real measure of control in industry and participation by the workers in the management, in the interests of labour and the general community.

(j) The furthering of any other action or purpose, or the participation, financial or otherwise, directly or indirectly, in any other purpose, so far as may be lawful, which is calculated, in the opinion of the Union or the General Executive Council, to further the interests of labour, trade unionism, or trade unionists.

(k) The provision of opportunities for social intercourse and promotion of sport and social events amongst the members.

3.—In order to achieve the above objects the Union shall have power, in addition to any other powers given them by law or by these rules, to impose such restraints upon the labour of its members or generally to interfere, whether such interference is in restraint of trade or not, but so far only as may otherwise be lawful, with the trade or conduct of such industries, businesses, and occupations as may be deemed expedient.

4.—The Union shall undertake the employment of the permanent officers of the amalgamated unions.

In the case of the unions which amalgamated in October 1921, if salaries or conditions have been altered after October 6, 1920, and prior to the registration of this Union, such alterations shall be taken into consideration and this Union shall grant out of its funds, pensions and/or gratuities to full-time officers of this Union and/or of any of the amalgamated unions, and generally, honour all obligations of the amalgamated unions or any of them in respect of pensions, grants, etc., to retired officers, which were granted prior to October 6, 1920.

In the case of unions amalgamating since October 1921, the conditions, terms and obligations shall be such as are agreed upon between this Union and the unions desiring amalgamations, and upon ratification shall form an integral part of these rules.

5.—In particular, the Union shall have power to provide funds, by subscription, levy, or otherwise, as the Union or the General Executive Council may direct, for maintaining all or some of the benefits from time to time authorised in pursuance of these rules, and for the establishment or maintenance of any undertaking of any kind, financial or otherwise, authorised by the Union, and for any action, including collective bargaining, striking, withholding of labour, taking action under the Wages Councils Act or other statutes, either severally or jointly, or the securing of agreements concerning wages or other conditions of employment, whether in defence of the members or in support of other workers of allied or other industries, which may, in the opinion of the Union or of the General Executive Council, be deemed to be calculated to further the interests of the Union, or of the Trade Union Movement generally. No levy shall be imposed until a vote of members concerned has been taken.

6.—There shall be an Officials' Superannuation Fund and a Staff Superannuation Fund to which the Union shall contribute an amount not less than that contributed by the officials and the staff, and the liabilities of the funds shall be guaranteed by the Trade Union funds of the Union, which may vary its contributions to the funds as and when found to be necessary following an examination of the funds.

Such provision shall apply to all contributions to the Funds and to Officials and Members of the Staff who joined the service of the Union up to and including December 31, 1962, or on a date to be decided by the General Executive Council, whichever is the later.

As from the date of commencement of the combined Superannuation Fund mentioned in the next succeeding paragraph no further entrants shall be accepted to either of the above Funds.

7.—There shall be a combined Superannuation Fund and on and after January 1, 1963, or such later date as shall be appointed for the commencement of the Fund, Officials and Members of the Staff who are not members of either of the Funds mentioned in the preceding paragraph shall contribute to such combined Fund as from the date of becoming eligible for membership thereof.

The Union shall contribute to the said Fund an amount not less than that contributed by Officials and Staff and the liability of the Fund shall be guaranteed by the Trade Union Funds of the Union, which may vary its contributions to the Fund as and when found to be necessary, following an examination of the Fund.

8.—For all or any of the above objects the Union and the General Executive Council shall have power (*inter alia*):

(*a*) To hold, purchase, lease, mortgage, or otherwise deal with land.

(*b*) To erect and furnish such buildings as may be considered necessary or desirable.

(*c*) To raise funds by borrowing money on any real or personal property of the Union, or by levies on its members or any class thereof (subject to proviso in preceding clause 5).

(*d*) To establish superannuation schemes, contributory or otherwise, for officers and for servants of the Union.

Source: TGWU. *Rules* (revised 1971), rule 2

6 NATIONAL UNION OF MINEWORKERS
OBJECTS

. . .

(*e*) To promote legislation in the interests of members and the Coal Mining Industry.

(*f*) To act as an association, organisation or intermediary for the purposes of any Conciliation Scheme for the Coal Mining Industry of Great Britain.

(*g*) To employ and organise the appointment of persons on the workmen's behalf to make inspection under the provisions of the Coal Mines Act, 1911 (and any other enactments which may be for the time being in force) or in pursuance of any agreement or arrangement with mineowners or association of mineowners of any coal mines.

(*h*) To represent members of the Union and the interests of the Coal Mining Industry before and present evidence and information to Government, Parliamentary, Municipal, Local Government, Official and other Commissions, Committees and bodies of Enquiry or Investigation or authorities . . .

(*s*) To promote and secure the passing of legislation for improving the condition of the members and ensuring them a guaranteed week's wage with protective clauses for the miners even when they cease work, when cessation is due to causes beyond the immediate control of the members and to join in with other organisations for the purpose of and with the view to the complete abolition of Capitalism . . .

SOURCE: NUM. *Rules* (1947), rule 3

7 NATIONAL UNION OF JOURNALISTS
CODE OF PROFESSIONAL CONDUCT

Like other trade unions, formed for mutual protection and economic betterment, the National Union of Journalists desires and encourages its members to maintain good quality of workmanship and high standard of conduct.

Through years of courageous struggle for better wages and working conditions its pioneers and their successors have kept these aims in mind, and have made provision in Union rules not only for penalties on offenders, but for the guidance and financial support of members who may suffer loss of work for conforming to Union principles.

While punishment by fine, suspension or expulsion is provided for in cases of 'conduct detrimental to the interests of the Union or of the profession' any member who is victimised (Rule 20, clause (f)) for refusing to do work . . . 'incompatible with the honour and interests of the profession', may rely on adequate support from Union funds.

A member of the Union has two claims on his loyalty—one by his Union and one by his employer. These need not clash so long as the employer complies with the agreed Union conditions and makes no demand for forms of service incompatible with the honour of the profession or with the principles of trade unionism.

1. A member should do nothing that would bring discredit on himself, his Union, his newspaper, or his profession. He should study the rules of his Union, and should not, by commission or omission, act against the interests of the Union.

2. Unless the employer consents to a variation, a member who wishes to terminate his employment must give notice, according to agreement or professional custom.

3. No member should seek promotion or seek to obtain the position of another journalist by unfair methods.

4. A member should not, directly or indirectly, attempt to obtain for himself or anyone else any commission, regular or occasional, held by a freelance member of the Union. A member should not accept a commission normally held by a freelance member of the Union without reasonable cause.

5. It is unprofessional conduct to exploit the labour of another journalist by plagiarism, or by using his copy for linage purposes without permission.

6. Staff men who do linage work should be prepared to give

up such work to conform with any pooling scheme approved by the National Executive Council, or any Union plan to provide a freelance member with a means of earning a living.

7. A member holding a staff appointment shall serve first the paper that employs him. In his own time a member is free to engage in other creative work, but he should not undertake any extra work in his rest time or holidays if by so doing he is depriving an out-of-work member of a chance to obtain employment. Any misuse of rest days—won by the Union on the sound argument that periods of recuperation are needed after strenuous hours of labour—is damaging to trade union aims for a shorter working week.

8. While a spirit of willingness to help other members should be encouraged at all times, members are under a special obligation of honour to help an unemployed member to obtain work.

9. Every journalist should treat subordinates as considerately as he would desire to be treated by his superiors.

10. Freedom in the honest collection and publication of news facts, and the rights of fair comment and criticism, are principles which every journalist should defend. Journalists should strive to eliminate distortion, news suppression, and censorship.

11. A journalist should fully realise his personal responsibility for everything he sends to his paper or agency. He should keep Union and professional secrets, and respect all necessary confidences regarding sources of information and private documents. He should not falsify information or documents, or distort or misrepresent facts.

12. In obtaining news or pictures, reporters and Press photographers should do nothing that will cause pain or humiliation to innocent, bereaved, or otherwise distressed persons. News, pictures, and documents should be acquired by honest methods only.

13. Every journalist should keep in mind the dangers in the laws of libel, contempt of court, and copyright. In reports of law court proceedings it is necessary to observe and practise the rule of fair play to all parties.

14. Whether for publication or suppression, the acceptance of a bribe by a journalist is one of the gravest professional offences.

15. A journalist shall not, in the performance of his professional duties, lend himself to the distortion or suppression of the truth because of advertising considerations.

16. Except in the case of freelances, reporters should not take photographs and photographers should not report other than in exceptional circumstances.

SOURCE: NUJ. *Rules* (1972), Appendix A

PART THREE

Trade Union Methods 1

(a) MEMBERSHIP AND EDUCATION

Trade unions, then, have a number of objectives which in employment are nowadays given the prosaic title of job regulation. Employment, that is to say, is carried out by people following rules determining their behaviour: how much work they are to do, how many hours, the type of work, the remuneration, etc. The authorship of the rules is crucial. It can be done by the employer alone; by the state; by the union; by groups of workers; by some form of joint activity, eg union and employer; or even by some tripartite system, with the state, employees and employers all involved.

The whole history of industrial relations can be summed up as attempts by both government and unions to reduce the ability of the employer to act unilaterally. More recently this has been complicated by the efforts of government to involve itself more in the process, whether by incomes policies or by legislation to regulate the industrial relations system. The actual method a union will use in a particular situation will depend on many factors: for example, its history; the relative strength or weakness of its membership; and the strategy which it thinks appropriate to the circumstances. In a broad sense the main aim of most unions has been to develop joint job regulation, that is, collective bargaining; but they will also act unilaterally or use their influence on government where suitable. Most attention in this section will be devoted to collective bargaining, especially to some newer developments. But there are some essential prerequisites.

The first is that, whatever method is used, unions need members. It *may not be strictly true that unions have always had to demand the right to represent their members. The Webbs have been rightly criticised for neglecting to draw attention to the fact that others besides unions are involved in collective bargaining and that some employers have argued in favour of unions.* Nevertheless there is sufficient truth in the proposition that employers are more ready to recognise and treat with unions if they can count on sufficient numbers of members. Indeed all unions aim to recruit all appropriate employees. It is by no means the case that all unions have consciously aimed at the closed shop, the situation where employees have to join a union as a condition of employment. Many prefer to speak of 100-per-cent unionism, achieved by people joining because they find it in their best interest to do so. Under the Industrial Relations Act, 1971 this is all changed, at least in law. No one can put pressure on another either to join or not to join a union. The closed shop is not permitted, except in very special circumstances. Instead there is the agency shop whereby the relevant employees may vote to require people to join a union, but even if the vote is favourable those who object to joining may still retain their employment and pay a sum of money to a charity in lieu of union contribution. Despite these changes, we include an extract from the standard work on the subject by McCarthy, written before the Act, which provides a justification for the closed shop.*

However, these simple statements conceal other matters. Unions do not necessarily argue that workers should join any union but rather that they should join a particular one. Unions sometimes act as do professional associations and assert that a job can be performed only by members of their organisation. One consequence of this is the possibility of demarcation problems, sometimes within unions—especially those with a craft tradition—and these often determine the types of work which different sections of the membership can perform. There are also disputes between unions which become acute when changes in materials upset any agreed allocations. In essence this can best be regarded as the union trying to maintain the interests of the members, notably the safeguarding of jobs.

A second prerequisite is the need to have members who understand

---

* See Flanders, A. 'The Nature of Collective Bargaining' in his *Collective Bargaining* (1969).

what it is they are being called upon to do. Much attention is paid to educational work. The government, the Confederation of British Industry (CBI), the TUC and individual unions all speak loudly of the need for more training for shop stewards. A great deal of effort is put into educational provision for others besides stewards. We give two out of many possible examples. One is a description of the educational programme of the Post Office Engineering Union, which demonstrates its comprehensiveness. The other is from the TUC, part of its Training Kit for the understanding of the Industrial Relations Act.

8 INDUSTRIAL RELATIONS ACT, 1971
APPROVED CLOSED SHOP AGREEMENTS

Special provisions for approval of closed shop agreement

17.—(1) In this Act 'approved closed shop agreement' means an agreement which—

(a) is made between one or more employers and one or more trade unions, or between an organisation of employers and one or more trade unions;

(b) is an agreement whereby it is agreed, in respect of workers of one or more descriptions specified in the agreement, that their terms and conditions of employment shall include a condition that every such worker, if he is not already a member of that trade union or of one of those trade unions, as the case may be, must become such a member unless specially exempted; and

(c) is made in accordance with proposals approved by an order of the Industrial Court made under Schedule 1 to this Act which is for the time being in force.

(2) Where an approved closed shop agreement is for the time being in force, the following provisions of this section shall have effect notwithstanding anything in section 5(1)(b) of this Act.

(3) A worker to whom the agreement applies, and who is not specially exempted, shall not have the right, as between himself

and an employer to whom the agreement applies, to refuse
to be a member of the trade union, or (as the case may be)
of one of the trade unions, with which the agreement was
made.

(4) A worker to whom the agreement applies, and who is
specially exempted, shall not have the right, as between himself
and an employer to whom the agreement applies, to refuse to
be a member of that trade union, or of one of those trade
unions, as the case may be, unless he agrees to pay appropriate
contributions to a charity.

(5) In accordance with subsections (3) and (4) of this section,
it shall not be an unfair industrial practice for an employer to
whom an approved closed shop agreement applies, or for a
person acting on behalf of such an employer—

(a) to dismiss, penalise or otherwise discriminate against a
worker to whom the agreement applies, on the grounds that
he is not a member of the trade union, or (as the case may
be) of one of the trade unions, with which the agreement
was made and has refused to become or has been excluded
from being such a member, or, if specially exempted, has
refused or failed to pay appropriate contributions to a
charity, or

(b) to refuse to engage a worker who, if engaged by him, would
be a worker to whom the agreement applies, on the grounds
that he is not a member of that trade union or of one of
those trade unions, as the case may be, and refuses to become or has been excluded from being such a member.

(6) Where a worker to whom the agreement applies, and
who is specially exempted, has agreed to pay appropriate contributions to a charity, and requests his employer to deduct the
contributions from his remuneration and pay them on his behalf, then so long as that request remains in force—

(a) he shall not be regarded for the purposes of subsection
(5)(a) of this section as having refused to pay the contributions to the charity, and

(b) any failure on the part of the employer to comply with the

request shall not be regarded as a failure on the part of the
worker to pay the contributions . . .

SOURCE: Industrial Relations Act, 1971 (c 72)

9 W. E. J. McCARTHY: THE CONTINUED JUSTIFIABILITY OF THE CLOSED SHOP

. . . It seems to me that, in general terms, the closed shop is
justifiable—although it is sometimes used unnecessarily and is
liable to abuse. It is usually demanded where unions face problems of organization and control which are insoluble without
its aid. Unless such problems can be solved three things may
happen:

(1) It may be impossible to develop enough collective strength
either to secure recognition, and the right to participate in
bilateral job regulation, or to impose any sort of unilateral
regulation;

(2) even if recognition can be secured the union may still be too
weak to take effective action if individual employers refuse
to observe agreements;

(3) even if this is possible, it may still not be strong enough to
secure any 'improvements' in wages and conditions.

Where either of the first two situations are likely, the justification of the closed shop can be based on the argument that unless
workers are free to demand and obtain it they will be unable to
sustain a system of visible job regulation. In Chamberlain's
words the employer will be free to 'force obedience to his laws'
and the system of 'self-government' which trade union participation in job regulation represents will no longer be possible. In
such a situation the only alternative to surrendering to the
arbitrary rules of the employer is an extension of state intervention . . .

It is not easy to list all the groups in which the closed shop is
essential, if the choice between state regulation and the arbitrary rule of the employer is to be avoided. However, it seems

reasonable to suppose that comprehensively closed groups like merchant seamen and musicians would find it impossible to maintain effective organization without its aid, and several less organized groups, such as builders' labourers and distributive workers, depend on it for the limited degree of organization which they have achieved. Nor is this all. It is not too much to argue that the only hope which most of the more weakly-organized groups have of dispensing with the 'prop' of minimum wage legislation, and the 'Wages Council System' is the attainment of the closed shop. The fact that at the moment there are no closed shops among groups like laundry workers or agricultural labourers, does not mean that they would not benefit if there were. Nor does it mean that if the level of unionization rises in these groups demands for the practice will not be made; the reverse is probably the case. I would regard this as a welcome development, and would consider the growth of actual closed shops in these industries as a sign that their industrial relations were advancing to what Professor Kahn-Freund has termed a more 'mature' stage.

But such arguments can only be used to justify the closed shop where the conditions set out in (1) and (2) above apply. This is not always the case. A few printers, and many engineers, sustain a viable system of job regulation without the aid of the closed shop, although they would be in a better position to defend and improve their position if they could obtain it.[1] To maintain a *general* justification of the practice it must be assumed that it can be justified in these instances as well, by reference to the benefits it ensures. It must also be assumed that it does not result in disadvantages to others, or to the general interest, which outweigh these advantages.

Any decision on questions of this sort must be very much a

---

[1] Of course it is often argued, by trade unionists, that groups of this sort depend on, and even batten off, the more highly organised groups in their industry who usually have obtained the closed shop. In other words, that the wages and conditions which have been established in the industry are largely the result of the efforts of the better organised sections. To the extent that this is admitted it may be argued that *all* workers in the industry are benefiting from the closed shop.

matter of personal judgment, but I would maintain that a general justification for the closed shop can be made in this way. Despite the extra bargaining position which individual workers now enjoy as a result of a high level of employment; despite the extension of social security provisions (despite, in short, all that has happened since 1867), I believe that workers still need to combine to match the power of employers . . . To me it seems that despite the very considerable powers which unions now enjoy, the power from which most workers still need to be protected is that of the employers. Despite union participation in job regulation the initiative in decision taking remains with employers. Generally, unions can do no more than try to influence those managerial decisions which vitally affect their members. If they feel that to do this more effectively they need the extra strength and discipline which only the closed shop can provide, I do not feel that the existing balance of power in industry justifies the law in trying to prevent them.

Nor do I accept that there is any essential difference between allowing unions to use collective sanctions in an attempt to regulate wages and conditions, and permitting the enforcement of entry control via the closed shop. The scope of union interest in entry control is, in any case, largely determined by the extent to which it is felt to be necessary to maintain effective job regulation. Whether entry control is more justifiable when enforced unilaterally, via a union imposed closed shop, or bilaterally, via a collective agreement, seems to me impossible to say. But there would appear to be no good reason why, in itself, the attempt to control entry should be regarded as especially unjustifiable—although entry control for certain purposes might be objectionable . . .

It should . . . be clear that what follows is written from the viewpoint of one who accepts the general justifiability of both the pre- and post-entry shop. Undoubtedly the practice sometimes results in a restriction of individual liberty, and probably it sometimes has disadvantageous economic effects. Nonunionists and employers are often coerced, and existing members are forced to obey union rules and orders by means of the threat of exclusion from the job. In its pre-entry form the practice is sometimes used to deny whole classes of workers the right to compete for particular jobs. But, in the great majority of cases, these things are done in order to assist in the maintenance and improvement of the unions' powers of job regulation, and in order to make possible greater opportunities for group protection and advancement. The inevitable restrictions on personal liberty they involve, and even the possible maldistribution of economic resources which result, seem to me to be the price which must be paid if the unions are to be allowed the freedom they require in order to pursue such objectives in the most effective way.

But I would seek to draw a line between acceptance of the general justifiability of the closed shop and approval of the use of the exclusion sanction in any particular instance. A general case must be made out against the closed shop before one can support legislation the intention of which is to suppress it by law. A general case must also be made out against the use of any one of the functions of the practice—say entry control—before one can approve of legislation aimed at striking at this function alone. I do not think such general arguments can be sustained.

But it does not follow from this that the powers which the closed shop confers are never abused. Nor does it mean that nothing ought to be done to try to prevent this. One may distinguish between the acceptance of a general right and approval of the way in which it is used in exceptional cases. One may say that men ought to be allowed to campaign for and obtain the closed shop and yet want to bring its use under public control. I would argue that while the closed shop should continue to be recognized as a lawful and 'legitimate' trade union objective, the actual imposition of the exclusion sanction requires some degree of justification in each specific case. In short, I think it ought to be plausible to argue that it was *functionally necessary*. This implies:

(a) that the enforcement of the closed shop results in certain
benefits to those who combine to impose it;

(b) that its enforcement was necessary in order to secure this
result;

(c) that the benefits resulting outweigh the losses suffered by
those who are damaged as a result of its enforcement.

Benefits and losses may be measured either in economic terms,
or in terms of individual liberty, but it must be stressed that to
feel that the benefits, on balance, 'outweigh' the losses, it is not
necessary to believe that those who impose the closed shop gain
more *in toto* than those who lose. This need only be the case where
one approves of the existing distribution of advantage and disadvantage. One might feel that the group who gains is more in
need, or deserves to gain more, than the group which loses. One
would then want to approve of the attainment of a closed shop
which produced such a result even if it could not be shown that
it produced a net gain. What is meant by saying that benefits
'outweigh' disadvantages is merely that on balance this results
in a redistribution of advantage and disadvantage, however
measured or judged, which is preferable to that existing before.
Unless the enforcement of the closed shop sanctions could be so
justified in a particular instance then I, for one, would not
approve of their employment.

Yet it is not suggested that the *legal* right to employ such
sanctions should be made dependent upon advance proof, in each
instance, of *functional justification*. Quite apart from the practical
difficulties this would involve, in strict logical terms, as was
argued throughout Chapter 10, a detailed weighing of advantage and disadvantage which is not possible in matters of this
sort. It is difficult to determine what constitutes a given degree
of advantage, and impossible to measure this against other advantages and disadvantages in any objective way. Any attempt
to enforce such a principle would constitute, in effect, a sur-
render to the judgements of those empowered to interpret the
principle. The consequences, from the union point of view,
would be as uncertain, and therefore as unacceptable, as pro-

posals to extend the scope of judicial control by developing new forms of common law liability. But this does not mean that nothing can be done to narrow the existing degree of immunity along lines suggested by the principle of functional justification . . .

SOURCE: McCarthy, W. E. J. *The Closed Shop in Britain* (1964), 259–62

10 TUC: DISPUTE OVER JOB CONTROL

(15) National Union of Sheet Metal Workers, Coppersmiths, Heating & Domestic Engineers; Amalgamated Union of Engineering and Foundry Workers and Transport & General Workers' Union

A Disputes Committee composed of Mr. S. A. Robinson (Chairman), Mr. W. Hogarth and Mr. T. Parry, with Mr. K. Graham as secretary, met in Congress House on Thursday, June 12, 1969, to consider a dispute over the allocation of certain work at Pressed Steel Fisher Ltd., Oxford, between the National Union of Sheet Metal Workers, Coppersmiths, Heating & Domestic Engineers on the one hand and the Amalgamated Union of Engineering & Foundry Workers and the Transport & General Workers' Union on the other . . .

For the National Union of Sheet Metal Workers, Coppersmiths, Heating & Domestic Engineers it was said that for many years their members who were employed as pipe fitters at Pressed Steel Fisher Ltd., Oxford, had undertaken repair work on air valves used on various types of machinery. As the design of air valves became more sophisticated and demanded more skill, the pipe fitters continued to undertake this work, and it was generally understood that such repair and maintenance work as was required was exclusively proper to the pipe-fitting department, although it was recognised that certain simpler air valves used on welding equipment in the welding maintenance department might be maintained and repaired by the

C

welding mechanics who were members of the TGWU or AEF.

In 1964, certain types of sophisticated air-valve (such as Lucifer and TAL valves) were introduced into the welding maintenance department for use on welding equipment. The NUSMWCHDE Shop Steward had then approached management and asked that the repair and maintenance of such valves should be undertaken by the pipe-fitters. This request was conceded and a minute of the meeting at which this was agreed had been signed as a correct record by the NUSMWCHDE Shop Steward and the Works Engineer who had informed the shop stewards that all other relevant departments and shop stewards had been informed.

It was said that during the course of 1968, however, the management had, in consultation with all of the unions, consolidated and re-drafted in greater detail the job specifications which had been drawn up during the course of a job-evaluation scheme which had been negotiated during 1965 and 1966. The new and more detailed job-specifications had been made generally available to union representatives and the NUSMWCHDE. Shop stewards had therefore gained copies of the job-specifications for the welding mechanics in the welding maintenance department, who were members of the AEF and TGWU. It had then been noticed that the job description included a reference to the maintenance and repair of air-valves of the TAL and Lucifer types. These were the type of air-valves which had been designated as pipe-fitters' work by the 1964 agreement. It was explained that the Pressed Steel Fisher works spread over several acres of land, and that it was not until 1968 that the pipe-fitters or their representatives had been aware that this work was being carried out by the AEF and TGWU members. The NUSMWCHDE representatives had immediately complained to the management that work which was the rightful prerogative of their members was being undertaken by the members of other unions and had reminded them of the agreement reached in 1964.

The management had then stated that the agreement had been purely informal and that anyway, they were unable to find it. This resulted in a stoppage of work by the pipe-fitters during which the management succeeded in locating the lost agreement, after which the pipe-fitters had returned to work with an undertaking from the management that the work would be given to them in future. The result of this was that the members of the TGWU and the AEF had taken strike action against the terms agreed between the management and the NUSMWCHDE. Negotiations were resumed but had proved unsuccessful, and the pipe-fitters had again stopped work. Earlier in the week, however, the members of all three unions had returned to work pending the TUC's investigation of the matter and the work in question had been frozen pending the outcome of the investigations.

In answer to a question from the Committee it was said that the work at issue was the repair and maintenance of the air valves and not the removal or fitting of them. When a valve-unit required maintenance or ceased to function correctly members of any of the three unions were entitled to remove the unit and replace it with another. The displaced valve-unit, however, should, in the opinion of the NUSMWCHDE members, be passed to the pipe-fitting department for repair. The TGWU and AEF members had maintained that they were entitled to repair the displaced unit in their own repair shop in the welding maintenance department.

The NUSMWCHDE representatives wished to emphasise that although their view differed from that of the AEF and TGWU, they regarded themselves as in dispute with the management and not with the other two unions, with whom they had always enjoyed cordial relations. The management were at fault for failing to observe an agreement and this was why the NUSMWCHDE members had taken strike action and the union had declared it official.

For the TGWU and the AEF it was said that the dispute had originated several months previously when a claim had been

made by the NUSMWCHDE that their skilled members had
the exclusive right to repair air-valves on welding equipment
under the terms of an 'agreement' dated January 28, 1964. It
was said that the TGWU and AEF representatives at Pressed
Steel Fisher had first heard of this 'agreement' during the course
of a meeting which took place during negotiations about the
wages structure on May 8, 1969, when the Senior Shop Steward
of the NUSMWCHDE referred to it in the course of discussions,
and stated that it had been drawn up by the then works engineer and agreed between him and the NUSMWCHDE.

The TGWU and AEF representatives challenged the validity
of this agreement on the following grounds: first, they held that
three unions were involved on the job in dispute (the TGWU,
the AEF and the NUSMWCHDE) and neither the AEF nor
the TGWU were at any time invited to participate in the discussions, despite the fact that the job opportunities of their
members were affected by the 'agreement'. For this reason
alone, the 'agreement' could not be accepted as valid. Second,
however, they stated that at no time had the management or
the NUSMWCHDE advised either the TGWU or the AEF of
the existence of the 'agreement', or, earlier, of their intention to
negotiate it. Third, even if the 'agreement' had been valid,
it must surely have been invalidated by the fact that the
NUSMWCHDE had at no time since January 1964, or previously, exercised the exclusive right which the purported
'agreement' bestowed upon them. Members of the TGWU and
of the AEF had in fact consistently repaired and maintained air-
valves on welding equipment since 1926. Fourth, throughout
the negotiations which had taken place from 1965 onwards,
about the job-evaluation scheme and the new wages structure,
neither the Company nor the NUSMWCHDE had at any time
referred to the 'agreement' or attempted to incorporate such a
provision into the new scheme. In addition, the job specifications for the repair section of the Welding Department which
had been drawn up in November 1966 had quite clearly included in the description of duties—repairing and fitting new

parts to various types of air-valve, i.e. British Federal, Igranic, Kempton and Lucifer.

It was said that during the wage-structure negotiations it had been agreed that this, along with three other jobs within the welding equipment department, would be consolidated into a comprehensive job description with the job title amended to Welding Equipment Mechanic. The consolidated job description had been in broader terms and it had no longer specifically referred to the repair of air-valves. All the unions in the plant had agreed to this procedure being adopted.

The TGWU and AEF representatives expressed their concern at the fact that the NUSMWCHDE were acting in breach of the procedural arrangements which were incorporated in the new wage structure agreement, and in breach of the National Engineering Procedure Agreement. They pointed out that the TGWU had two references in procedure at the time and if the NUSMWCHDE were permitted to act outside the procedure, there would inevitably be some pressure from the other unions' members to ignore the procedure.

The TGWU and the AEF both considered that it would be extremely unjust if the NUSMWCHDE were permitted to reach any agreement which severely affected the job-opportunities of their members. They contended that members of all three unions should retain the right to carry out repair work on the disputed valves.

The TGWU and AEF representatives said that they had to date seen no agreement between the management and the NUSMWCHDE which gave that union exclusive rights to the disputed work. They had seen an unsigned photostat copy of the minutes of a meeting at which it had been agreed that the NUSMWCHDE members could do the disputed work, but as they interpreted the wording of this document the rights agreed upon were purely permissive and in no way exclusive to the NUSMWCHDE.

At this point the NUSMWCHDE representatives showed to the Committee a copy of the 'agreement' which was signed by a shop steward and a representative of management and stated that in their view the wording of the minute implied an exclusive right for their members to carry out the disputed work. The TGWU and AEF representatives did not accept this view.

The Committee examined the 'agreement' which took the form of a signed minute of a meeting which had taken place in January 1964, between the NUSMWCHDE Shop Steward and the Works Engineer about the TAL valves which were then being introduced in the welding maintenance department. The Shop Steward had pointed out that the new valves were connected with copper piping rather than rubber hose as the older type had been, and had reminded the Works Engineer that the pipe-fitters' responsibility had traditionally ceased at the hose and that the new valve should therefore be fitted or removed by a pipe-fitter. The Works Engineer had refused to accept this on the grounds that a welding mechanic was always available and that he was quite capable of fitting or removing the air-valve. He had conceded however that once the valve was removed it could be repaired by the pipe-fitters if they so wished. The minute was signed by the then Works Engineer and the Shop Steward concerned.

The NUSMWCHDE considered that this report gave the pipe-fitters the exclusive right to undertake repair and maintenance work on the TAL and Lucifer valves, but the TGWU and AEF considered that the document was permissive rather than mandatory, and that the NUSMWCHDE was one of three unions whose members could carry out this work.

So far as communication with other unions about the agreement was concerned, the NUSMWCHDE representatives reiterated that the management had, at the operative time, informed the shop stewards that they had made the agreement known to representatives of the unions involved. In addition, the NUSMWCHDE shop stewards had informally approached shop stewards of the other unions before commencing negotiations with management and informed them of their intentions.

The TGWU and AEF representatives said they could not re-
collect any such meeting taking place. However, they pointed
out that the job specifications had, in 1966, quite specifically
included the job of repairing air-valves for one of the jobs which
had later been consolidated into the job description of a welding
equipment mechanic. They proffered copies of the job specifications for examination by the Committee and the NUSMWC-
HDE.

The NUSMWCHDE representatives said that they had not
seen the earlier job-specifications before but had only seen the
consolidated job-specification which had not stated specifically
that the welding equipment mechanic had the responsibility of
maintaining and repairing air-valves.

In answer to questions from the Chairman and Committee,
the NUSMWCHDE representatives said that if they had not
exercised the prerogative given them by the 1964 agreement,
this was simply because they had been under the misapprehen-
sion that no other workers had been doing the disputed work. In
answer to further questions, it was said that all of the unions had
been involved in the negotiations during 1965 and 1966 about
the job-evaluation scheme. It was also said that Lucifer and
TAL valves were used on other type of machinery in other parts
of the factory and they were normally maintained or repaired
exclusively by NUSMWCHDE members. The NUSMWCHDE
considered that the same conditions should apply in the welding
maintenance department although they were, and always had
been quite prepared to allow TGWU and AEF members to
repair the older types of valve on the welding equipment.

The TGWU and AEF representatives said that their
members had been undertaking work of this nature for more
than 19 years. The NUSMWCHDE were now attempting to
take it away from them. The NUSMWCHDE representatives
said that this was not so. They accepted that throughout the
past two decades the TGWU and AEF members had repaired
air-valves on welding equipment, but these were only the older
types of air-valve. Technological advance had changed the job

completely in recent years, and TAL and Lucifer type valves had been introduced for use on welding equipment. The repair and maintenance of these newer air-valves was quite clearly pipe-fitters' work. The pipe-fitter had always repaired these valves wherever they were used on other types of machinery in the factory.

The Chairman, in summing up the matter, said that as he understood the situation, the repair of air-valves on welding equipment (which had been fitted with rubber hose) had always been the work of the TGWU and AEF members, and that the repair of the newer types of air-valves (e.g. TAL, Lucifer, Weldman Ross which had been fitted with copper pipes) which were used elsewhere in the factory had always been the work of the NUSMWCHDE members, who were employed as pipe-fitters in the factory. The point of issue arose when the newer types of air-valves were fitted into welding equipment. The TGWU and AEF members considered that the repair of these valves was their work because they had always repaired air-valves on welding equipment. The NUSMWCHDE members said that it was their work as they had always maintained or repaired this type of valve. The NUSMWCHDE had made an agreement with management which they considered gave them the exclusive right to this work and had understood that the other unions were aware of this. The TGWU and AEF members had not been aware of this agreement and on becoming aware of it, challenged its validity.

Representatives of all three unions agreed that this was a fair statement of the position.

The Chairman then suggested that the hearing should adjourn and that the three unions should meet to discuss the matter among themselves with a view to reaching some agreement. It was noted that the NUSMWCHDE members had the right to repair and maintain air-valves of this type everywhere else in the factory and it might be that their main concern was that if the work was conceded in the welding maintenance department, it might then be taken from elsewhere also. The unions might consider some sort of agreement which gave adequate protection to the interests of the NUSMWCHDE members elsewhere in the factory.

The unions' representatives agreed to the Chairman's suggestion. The Chairman indicated that the Committee or the TUC staff would be at hand if assistance of any kind was required. The meeting adjourned at 1.30 p.m.

At 2.30 p.m. the representatives of all three unions met together to discuss the problem between themselves.

At 4 p.m. they separated and each side proceeded to draw up their proposals for agreement, which were then presented to the Chairman, who after examining the two sets of proposals, called the union representatives together again in the presence of the Committee.

The Chairman noted that the two sets of proposals appeared to be substantially the same in their intent, but differed in wording: it was necessary for them to be examined closely so that all were fully aware of what was intended. The proposals were discussed in detail and then amalgamated into a draft agreement, copies of which were circulated to all present. There followed a lengthy discussion about the wording and effect of the agreement during which it was redrafted on several occasions. After exhaustive discussions, the final agreement was drawn up and was signed by representatives of all three unions and by the Committee: (Mr. W. Hogarth was present until the agreement was concluded, but had to leave on union business before the copies were ready for signing).

Agreement

The agreement is set out below:

Agreement between the National Union of Sheet Metal Workers, Coppersmiths & Heating & Domestic Engineers and Amalgamated Union of Engineering & Foundry Workers and the Transport & General Workers' Union, relating to Pressed Steel Fisher Ltd., Oxford

1. It is agreed that all three unions shall retain the right to

carry out repair and maintenance work on the following types
of air-valve:

Lucifer; Igranic; British Federal; TAL pneumatic; Kemp-
ston; Ross; Skiaky

which are at present used on the welding equipment designated,
i.e. VEWs and portable equipment (transformer) in the welding
maintenance department.

2. In respect of all other places and all other work for which
the NUSMWCHDE have exclusive rights at the present time
such rights will in no way and at no time be varied by the
members of either of the other two unions other than with the
consultation and agreement of all unions concerned.

3. Where any variation of this agreement appears likely to
occur due to the introduction of other types of valve, as a result
of any technological change or action by management it shall
be incumbent upon the three parties to this agreement to commence consultation jointly with management at the earliest
possible opportunity.

4. In the event of failure to agree about the interpretation or
application of any clause of this agreement the issue shall be
referred to the TUC Disputes Committee for adjudication.

The representatives of the three unions thanked the Chairman
and Committee for the way in which they had been received
and for their assistance in achieving a solution to the problem.

SOURCE: Report of the 101st Annual Trades Union Congress
(1969), 110–16

11 POST OFFICE ENGINEERING UNION
THE UNION'S EDUCATION SCHEME

The Post Office Engineering Union places a high priority on
Union education. An Assistant Secretary has special responsibility for education and indeed devotes all of his time to the
development and administration of the Union's educational
schemes.

In 1965, £10,135 (4·3% of the total budget) has been allocated to education from the General Fund of the Union (this does not include expenditure on salaries). The general objectives of the Union's education scheme are as follows:

1. To train Branch Officers to perform their Union duties as effectively as possible.
2. To increase the knowledge, self-confidence, and the ability to express themselves of individual members so that they may feel ready and competent to take Branch office.
3. To create a well-informed and knowledgeable membership capable of playing an effective part in the making of Union policy.
4. To help members play an effective part in the wider local, national and international Trade Union and Labour Movement.
5. To bring about a greater understanding of national and international problems among the membership.
6. To encourage and assist members to be active in community life.
7. To help and encourage the membership to use their leisure more profitably thereby getting more satisfaction and pleasure from life.

To achieve its objects the Union runs general linked week courses, training courses for Branch Officers and Political courses. Our members also derive benefits from the Union's affiliation to the Workers' Educational Association and the Trades Union Congress.

The general linked scheme
All members of the Union are entitled to attend the Union's linked courses. These consist of a short Induction Course (either day or weekend), a Basic Course, an Intermediate Course and an Advanced Course.

Short induction course
All members must (except in the most exceptional circum-

stances) go through each stage of the linked scheme in order.
This means that before any student can attend a week course he
must attend a weekend or day course. At an Induction Course
the members study 'The Purpose and Structure of the Union'
using the Course Papers. An 'Any Questions Session' is held at
every Course that is run by the Union so that members can be
kept informed of current developments in every field. The Day
Courses are held on a Saturday between 10 a.m. and 5.30 p.m.,
generally in a comfortable hotel in a large town. During 1965,
about 420 members have attended one of 20 or so Day Courses.
Thirteen members have attended a Weekend Course. These
members attending an Induction Course will mainly be attending a trade union course for the first time.

Basic courses
Members who have attended an Induction Course may be
nominated by their Branches to attend a Basic week Course at
the Post Office Fellowship of Remembrance Centre at West-
gate-on-Sea, Kent. The members' pay and travelling expenses
are generally met from Branch funds. Special Leave (without
pay) is granted by the Post Office for the purpose of attending.
The General Fund of the Union meets the expense of tuition,
accommodation and books. It is a feature of Post Office Engineering Union Courses that the Union lends a copy of each book
used to each student. This means buying books in sets of 40. Two
Courses—attracting 65 members—have been held this year.
Tuition is given both by Workers' Educational Association
tutors, permanent Officers of the Union and members of the
National Executive Council. At these courses the students study
the National Trade Union Movement, the relationship of the
Post Office Engineering Union to the Civil Service, National
and International Trade Union Movement, the Art of the
Cinema and how to appraise literature critically, take notes,
write an essay and make a speech. Great emphasis is placed on
expression and participation. Before coming on a Course each
student is required—as a condition of acceptance—to answer a

questionnaire on the Structure of the Union. During the Course each student writes an essay on the topic 'How far does the Structure of the Post Office Engineering Union meet the needs of its members?' These are marked by the Workers' Educational Association tutors and then commented on by Union Officers and National Executive Council members, responsible for organisational matters. Students also make a four minute speech on a topic which is controversial within the Union.

By arrangement with the British Film Institute, a film is introduced and shown on Sunday evening by a lecturer from the British Film Institute. On the Monday evening a discussion —conducted by the lecturer—takes place on the film. This has proved to be of great interest.

Intermediate course
Three Intermediate Courses have been held in 1965, which were attended by about 79 members. The same general arrangements apply to the Intermediate Course as to the Basic. The syllabus is, of course, different. The students before coming have to answer a questionnaire to show that they have read and understood selected passages of J. Blondel's 'Voters, Parties and Leaders'. At the course the members study some British Social and Political Institutions including social class and the distribution of income, electors and elections, parties and pressure groups, the 'Establishment', and the press and T.V. An essay on the topic: 'How important is "class" in British politics? What can be done to reduce its influence?' is written by each student. Each student also makes a speech of four minutes. This study is done under the guidance of Workers' Educational Association tutors. Union Officers and National Executive Council members give lectures on the Union's Personal Services, the Social Role of the Union, the Structure of the Post Office and the future problems of the Union. A session on 'The Art of the Painter' is also included.

Advanced course

One Advanced Course for 35 members has been held in 1965. Advanced Courses have been held in the past at both Ruskin College and Rewley House, Oxford. The topic of this week course is wages. Students are asked to prepare a policy document on the topic 'What are the best methods in the circumstances of today for raising the real pay level of members of the Post Office Engineering Union?' They are required to answer a questionnaire after reading three books, i.e. 'Royal Commission on the Civil Service, 1953–1955', the 'Fawley Productivity Agreements' by Allan Flanders and the Trades Union Congress pamphlet on 'Productivity, Prices and Incomes', before attending the Course. In order to assist them write their policy document, the Workers' Educational Association lecturers and members of the Union's Wages and Allowances Committee take sessions on wage determination in the Civil Service, productivity bargaining and national incomes policy. The policy documents are marked by the Workers' Educational Association tutors and discussed in a final session with members of the Wages and Allowances Committee. Students at this course also make a seven minute speech supporting a proposition selected from the agenda of the Annual Conference and a four minute speech opposing another proposition. A visit to the theatre and subsequent discussion has been arranged with the Royal Shakespeare Theatre. It will be seen that there is a fairly common pattern in the linked Week Courses. This pattern deliberately excludes all elements of training (with the exception of the making of speeches). Training programmes are being developed separately.

Impact of linked courses

In September 1965 a questionnaire was sent out to 105 students who had attended the four linked Courses. These members have gone through a programme which was similar in many respects to that which has been outlined above. The Intermediate

Course that they had attended, however, was very different in that social and political institutions were not discussed. Less emphasis was placed on written work. To date, 67 students have replied. It is interesting to note that of these, 17 are Branch Secretaries, 8 Branch Chairmen and 4 Financial Secretaries. Only three hold no Branch office. Of the Branch Secretaries, Chairmen and Financial Secretaries, 24 have taken higher office after attending Union Courses. Twelve of those who replied are active in political parties, 26 others are engaged in active work in other organisations (particularly the church) and 27 have no officerships in outside organisations. Only 17 of those who replied have taken no other general Courses than those organised by the Union and the Post Office. The bulk of those who have attended have interested themselves in the educational work of the Workers' Educational Association and the Trades Union Congress. From the replies it is clear that the Courses give members more confidence and help them to express themselves more readily and clearly. As a result of the Courses, members appear to become better informed of what the Union is doing and in some cases more critical.

Training
Branch secretaries' courses
In 1965, two Branch Secretaries' Courses were held. These were attended by 45 Branch Secretaries. It is now our practice to invite all newly elected Branch Secretaries, within six months of their election, to a three-day Course held at the moment at Union headquarters. During this Course, guidance is given by permanent officers of the Union and members of the National Executive Council on the importance of Branch Secretaries, meetings, minutes and filing, discipline cases, the art of negotiating, industrial injuries law and the provision of the Union's Personal Services. Role playing plays an important part of the Course and is popular with the students.

Financial secretaries' courses

During 1965, four Day Courses for Branch Financial Secretaries have been introduced. Ninety-eight Branches have responded by nominating their Financial Secretary for a place on the Courses to be held in Sheffield, London, Edinburgh and Bristol. These Financial Secretaries will receive tuition from the General Treasurer or a National Organiser and a Trustee. The subjects to be covered will include the 'Financial Arrangements of the Union', the 'Branch Fund' and 'Deductions from Source'.

Political courses

Two Political Courses, attracting 42 members, were arranged at Birmingham and London during 1965. These were open to all members of the Union. The lecturers were all drawn from within the Union and included members on the Parliamentary Panel, members of the National Executive Council and permanent Officers of the Union. The subjects covered were the Union's place in the Labour Party, problems facing the Government, the National Plan, Education Policy and Housing Policy. The Courses are concerned more with the broad background to policy making rather than with the Labour Party's programme. A residential weekend Political Course was held in Northern Ireland which attracted 33 members. This dealt with the Northern Ireland economy.

Full-time scholarship to Ruskin College

Provision is made for the award of a Charles Howard Smith Scholarship each year. These enable a member to study full time for three terms at Ruskin College. The amount of the scholarship varies according to the domestic circumstances of the individual awarded it. This was not, however, awarded in 1965.

Educational facilities obtained outside the union

Several members are awarded Scholarships by the Trades

Union Congress each year to attend courses held at their Training College and Summer Schools. Members are also sent to the Labour Party Summer School. Many members take advantage of the Correspondence Courses now administered by the Trades Union Congress. They also attend, without incurring any expense, courses on trade unionism and related subjects organised by the Trades Union Congress Education Service. Certain evening class fees (Workers' Educational Association University Extra-mural) are refunded by the Union. In addition, the Union has organised joint schools with Unions abroad. A group of young members were sent to Germany in 1965 and we will be receiving some young Europeans here this year.

Conclusion

It will be seen that strenuous efforts are being made to educate the membership of the Union and train its Officers.

There is only one major barrier to a very great advance and that is our inability to meet the cost of paying wages and salaries. At the moment, students attending the Linked Courses receive their pay from Branch funds. In the case of small Branches, assistance is given from the General Fund. Branch Secretaries when attending Branch Secretaries' Courses are paid from the General Fund. Many Branches find that they cannot afford to send members on Union Courses—certainly not as many as are willing to attend. Likewise at headquarter level a restriction has had to be placed on the number and length of the training courses owing to the heavy cost of the payment of wages and salaries. If the Post Office were to grant Special Leave with pay to members attending Union Courses great benefits would accrue both to the Post Office and the Union.

SOURCE: *Evidence of the Post Office Engineering Union to the Royal Commission on Trade Unions and Employers' Associations* (1966), Appendix H (i), 80–3

12 TUC : TRAINING ON THE INDUSTRIAL RELATIONS ACT

Trade Union government and structure

The legislation seeks to interfere with the principles of trade union structure and government principally through the process of registration. The Chief Registrar is given wide powers to demand general or specific changes in union rule books. He may make investigations into a registered union's affairs, and may apply for a winding-up order against a union he believes to be insolvent.

The Registrar has no control at all over the affairs of an unregistered union. But the Act does seek to regulate the internal affairs of unregistered unions in two ways.

1. Principles are laid down in the Act to regulate the conduct of 'organisations of workers' in relation to internal union discipline; voting in elections; admission to membership and resignation; participation in union meetings; nominations for union office and termination of membership. Members (or potential members, or ex-members) may raise grievances on these subjects in the Industrial Tribunals and possibly the NIRC. The Tribunals' attitude to such cases will be determined by the principles in the Act—the contravention of which would constitute an 'unfair industrial practice'.

2. The Act provides a new method for members to challenge their union about the application of union rules. It permits individuals to appeal to an Industrial Tribunal where a breach of the union's rules is alleged.

In addition the Act could undermine the Movement's own procedures for ensuring orderly inter-union relationships. By seeking to restrict severely a union's freedom of action in regard to membership questions, the Act could make the

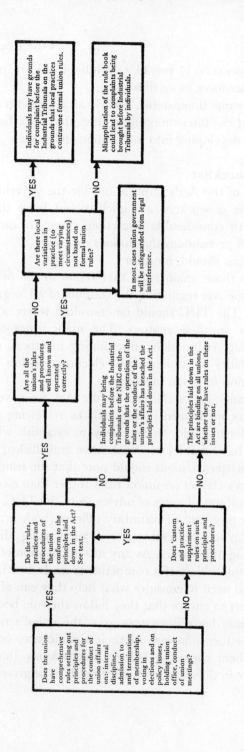

smooth operation of the TUC Bridlington Principles and Disputes Procedures more difficult.

At the same time, stable, orderly arrangements are essential to prevent the inter-union difficulties that arise because of the Act from developing into inter-union strife . . .

Action checklist

As many of the Act's implications for the government of 'organisations of workers' are unclear and leave the industrial courts with considerable discretion, there are only a limited number of precautions that unions can take.

All unions should, however:

Review those union rules that relate to the principles laid down in the Act regulating the conduct of all 'organisations of workers'. The TUC should be consulted where a union faces difficulties on these matters. The main issues covered are: membership, resignations, disciplining members, nominations and eligibility for union office, elections, ballots and voting, participation in union meetings.

The principles established in the Act for governing these matters are mentioned in the text. In reviewing the relevant union rules it might be necessary to establish whether local practices have developed which have embellished union rules on such matters. Unions should note that the issues dealt with by the Act's clauses on union rules (other than elections) have been the subject of notes of advice from the TUC.

Review problems of voluntary officers (both branch officers and workplace representatives) experiencing difficulties in interpreting union rules. As any mis-application of union rules could be the subject of a complaint to an Industrial Tribunal, unions will need to consider what help they can give to voluntary officers to ensure that they follow the rule book.

Sometimes lay officers transgress the union's rules because they are either unaware of their significance, or of how to operate them correctly. Where unions know that voluntary officers are in difficulty, assistance needs to be given, possibly in the form of guides and checklists on the necessary action that has to be taken on the issues covered by rules.

Training checklist

Training concerned with trade union government will probably be most effective where it concentrates on the efficient operation of the existing union constitution, thus minimising the possibility of legal challenges being made against the union on the grounds of the mis-application of union rules.

Advice should be given to officers and representatives whenever any changes are made to the rule book, to ensure the rapid implementation of changes in line with the new rules.

Information should be supplied to officers and representatives on the precise importance of ensuring a correct application of the rule book.

Training should accompany the introduction of any form of guides or checklists produced by the union to ensure the efficient and equitable application of union rules.

SOURCE: TUC Education Service. *Industrial Relations Act, TUC Training Analysis Kit* (1971), 23–6

(b) POLITICAL LOBBYING AND CAMPAIGNING

Trade unions are part of the political process. The TUC plays a particularly important role. It came into existence primarily to represent the views of its affiliated unions to government and to Parliament, to keep surveillance over intended legislation and to act as a pressure group to safeguard the interests of trade unionists and work people generally. Its annual report is to a large extent an account of the diverse matters which bring it into close contact with government. A traditional stance of the TUC is that, whatever party is in power, it remains independent and puts forward its own policies and ideas, however discomforting to the government of the day. Thus in 1969 and 1970 it opposed the Labour Govern-

*ment's prices and incomes policy and helped to bring it to an end. Simi-
larly, the Conservative Government's Industrial Relations Bill was
opposed and at a Special Congress in March 1971 a policy of non-
registration and non-co-operation was agreed.*

*Yet it is not as simple as that. The Labour Party came into existence in
the first place through trade union initiative and its constitution
clearly spells out the formal significance of the trade union movement.
Moreover, since the Trade Union Act of 1913, as amended by the Industrial Relations Act 1971, the role of individual unions within the
political process has been accepted and legitimised. The law permits
unions to apply to political purposes funds raised and expended according
to certain safeguards. Sixty-seven unions are affiliated to the Labour
Party. None is affiliated to the other major political parties, whose constitutions in any case do not allow for membership by organisations.
Many trade unionists do not support the Labour Party, as the surveys of
voting at general elections show quite clearly, and there are organisations
for trade unionists within the Conservative and Liberal parties. But it is
right and proper in the consideration of trade unions in politics to equate
their formal association with the Labour Party.*

*Unions sponsor and provide financial support for candidates at both
local and parliamentary elections. The number of trade union MPs has
been declining in recent years, but unions still pay a great deal of attention to this area of activity. The report by Fred Lee gives an indication of
the work of one group of trade unionist MPs. Similarly, the report by the
Union of Shop, Distributive and Allied Workers of its opposition to the
Sunday Trading Bill in 1968 illustrates union activity in Parliament by
union-sponsored MPs.*

*This report also refers to 'an active campaign in opposition to the
Bill', including protest meetings throughout the country. Unions, that is
to say, are ready to undertake political activity outside the established
political machinery and perhaps none has been as significant as the
TUC's campaign against the Industrial Relations legislation since 1970.
The protest march through London in 1971 is described in the TUC's
report as 'the largest and most representative demonstration against
government legislation to take place in Great Britain in the twentieth
century'. This was clearly an attempt by the unions to alter proposed*

legislation; in this there was nothing unusual—all pressure groups do it, even using the same non-parliamentary methods. The unions were un- successful; the Act was passed, but opposition to it continued. The Times *in an editorial, 'Yes, We are in danger' on 28 July 1972, lamented the threats to democracy including that which came 'from the refusal of the trade union movement to accept the existence of a law covering trade union affairs, and industrial relations, or indeed to accept the legitimacy of passing any such law, whatever it might be'.* This was at the end of a week of hectic activity when the General Council took the unprecedented step of calling a general strike—the first since 1926—over the issue of five trade unionists imprisoned for contempt of court.* The Times *naturally enough deplored the unions' attitudes and actions, but at the same time castigated the government for failing 'to understand the rule of consent', and for failing to seek 'wholeheartedly and consistently . . . the consent of those parts of the nation which disagreed with them'. In such a situation it may well be argued that the only way to effect change is to adopt extra-parliamentary political action.*

13 TRADE UNION ACT, 1913 : POLITICAL FUND

3.—(1) The funds of a trade union shall not be applied, either directly or in conjunction with any other trade union, associa- tion, or body, or otherwise indirectly, in the furtherance of the political objects to which this section applies (without prejudice to the furtherance of any other political objects), unless the furtherance of those objects has been approved as an object of the union by a resolution for the time being in force passed on a ballot of the members of the union taken in accordance with this Act for the purpose by a majority of the members voting; and where such a resolution is in force, unless rules, to be approved, whether the union is registered or not, by the Registrar of Friendly Societies, are in force providing—

(a) That any payments in the furtherance of those objects are to be made out of a separate fund (in this Act referred to as the political fund of the union); and for the exemption in

---

* Some union reactions are given in Parts Four (c) and Seven.

accordance with this Act of any member of the union from any obligation to contribute to such a fund if he gives notice in accordance with this Act that he objects to contribute: and

(b) That a member who is exempt from the obligation to contribute to the political fund of the union shall not be excluded from any benefits of the union, or placed in any respect either directly or indirectly under any disability or at any disadvantage as compared with other members of the union (except in relation to the control or management of the political fund) by reason of his being so exempt, and that contribution to the political fund of the union shall not be made a condition for admission to the union . . .

(3) The political objects to which this section applies are the expenditure of money—

(a) On the payment of any expenses incurred either directly or indirectly by a candidate or prospective candidate for election to Parliament or to any public office, before, during, or after the election in connection with his candidature or election; or

(b) On the holding of any meeting or the distribution of any literature or documents in support of any such candidate or prospective candidate; or

(c) On the maintenance of any person who is a Member of Parliament or who holds a public office; or

(d) In connection with the registration of electors or the selection of a candidate for Parliament or any public office; or

(e) On the holding of political meetings of any kind, or on the distribution of political literature or political documents of any kind, unless the main purpose of the meetings or of the distribution of the literature or documents is the furtherance of statutory objects within the meaning of this Act.

The expression 'public office' in this section means the office of member of any county, county borough, district, or parish council or board of guardians, or of any public body who have power to raise money, either directly or indirectly, by means of a rate.

(4) A resolution under this section approving political objects as an object of the union shall take effect as if it were a rule of the union and may be rescinded in the same manner and subject to the same provisions as such a rule . . .

4.—(1) A ballot for the purposes of this Act shall be taken in accordance with rules of the union to be approved for the purpose, whether the union is registered or not, by the Registrar of Friendly Societies, but the Registrar of Friendly Societies shall not approve any such rules unless he is satisfied that every member has an equal right, and, if reasonably possible, a fair opportunity of voting, and that the secrecy of the ballot is properly secured.

(2) If the Registrar of Friendly Societies is satisfied, and certifies, that rules for the purpose of a ballot under this Act or rules made for other purposes of this Act which require approval by the Registrar, have been approved by a majority of members of a trade union, whether registered or not, voting for the purpose, or by a majority of delegates of such a trade union voting at a meeting called for the purpose, those rules shall have effect as rules of the union, notwithstanding that the provisions of the rules of the union as to the alteration of rules or the making of new rules have not been complied with.

5.—(1) A member of a trade union may at any time give notice, in the form set out in the Schedule to this Act or in a form to the like effect, that he objects to contribute to the political fund of the union, and, on the adoption of a resolution of the union approving the furtherance of political objects as an object of the union, notice shall be given to the members of the union acquainting them that each member has a right to be exempt from contributing to the political fund of the union, and that a form of exemption notice can be obtained by or on behalf of a member either by application at or by post from the head office or any branch office of the union or the office of the Registrar of Friendly Societies.

Any such notice to members of the union shall be given in accordance with rules of the union approved for the purpose by the Registrar of Friendly Societies, having regard in each case to the existing practice and to the character of the union.

(2) On giving notice in accordance with this Act of his objection to contribute, a member of the union shall be exempt, so long as his notice is not withdrawn, from contributing to the political fund of the union as from the first day of January next after the notice is given, or, in the case of a notice given within one month after the notice given to members under this section on the adoption of a resolution approving the furtherance of political objects, as from the date on which the member's notice is given.

SOURCE: Trade Union Act, 1913 (2 & 3 Geo 5, c 30). The Industrial Relations Act 1971 (c 72), Schedule 8 amends the above sections as follows: In sections 3 to 6, for the words 'a trade union', wherever they occur, there shall be substituted the words 'an organisation to which this Act applies', and for the word 'union' or the words 'a union', wherever it or they occur (except as part of the expression 'trade union'), there shall be substituted the words 'organisation to which this Act applies' or 'an organisation to which this Act applies', as the case may be; and for the words 'Registrar of Friendly Societies' there shall be substituted the words 'the registrar'.

14 THE CONSTITUTION OF THE LABOUR PARTY
. . .

Clause II. Membership
1. There shall be two classes of members, namely:
(a) Affiliated Members.
(b) Individual Members.
2. Affiliated Members shall consist of:
Trade Unions affiliated to the Trades Union Congress or recognised by the General Council of the Trades Union Congress as *bona fide* Trade Unions . . .

Clause III. Conditions of membership

1. Each affiliated organisation must
(a) Accept the Programme, Principles, and Policy of the Party.
(b) Agree to conform to the Constitution and Standing Orders of the Party.
(c) Submit its Political Rules to the National Executive Committee ...
3. Each individual member must ...
(b) If eligible, be a member of a Trade Union affiliated to the Trades Union Congress or recognised by the General Council of the Trades Union Congress as a *bona fide* Trade Union ...

Clause IV. Party objects
National
...

2. To co-operate with the General Council of the Trades Union Congress, or other Kindred Organisations, in joint political or other action in harmony with the Party Constitution and Standing Orders ...

Clause VI. The party conference
...

2. The Party Conference shall be constituted as follows:
(a) Delegates duly appointed by each affiliated Trade Union or other organisations to the number of one delegate for each 5,000 members or part thereof on whom affiliation fees, by-election insurance premiums and any levies due were paid for the year ending December 31 preceding the Conference.
(b) Delegates duly appointed by Constituency Labour Parties (or Trades Councils acting as such) to the number of one delegate for each 5,000 individual members or part thereof on whom affiliation fees, by-election insurance premiums and any levies due were paid for the year ending December 31 preceding the Conference; where the individual and

affiliated women's membership exceeds 2,500 an additional
woman delegate may be appointed; where the membership
of Young Socialists Branches within a constituency is 200 or
more an additional Young Socialist delegate may be
appointed.

(c) Delegates duly appointed by Central Labour Parties or
Trades Councils acting as such in Divided Boroughs not
exceeding one for each Central Labour Party provided the
affiliation fees, by-election insurance premiums and any
levies due have been paid for the year ending December 31
preceding the Conference.

15 AMALGAMATED ENGINEERING UNION
THE AEU PARLIAMENTARY GROUP

by Bro Rt Hon Fred Lee, MP, chairman

The AEU Group of Labour MPs is now celebrating 25 years of
active life, and a few facts about it may not be out of place.
After the General Election of July, 1945 there were 3 AEU
sponsored MPs in the Commons. They were David Kirkwood,
Sir Robert Young and myself. In those days aspiring members
had to win a place on the panel of AEU Parliamentary Candidates through a national ballot of members of the union. To
stand much chance of success in this, one had to be pretty well
known at national level in the union and to come from a large
engineering centre. In consequence, many very able members
who had given outstanding service to the AEU, found it impossible to secure the union's financial support for a parliamentary candidature. My two colleagues having reached the
veteran stage, I took it upon myself to seek out members of the
Parliamentary Labour Party who, although in the Commons as
constituency supported MPs, were also AEU members, who
were prepared to render service to the union in their new
capacity as Members of Parliament. I eventually came up with
six of these and was able to convene a meeting between them
and the three sponsored members.

The names of the six will still ring a bell with many older AEU members. They were: Walter Ayles, Harry Berry, Charles Hobson, Bert Medland, George Pargiter and John Forman. John agreed to help until we got on to our feet, despite the fact that he was sponsored by the Co-op.

We then set about the task of establishing a working relationship between ourselves and the Executive Council of the AEU —a vital consideration, if we were to fulfil our objective of providing maximum assistance in contacts with Government, while avoiding the danger of taking up issues upon which they were already engaged through industrial channels. Jack Tanner and Ben Gardner were as keen about getting this right as we were, and agreement that we would function only on cases referred to us by Executive Council was reached and is still the basis of our joint arrangements.

Regular quarterly meetings between the two bodies were initiated with both placing on the agenda items of importance for decision and action. At our suggestion, Executive Council took up with the Rules Revision Committee the question of changing the system of having a national ballot to secure membership of the panel of parliamentary candidates, and this was changed to nomination by District Committees and Executive Council, and acceptance by National Committee—a method which has yielded much better results.

The maximum number we have had in the Group was 17, during the 1966–1970 Parliament—one more than the present figure.

The arrangements by which our union trains and examines its new candidates in order to fit them for life at Westminster are, in my opinion, the best ever devised by any trade union. We have never tried to use the prospect of financial support as the major incentive for Constituency Labour Parties to accept our nominees, and the work of the Group has benefited appreciably as a result of this policy.

Over the years our MPs have taken the initiative in successful attempts to improve industrial legislation, such as the Factory

Acts, Workmen's Compensation, Industrial Injuries Acts, Employers' Liability (Compulsory Insurance) Bill 1968–9, and many other improvements of great benefit to factory workers, which are now on the Statute Book.

We have played a prominent part in the work of the Trade Union Group of the Parliamentary Labour Party and have provided it with a number of its officials.

When the Labour Party has formed the Government, some of our members have been called to ministerial positions of considerable importance, including membership of the Cabinet, and, in Opposition we have had Front Bench spokesmen on a wide variety of subjects.

The number of cases referred to us by Executive Council on which we have secured satisfaction for the Union, must run into many thousands, and we have lectured at the Union's Summer Schools, etc to a large number of AEU members who have been desirous of learning more about national problems and the working of the British parliamentary institutions.

Our members have not confined themselves to purely industrial subjects. We have become an important cross-section of the Parliamentary Labour Party with points of view on practically every subject which has been debated in Parliament. Every one of our MPs has graduated through the Shop Stewards Movement, or through work on national, district and branch committees, and we try to bring to our work in the Commons the results of our experience in the workshop.

Members of Parliament are not delegates from any organisation, including their constituency parties. They are representatives of the people as a whole and, inevitably, policy issues arise during the life of any Parliament on which they must use their own judgment.

Looking back over a quarter of a century of membership of the House of Commons, and over a similar period as an official of the AEU Group, I am agreeably surprised at the degree of unanimity which has existed among the Members of the

Group, and also between the Group as a whole, the policy making body of the Union and Executive Council.

I do not claim that, as yet, our organisation is as effective as we all desire it to be. I do claim that we are the most efficient grouping on the political side of the work of any trade union, and I believe that the benefits our work brings to the members of the union as a whole, are far greater than even those of us who pioneered it, could have hoped for.

Here's to the next twenty-five years!

SOURCE: *AEU Journal* (August 1970), 37, No 8, 346

16 DRAUGHTSMEN'S AND ALLIED TECHNICIANS ASSOCIATION : LOBBYING PARLIAMENT

Those who studied the election results will be aware that DATA's three sponsored MPs, Joe Ashton, Ted Bishop and Albert Booth were all returned.

It was not a belief that the House of Commons can solve our problems which prompted the Executive Committee to produce a guide on lobbying. The knowledge that this activity is often carried out as part of wider campaigns prompted an examination with our MPs' advice, on the way to achieve the best results. The resulting statement is reproduced below.

Members frequently find that Government or Parliamentary influence or investigation may be necessary in their relationship with employers and send deputations to meet DATA MPs in Parliament.

This is a time honoured tradition which is a valuable contact and can result in favourable publicity and pressure being placed on employers or Government.

Recent lobbies to Parliament have not had the maximum impact because of lack of co-ordination and information.

The three DATA MPs are only too anxious to help members,

but unless the necessary ammunition is given to them they are
at a disadvantage, and therefore it is essential that the following
procedure should be observed:

(1) Head Office, Divisional Office and the MPs must be informed seven days in advance, and it is advised that the
MPs for the area concerned should also be approached.
MP's offices are frequently not in the House of Commons
and often they are on Parliamentary business outside
London or in their constituencies. Members should also
ensure, as necessary depending on the subject matter, full
consultation and co-ordination with the other trade
unionists directly involved.

(2) Lobbyists should send in advance a brief giving facts and
figures concerning their dispute and indicate whether this
is for press release or not, with copies to the Divisional
Organiser concerned with Head Office, and bring spare
copies with them when they arrive for further distribution.

(3) The best time for lobbying Parliament is in the morning.
The press and interview rooms are more available then and
it is easier to get space in the evening newspaper. This also
prevents the awkward situation of MPs waiting to ask a
question or speak on another important topic on DATA's
behalf suddenly being called out and forfeiting their opportunity.

This guide is designed to help DATA and other trade unions
to make their influence felt to the maximum degree.

SOURCE: *DATA Journal* (August 1970), 25

17 UNION OF SHOPS, DISTRIBUTIVE AND ALLIED WORKERS : SUNDAY TRADING

A Private Member's Bill was introduced in the House of
Lords by Lord Derwent to amend the Shops Act, 1950–1965;
in relation to the provisions as to trading on Sundays and for

related purposes thereto. An amended No. 2 Bill subsequently came before the House of Commons at the end of May.

One of the main objectives of this Bill was to make provision for the registration by the local authority of shops wholly or mainly engaged in the sale of food or drink in order that they may be open for business at any time on any Sunday and also sell on a Sunday any articles forming part of their regular stock.

An active campaign in opposition to the Bill was mounted by the Union in association with the Union's branches and in collaboration with the Union's Panel of Members of Parliament.

The co-operation of branches was sought for the initiation of maximum activity within the localities in opposition to the Bill by the organising of protest meetings, approaches to the members of Parliament for the local Constituencies, contacting Trades Councils and securing the widest possible measure of support and publicity for the Union's viewpoint.

Branches responded magnificently to this request. Successful and well-attended meetings of shop workers were held throughout most parts of England and Wales, extensive Press, radio and television coverage was obtained publicising the Union's case in opposition to the Bill, and commitments of support were secured from Constituency Members of Parliament, Trades Councils, Trade and Religious organisations and other bodies.

In the House of Commons, close liaison and consultations were maintained with the Union's Panel of Members of Parliament, and activities co-ordinated directed to ensuring that each time the Bill came before the House, it failed to secure a Second Reading.

Under Parliamentary procedure, all uncompleted legislation falls at the end of each session. The appropriate session of Parliament ended on 26th July, by which date the Bill had failed to receive the consent of Parliament for a Second Reading and consequently fell.

Whilst the Shops (Sunday Trading) (No. 2) Bill as a legislative measure has, as a result of the Union's activities, been

D

killed, the probability cannot be ignored, occasioned by the very real anomalies relating to the Sunday Trading provisions which exist in the current Shops Act, that there will be a return to this subject in some future session of Parliament.

SOURCE: USDAW. *22nd Annual Report* (1968), 21–2

18 TUC : PRICES AND INCOMES LEGISLATION

(381)

In October 1968 the General Council considered a letter from the Secretary of State for Employment and Productivity in which she said that she wished to enter into consultation with the TUC, CBI and NBPI about the future of incomes policy after the present statutory powers had elapsed at the end of 1969. The General Council took the view that such discussions should be on the basis of defined objectives related to the economic situation and they wrote accepting the invitation, but suggesting that the best time would be after the General Council had examined the future of incomes policy in the context of their 1969 Economic Review. . .

(382) Government proposals

In February [1969] the General Council reviewed the provisions of the existing Prices and Incomes Acts and considered whether, taking into account the views expressed by the 1968 Congress, they should advocate the outright repeal of the legislation as a whole or confine their demands to the wages and salaries aspects. They decided that, at least initially, they should adopt the latter course, and that, in order to clarify the issues they should as a first step seek legal opinion on what amendments this would require to the Acts.

While this legal opinion was being obtained, the Government announced, during the Parliamentary debate on the Budget, that it proposed to allow the 1967 and 1968 Acts to expire at the end of 1969 and to revert to the powers contained in Part II of the 1966 Act. This would enable the Government to impose a standstill of up to three months on a reference to the National Board for Prices and Incomes and would provide for penalties on trade unions and employers who took or threatened to take action to induce an employer to break the standstill. The Government promised that full consultation would take place on the content of a White Paper on the principles of incomes policy, which it proposed to issue later in the year. Counsel took this proposal into account in drawing up his Opinion.

In June the General Council examined this issue in the light of the Government's announcement and of Counsel's Opinion. They agreed that it would be desirable to defer discussing the future of incomes legislation with the Government until after the outcome of discussions which were then taking place with the Government about the proposed Industrial Relations Bill. They recognised however that it would be necessary for them to clarify their views on this matter well before discussing incomes policy with the Government, and decided that the starting point for their examination should be the proposition that Part II of the 1966 Act, containing standstill powers and penalties, should be repealed, but that Part I of the 1966 Act (which establishes the NBPI on a statutory basis and gives it power to consider references but does not provide for the imposition of a standstill) might be retained. They took the preliminary view that this was likely to be compatible both with their opposition to penal sanctions on trade unions and with the views of many unions that the NBPI is capable of performing a useful and constructive role and should be maintained.

When the General Council gave further consideration to the situation at their July meeting, they confirmed that they should press the Government to repeal Part II of the 1966 Act, together with the 1967 and 1968 Acts. They decided to seek a meeting with the Secretary of State for Employment and Productivity to put their case against the retention of Part II of the 1966 Act, and to ascertain the Government's intentions in relation to the publication of a new White Paper . . .

(420) Prices and incomes legislation

In July 1969 the General Council met the Secretary of State for Employment and Productivity with the aim of ascertaining her intentions in relation to Part II of the Prices and Incomes Act 1966 (which would enable the Government to delay wage settlements for up to three months while a reference to the National Board for Prices and Incomes was being examined). They informed her that the TUC was opposed to the maintenance and extension of these powers. The Employment Secretary replied that the Government's position with regard to legislation had been made clear by the Chancellor in his 1969 Budget statement and amplified by her the following day: the Government were committed to reactivating Part II of the 1966 Act when the present powers over wages embodied in the 1967 and 1968 Acts came to an end at the end of 1969. She would, however, be pleased to discuss any proposals the General Council might wish to make on the longer term future of prices and incomes policy in the context of discussions on the Government's proposed White Paper.

At a special meeting before the 1969 Congress the General Council decided to reaffirm their fundamental opposition of Part II of the 1966 Act, but to suspend judgment on the question whether Part I of the Act, which established the National Board for Prices and Incomes on a statutory basis, might be maintained; on the latter point they would wish to discuss with the Government its intentions in relation to Part II and the future development of incomes policy.

The 1969 Congress carried a motion which re-affirmed opposition to anti-trade union legislation and demanded the total repeal of the 1966 Act.

The General Council met the Employment Secretary again in October in order to inform her of the Congress decision on legislation and to ascertain the Government's intentions in relation to the future of their policy generally. The Employment Secretary said that she was considering the extent of powers which would be necessary in the future and she promised to report the views of the TUC to her Government colleagues.

(421) White paper

In December the General Council met the Employment Secretary to discuss a draft of the White Paper *Productivity, Prices and Incomes Policy after 1969*, which proposed a norm for wage increases of $2\frac{1}{2}$ to $4\frac{1}{2}$ per cent based on a projected increase in national output of 3 per cent per annum; proposed that a new Commission for Industry and Manpower should be established by merging the NBPI and the Monopolies Commission; and stated that Part II of the 1966 Act would be brought into force for a year beginning on January 1, 1970, but that the Government hoped that it would not be necessary to perpetuate the delaying powers in new legislation. The General Council said that they did not wish to discuss the draft in detail as they did not wish the Government to think that there was any prospect of the General Council endorsing the draft White Paper in whole or in part. They argued that any attempt to impose a norm of $2\frac{1}{2}$ to $4\frac{1}{2}$ per cent was doomed to failure, except in so far as backward employers could impose it on weakly organised groups of workers. They repeated their view that the Prices and Incomes Act should be repealed and they asked if it was the Government's intention to drop statutory powers over wages when the new legislation setting up the Commission for Industry and Manpower was introduced. The Employment Secretary noted the General Council's view on the norm and the legislation. She said that she could not at this stage go further than repeat the White Paper's statement that the Government hoped it would not be necessary to perpetuate delaying powers in the new legislation: a decision on this would depend on the economic circumstances at the time and particularly on whether there was inflationary pressure.

The White Paper was published in December 1969 and the General Council issued a statement to the effect that they did not regard the proposals in it as acceptable to the trade union

Movement, because the policy envisaged would continue to be based on statutory interference in collective bargaining, which was at best irrelevant and would at worst hinder the development of a coherent policy for collective bargaining and incomes, and jeopardise good industrial relations. The General Council did not accept that the proposed norm—based upon an unduly cautious estimate of the nation's productive potential—provided a realistic policy basis. They pointed to the conspicuous contrast in the White Paper between the detailed treatment of wages and the absence of any reference to high salaries, unearned incomes and the incomes of highly paid professional and self-employed persons; and between the emphasis given to wages and that given to prices, in spite of the criticism that the NBPI itself had made of the effectiveness of prices policy. The statement concluded, however, that the General Council would welcome a longer-term approach which provided a radically different framework from the one into which the Government had hitherto forced an essentially restrictive incomes policy, and maintained that if this was the Government's intention it could count on the co-operation of the trade union Movement...

The Government confirmed in March that the proposed legislation to establish a Commission for Industry and Manpower would repeal the 1966 Prices and Incomes Act.

SOURCES: TUC. General Council's Report to the 1969 Congress, paras 381–2; and Report to the 1970 Congress, paras 420–1

19 TUC : CAMPAIGN AGAINST THE INDUSTRIAL RELATIONS BILL

(148)

The purpose of the General Council's campaign against the Industrial Relations Bill was two-fold. First, it was intended to explain clearly to all active trade unionists the dangers to the trade union Movement contained in the Government's legislation, to inform them of the reasons for the TUC's opposition to it, and to enlist their active participation in opposing it. Second, it was aimed at influencing public opinion generally against the proposals, in an attempt to persuade the Government to reconsider its intentions.

Conference on campaign strategy

As a first step the General Council decided to invite the principal officers of all affiliated unions to a conference to discuss policy in relation to the legislation and the strategy of the campaign of opposition. This was held in Congress House on November 12.

Training of union officers

In their initial consideration of the campaign, the General Council decided that it was essential that all union full-time officials should be equipped with the TUC's case against the legislation in a form which would enable them to explain to their membership the nature of the legislation and the reasons for trade union opposition to it.

Accordingly they arranged for a series of weekend conferences to be held for union full-time officers to acquaint them with the use of teaching notes and diagrams about the legislation which had been prepared in the TUC office. Details of this aspect of the campaign are given in Section F of this Report.

Regional and local meetings

In order to rally trade union opposition to the legislation and to provide an opportunity for the TUC's case to be explained in detail in a number of regional centres, the General Council decided to organise nine regional conferences in the first two months of 1971. These were held in London, Newcastle, Glasgow, Leeds, Liverpool, Cardiff, Bristol, Manchester and Birmingham. There was a capacity audience at each conference.

The TUC also offered to provide speakers on the Bill for meetings organised by trades councils and trade union branches and the TUC co-operated in arranging 118 meetings on this basis. Many hundreds of other meetings were arranged by unions and trades councils.

National demonstrations

The General Council considered that January 12 and February 21 should be set aside as days for national demonstrations against the Bill. For January 12 they invited all affiliated unions to organise local meetings about the legislation during meal breaks and after working hours, and to send representatives to a national rally at the Albert Hall in London in the evening. Several million workers took part in the local meetings during the day. The Albert Hall Rally in the evening was addressed by the Leader of the Opposition, Mr. Harold Wilson, Professor Wedderburn of London University and the TUC General Secretary.

For February 21 the General Council organised a national demonstration against the Bill which took the form of a march through London from Hyde Park Corner to Trafalgar Square and the Embankment. An estimated 140,000 people from all sections of the trade union Movement took part. It was the largest and most representative demonstration against Government legislation to take place in Great Britain in the twentieth century.

Petition

The General Council decided to organise a national petition, addressed to the House of Commons, calling for the withdrawal of the Bill. Supplies of petition forms were delivered to trades councils and union head offices by January 20. Because of the postal dispute, both the further distribution, and subsequent collection, of petition forms were severely impeded. Nevertheless, the petition obtained 549,391 signatures and was presented to the House of Commons on March 24, the day before the Industrial Relations Bill was given its Third Reading. On the same day a lobby of MPs took place calling for the Bill's withdrawal.

Advertising

In order to inform public opinion generally of the reasons for their opposition to the Bill the General Council decided to place advertisements in a number of national and provincial newspapers criticising some of the Bill's major aspects. A research survey indicated a high level of readership.

After consultations with an advertising agency the advertisements were placed in the *Daily Mirror*, *The Sun*, *The Guardian*, *Morning Star*, *The Times* and the *Daily Express*, in 21 provincial newspapers and in *Tribune*. Three advertisements were inserted —on January 11, February 4 and February 18—at a total cost of £51,000. The collective readership of the newspapers in which the advertisements were placed was approximately 30 million.

Publications and other publicity material

During the campaign a number of publications were produced attacking aspects of the Government's proposals which were circulated widely within the trade union Movement and elsewhere. Reference to these is made in Section J of this Report. In addition the TUC distributed a seven-minute film by the Freeprop Films Group satirising the Bill; produced a gramophone record containing a message by the TUC general secretary, *Time to Think Again* on one side, and a calypso *Co-operate not Legislate* by Horace James' Steel Band on the other; and distributed a 17-minute colour film of the February 21st Demonstration—also made by Freeprop Films—entitled *March*.

Advice to trades councils

In November all trades councils were advised by the General Council about the purpose of the campaign and how they might arrange campaign events in their area. A circular suggested twelve possible activities that trades councils might organise locally to rally trade union opposition to the legislation.

SOURCE: TUC. General Council's Report to the 1971 Congress, para 148, 96–8

20 TUC : CONGRESS MAKES POLICY ON THE INDUSTRIAL RELATIONS ACT

1 Registration

Affiliated unions shall be strongly advised not to become registered under the Act and before any union decides to apply to be entered on the provisional register, or to take any steps to remain on the provisional register, or thereafter to seek full registration, it shall inform the General Council of its reasons for doing so, and give the General Council the opportunity to express a view;

The General Council shall be empowered to render such assistance as it considers justified to a union which encounters difficulties as a result of not registering;

2 Repeal of the act

The General Council shall seek from the Parliamentary Labour Party an explicit and unconditional assurance on repeal of the Act.

3 Collective agreements

Affiliated unions should take steps to ensure that they do not enter into legally binding collective agreements and that any agreements which already exist or are currently being concluded should contain an adequate clause excluding legal enforcement;

Affiliated unions shall not apply for a CIR reference relating to procedure agreements, shall not co-operate with the CIR, and should use all lawful means to persuade employers not to apply to the NIRC for a legally binding order or to secure the revocation of any order that might be made.

4 The Bridlington principles and the TUC disputes procedure

The General Council will support affiliated unions who take steps to maintain and strengthen trade union organisation and existing TUC procedures;

Affiliated unions shall continue to observe strictly the requirements of the Bridlington Principles and the TUC Disputes Procedure, and shall consult the TUC if they find themselves in difficulties between the conflicting requirements of the Bill and the Bridlington Principles in respects of the admission of applicants or the exclusion or resignation of members;

An affiliated union shall not apply to an employer for recognition rights in respect of any grade or grades of worker in any establishment where any other affiliated union has membership in those grades without referring the question firstly to that union, and in the event of disagreement between the unions, to the TUC;

An affiliated union shall not, in any circumstances, apply to the NIRC for recognition rights or an agency shop;

Affiliated unions shall not co-operate with the NIRC and the CIR.

5 Statutory bodies

Trade unionists shall be advised not to serve on the National Industrial Relations Court;

In the event of the Bill becoming an Act, trade unionists should withdraw from the employed persons' panel of Industrial Tribunals;

Trade unionists shall be advised not to serve on the Commission on Industrial Relations, and affiliated unions shall not co-operate with it;

There should be no change in the present practice of affiliated unions with regard to references or claims under existing Acts to the Industrial Arbitration Board (the new title of the present

Industrial Court) and trade unionists should be advised to
continue to serve on that body.

6   Assistance to unions

The General Council shall be authorised to assist a union,
where they receive a request and are satisfied that assistance
from the Movement would be merited, to meet the costs of
defending an action taken against a union under the Industrial
Relations Act, and, in exceptional circumstances, to indemnify
the union against damages.

7   United action

Congress should concentrate its support behind the positive
recommendations in this Report and preserve its unity of purpose that has hitherto characterised the campaign of opposition.

SOURCE: TUC. General Council's Report to a Special Congress
on the Industrial Relations Bill, 1971

PART FOUR

Trade Union Methods 2

(c) COLLECTIVE BARGAINING

The focus of trade union activity is collective bargaining. Industrial relations consists largely of the creation and operation of mechanisms whereby the differences between employers and employees can be examined, discussed and resolved. The result of this form of activity is an agreement of some kind, written or not, which determines for the time being the wages, hours of work, conditions, <u>and whatever else the parties have agreed upon</u>. The underlined words are very important. There is in theory no topic, no situation affecting workers which could not be the subject of collective bargaining. Workers normally wish to negotiate about wages, holidays and so on, but questions of promotion, redundancy, and apparently trivial matters, such as a dispute in 1972 about the size of teacups used by workers in a Midlands factory, also occur. The secular extension of the area of negotiation might well begin to include such matters as finance and accountancy. The mineworkers' union was discussing the National Coal Board's pricing policy and its methods of depreciation in the 1950s. The limits to extension are set by the interests and desires of the unions, who may have no wish to be involved in many of them, and by management, which normally tries to prevent employees sharing in the decision making they have traditionally considered their prerogative.

Collective bargaining can be classified in a number of ways. One approach is to distinguish between process and substance. The first, the procedural aspect, consists of those agreements or understandings which lay down the rules of behaviour: who is to negotiate; when; where; on what subjects; how disputes are to be resolved. One view of industrial relations is that much progress and avoidance of conflict would result from improved procedures. The Commission on Industrial Relations was established as a result of the Donovan Commission's inquiries, with the function inter alia of encouraging such developments, especially at company and plant level. Most industries which undertake industry-wide bargaining possess procedural agreements. We print a section of the British Leyland Motor Company's procedure agreement, whose significance can be gauged by comparing its statement that 'no action or change shall be implemented until agreement has been reached . . .' with the long-drawn-out arguments about 'status quo' which by 1972 had led to the breakdown of the engineering industry's procedure agreement. The 'status quo' question relates to the claim by the unions that changes should not be put into operation until agreement is reached.

Substantive agreements contain the stuff of collective bargaining's outcome. They specify the wages to be paid, hours to be worked and so on. The national agreements in the railway industry are examples. The TGWU model for comprehensive plant agreements illustrates the point that an agreement may include both procedural and substantive sections. An example of a recent extension in bargaining is the British Actors' Equity Association agreement which aims to protect members in situations 'where nudity and/or acts of a sexual nature are required'. The Industrial Relations Act, as part of its tightening-up process, proposed that collective agreements should be legally binding, if the parties so wished. The TUC advised affiliated unions on the form of words which might be used to exclude them from the legal presumption that they were legally binding.

There are other ways of classifying collective bargaining. One is in terms of the level of activity: plant, company, industry, or national (TUC/CBI). Co-ordinated plant and company bargaining has been particularly important in extending both procedural and subject areas of collective bargaining. A further classification would consider all the various processes within it. A claim is made by the workers or a proposal comes from the management; there are discussions and negotiations. If no agreement is reached, some form of conciliation or arbitration may be used (sometimes with the aid of government agencies). Whatever the laid-down procedures, there may be overt industrial action at any stage. On the workers' side there may be a go-slow, a work to rule or a strike; on the employer's side, a lock-out or threat of dismissal. The long-term trend in industrial relations has been to create mechanisms to resolve disputes without recourse to overt action. In one sense this has happened. There were until the 'wages explosion' of 1970 very few official strikes in Britain. This remains true in terms of numbers of strikes, but official strikes are larger if measured in numbers of days lost.

During the 1960s there was much talk of 'disorder' in industrial relations, usually referring to the predominance of short, unpredictable, unofficial and often unconstitutional strikes. One aim of the Industrial Relations Act is to try to remedy this, but the obvious problem of the Act, in this context, is that it injects an additional element of disagreement. What is noticeable and fascinating is that after the events of early 1972, when the Act began to be operated in earnest and especially after the imprisonment of five dockworkers, a strong body of opinion began to move away from the extreme rigour of the Act. An editorial in The Times of 3 August 1972 was headed 'How the law should be Changed'. It argued among other things the virtues of conciliation, in this echoing a letter in the same issue from the Director of The Industrial Society, an employers' organisation. The previous day the TUC and the CBI had announced plans for establishing, from 1 September 1972, an independent conciliation service. A major object of the exercise will be to minimise the use of the Industrial Relations Act.

21 BRITISH LEYLAND MOTOR CORPORATION PROCEDURAL AGREEMENT

Procedure for settling issues
5.5 The management of change

The parties to this Agreement accept that the Corporation's ability to meet the aspirations of its employees depends substantially on its productive efficiency and that this, in turn, depends largely on the facility with which necessary changes of all kinds can be introduced in a harmonious manner. The Unions accept that management has the responsibility to manage. The Corporation, for its part, accepts that management should be conducted with due regard to the interests of its employees. There shall be included in procedure agreements in all establishments covered by this Agreement the following provisions for the management of change—

(a) It is accepted that effective joint consultation is vital to the successful and harmonious introduction of change.

(b) In order to avoid doubt as to their status it is desirable that all established customs and practices should, to the fullest extent practicable, be defined to the satisfaction of the parties who have to operate them, and codified in written agreements. Such agreements, together with any existing written agreements, will serve as agreed rules within which managers and employees can operate in the knowledge that their respective responsibilities, rights and obligations, in respect of the matters covered, are clearly laid down.

(c) Written agreements shall include a procedure for the maintenance of standards of conduct and a procedure for appeals against disciplinary decisions, and also a procedure for avoiding redundancies and handling unavoidable redundancies. These procedures shall be based on principles to be agreed by the Corporation and the Unions.

(d) Where an employee (or groups of employees) or the management of the establishment wishes—

  (i) to change the terms of a written agreement (provided that such change is not debarred by the agreement itself),

  (ii) to change an established custom and practice, or

  (iii) to introduce new terms,

a claim shall first be raised through the agreed procedure. No action or change shall be implemented until agreement has been reached or, alternatively, the procedure has been exhausted and five working days' notice has then been given of such action or change. If an employee considers that, in being required to comply with the terms of an existing agreement or an established custom and practice, he is affected unfairly, an appeal may be raised and considered under the agreed procedure but implementation of the agreement or practice need not be deferred pending that consideration.

(*e*) Where there is an urgent need for operations to continue and notwithstanding the other provisions of this Section, the parties shall endeavour to reach a temporary arrangement without prejudice to either side, pending a final determination of the question.

SOURCE: Memorandum of Agreement between British Leyland Motor Corporation Limited and Amalgamated Society of Boilermakers, Shipwrights, Blacksmiths and Structural Workers; Amalgamated Union of Engineering Workers (Engineering Section); Amalgamated Union of Engineering Workers (Constructional Section); Amalgamated Union of Engineering Workers (Foundry Section); Association of Patternmakers and Allied Craftsmen; Associated Metalworkers' Society; Birmingham and Midland Sheet Metal Workers' Society; Electrical Electronic and Telecommunication—Plumbing Trades Union; Furniture Timber and Allied Trades Union; General and Municipal Workers' Union; National Society of Metal Mechanics; National Union of Sheet Metal Workers and Coppersmiths, Heating and Domestic Engineers; National Union of Vehicle Builders; Transport and General Workers' Union; Union of Construction, Allied Trades and Technicians

22 ENGINEERING INDUSTRY : PROCEDURE— MANUAL WORKERS

Agreement between Engineering Employers' Federation and the Trade Unions
I.—General principles
   (*a*) The Employers have the right to manage their establish-

ments and the Trade Unions have the right to exercise their functions.

(*b*) In the process of evolution, provision for changes in shop conditions is necessary, but it is not the intention to create any specially favoured class of workpeople.

(*c*) The Employers and the Trade Unions, without departing in any way from the principles embodied in Clause (*a*) above, emphasise the value of consultation, not only in the successful operation of the Procedure set out in Section II but in the initial avoidance of disputes.

II.—Procedure for dealing with questions arising
(1) General

(*a*) The procedure of the Provisions for Avoiding Disputes so far as appropriate, applies to:

(i) General alterations in wages;

(ii) Alterations in working conditions which are the subject of agreements officially entered into;

(iii) Alterations in the general working week;

but such alterations shall not be given effect to until the appropriate procedure between the Federation and the Trade Union or Unions concerned has been exhausted.

(*b*) When the Management contemplates alterations in recognised working conditions which do not involve a change in material, means or method, and would result in work currently done by one class of workpeople in future being done by another class of workpeople in the establishment, the Management shall give the workpeople directly concerned or their representatives in the Shop intimation of their intention, and afford an opportunity for discussion with a deputation of the workpeople concerned and/or their representatives in the Shop. In the event of no settlement being reached, the Procedure outlined in Section (2)—provisions for Avoiding Disputes—shall be operated. The alterations concerned shall not be implemented until settlement has been reached or until the Procedure has been exhausted.

Where a contemplated alteration involves a change in the material, means or method and may result in one class of workpeople being replaced by another in the establishment, the Management shall as soon as possible notify their proposals to the workpeople directly concerned and/or their representatives in the Shop in order that there may be consultation between the parties concerned with a view to reaching agreement. If agreement is not achieved the workers concerned may give notice of an apprehended dispute, in which case the Management will not operate the proposed change for seven working days. The matter may be dealt with in accordance with the Provisions for Avoiding Disputes, the change being without prejudice to either party in any discussions which may take place.

(c) Where any class of workpeople is displaced by reason of any act of the Management, consideration shall be given to the case of workpeople so displaced with a view, if practicable, of affording them in the establishment work suitable to their qualifications.

(d) Questions arising which do not result in one class of workpeople being replaced by another in the establishment and on which discussion is desired, shall be dealt with in accordance with the Provisions for Avoiding Disputes and work shall proceed meantime under the conditions following the act of the Management.

(e) Where a change is made by the Management involving questions of money payments and as a result of negotiations in accordance with the recognised procedure, it is agreed that the claim of the workpeople is established, the decision so arrived at may be made retrospective on the particular claim to a date to be mutually agreed upon, but not beyond the date upon which the question was raised.

(f) Where any local agreement conflicts with the terms of this agreement, the provisions of this agreement shall apply.

(g) Nothing in the foregoing shall affect the usual practice in connection with the termination of employment of individual workpeople.

(2) Provisions for avoiding disputes

(a) When a question arises, an endeavour shall be made by the Management and the workman directly concerned to settle the same in the works or at the place where the question has arisen. Failing settlement deputations of workmen who may be accompanied by their Organiser (in which event a representative of the Employers' Association shall also be present) shall be received by the Employers by appointment without unreasonable delay for the mutual discussion of any question in the settlement of which both parties are directly concerned. In the event of no settlement being arrived at, it shall be competent for either party to bring the question before a Local Conference to be held between the Local Association and the local representatives of the Society.

(b) In the event of either party desiring to raise any question a Local Conference for this purpose may be arranged by application to the Secretary of the Local Association or to the local representative of the Society.

(c) Local Conferences shall be held within seven working days, unless otherwise mutually agreed upon, from the receipt of the application by the Secretary of the Local Association or the local representatives of the Society.

(d) Failing settlement at a Local Conference of any question brought before it, it shall be competent for either party to refer the matter to a Central Conference which, if thought desirable, may make a joint recommendation to the constituent bodies.

(e) Central Conference shall be held on the second Friday of each month at which questions referred to Central Conference prior to fourteen days of that date shall be taken.

(f) Until the procedure provided above has been carried through, there shall be no stoppage of work either of a partial or a general character.

(3) Shop stewards and works committee agreement

With a view to amplifying the provisions for avoiding disputes by a recognition of Shop Stewards and the institution of Works Committees.

It is agreed as follows:

(a) Appointment of Shop Stewards

(1) Workers, members of the Trade Unions, employed in a federated establishment may have representatives appointed from the members of the Unions employed in the establishment to act on their behalf in accordance with the terms of this Agreement.

(2) The representatives shall be known as Shop Stewards.

(3) The appointment of such Shop Stewards shall be determined by the Trade Unions concerned and each Trade Union party to this Agreement may have such Shop Stewards.

(4) The names of the Shop Stewards and the shop or portion of a shop in which they are employed and the Trade Union to which they belong shall be intimated officially by the Trade Union concerned to the Management on election.

(b) Appointment of Works Committee

(5) A Works Committee may be set up in each establishment consisting of not more than seven representatives of the Management and not more than seven Shop Stewards, who should be representative of the various classes of workpeople employed in the establishment.

The Shop Stewards for this purpose shall be nominated and elected by ballot of the workpeople, members of the Trade Unions parties to this Agreement, employed in the establishment.

The Shop Stewards elected to the Works Committee shall, subject to re-election, hold office for not more than twelve months.

(6) If a question failing to be dealt with by the Works Committee in accordance with the procedure hereinafter laid down arises in a department which has not a Shop Steward on the Works Committee, the Works Committee may, as regards that

question, co-opt a Shop Steward from the department concerned. An agenda of the points to be discussed by the Works
Committee shall be issued at least three days before the date of
the meeting if possible.

(c) Functions and procedure
  (7) The functions of Shop Stewards and Works Committee,
so far as they are concerned with the avoidance of disputes,
shall be exercised in accordance with the following procedure:
(a) A worker or workers desiring to raise any question in
    which they are directly concerned shall, in the first instance,
    discuss the same with their foreman.
(b) Failing settlement, the question shall be taken up with the
    Shop Manager and/or Head Shop Foreman by the
    appropriate Shop Steward and one of the workers directly
    concerned.
(c) If no settlement is arrived at the question may, at the re-
    quest of either party, be further considered at a meeting of
    the Works Committee. At this meeting the ODD may be
    present, in which event a representative of the Employers'
    Association shall also be present.
(d) Any question arising which affects more than one branch
    of trade or more than one department of the Works may be
    referred to the Works Committee.
(e) The question may thereafter be referred for further con-
    sideration in terms of the 'Provisions for Avoiding Disputes'.
(f) No stoppage of work shall take place until the question has
    been fully dealt with in accordance with this Agreement
    and with the 'Provisions for Avoiding Disputes'.

(d) General
  (8) Shop Stewards shall be subject to the control of the Trade
Unions and shall act in accordance with the Rules and Regulations of the Trade Unions and agreements with employers so
far as these affect the relation between employers and workpeople.

(9) In connection with this Agreement, Shop Stewards shall be afforded facilities to deal with questions raised in the shop or portion of a shop in which they are employed. Shop Stewards elected to the Works Committee shall be afforded similar facilities in connection with their duties, and in the course of dealing with these questions they may, with the previous consent of the Management (such consent not to be unreasonably withheld), visit any shop or portion of a shop in the establishment. In all other respects, Shop Stewards shall conform to the same working conditions as their fellow workers.

(10) Negotiations under this Agreement may be instituted either by the Management or by the workers concerned.

(11) Employers and Shop Stewards and Works Committee shall not be entitled to enter into any agreement inconsistent with agreements between the Federation or Local Association and the Trade Unions.

(12) For the purpose of this Agreement the expression 'establishment' shall mean the whole establishment or sections thereof according to whether the Management is unified or sub-divided.

(13) Any question which may arise out of the operation of this Agreement shall be brought before the Executive of the Trade Union concerned or the Federation as the case may be.

SOURCE: Engineering Employers' Federation and signatory unions' Agreement (2 June 1922. Amended 10 August 1955)

23 TGWU : NEGOTIATION OF COMPREHENSIVE PLANT AGREEMENTS

The Donovan Commission on Industrial Relations commenting on the growth of 'informal bargaining' at plant level recommended that employers and trade unions should negotiate formal comprehensive agreements at plant and company level.

The information provided is to give guidance to union negotiators at plant and local level on the subject matter for comprehensive plant agreements.

First is set out the form of an agreement that could be presented to an employer, followed by possible variations and points for guidance together with additions that might be considered in certain circumstances.

Agreement between the Transport and General Workers' Union and .... Company, dated .... hereinafter referred to as the Company and the Union.

(Section 1) Trade Union membership
(*a*) The Company recognises the Union as the exclusive representative of all its hourly rated and salaried employees including supervisors.
(*b*) All employees covered by this agreement shall maintain membership of the Union as a condition of continued employment.
(*c*) The Company will deduct all membership contributions from the pay of each employee covered by this agreement who has signed the necessary authorisation form and remit these in full to the union.

(Section 2) Representation
(*a*) Shop stewards shall be elected in each section or department to represent the employees as official representatives of the Union.
   Adequate facilities will be allowed to these representatives for consultations and to deal with matters arising without loss of payment or other rights.
(*b*) The shop stewards shall elect from amongst themselves three representatives who will be known as Senior Stewards. They will deal with matters that cannot be resolved at department level or matters of a general character.

(Section 3) Grievance procedure
(*a*) Any grievance arising in a department shall be raised with

the Shop Steward by the employee or employees concerned and the matter will be dealt with by the Steward and appropriate Foreman.

(b) If the matter is not satisfactorily settled the Shop Steward will seek to resolve the matter with the departmental head.

(c) If the grievance is still unresolved a meeting shall be arranged between the Senior Stewards and the Management who shall endeavour to satisfactorily settle the matter. In the event of continuing difficulty the Senior Stewards may call in the appropriate full-time Union Officer to assist.

(d) Until all the above stages have been exhausted the conditions applying immediately before the action leading to the dispute shall apply.

(e) It shall be the spirit and intention of both Company and Union that there will be no undue or unreasonable delay in progressing issues through the above procedure.

(Section 4) Employment security

(a) Both parties to this agreement recognise the importance of avoiding dismissals of employees for reasons of redundancy or other causes if this can be prevented by management planning or adequate consultation and negotiation. Where any disciplinary action is contemplated the decision will not be effected until the procedure in Section 3 has been fully used.

(b) Every endeavour will be made to avoid redundancy through careful forward planning of labour requirements and regular consultation with the shop stewards on production schedules, overtime, short-time working etc. Where redundancy is unavoidable employees will be selected on the basis of 'last in, first out' excepting by mutual agreement between the Company and the Union.

(c) Where the employment of an employee with less than one year's service is terminated by the employer the period of notice will be one week and for an employee with more than one year's service the minimum period will be four weeks.

(Section 5) Working hours

(*a*) The standard working week shall be 40 hours worked within five days Mondays to Friday. Shift workers shall work 37½ hour week on a 7½ hour five-day basis. Starting and finishing times shall be mutually agreed.

(Section 6) Tea breaks

(*a*) A minimum ten minute (10) paid tea break shall be allowed between starting time and meal break and a similar period between lunch time and finishing time.

(*b*) A five minute (5) paid washing period shall be allowed before lunch and finishing times.

(Section 7) Overtime

(*a*) All time worked before the normal starting time and after the normal finishing time shall be paid at the rate of time and one half from Monday to Saturday and double time for Sunday.

(*b*) The necessity for overtime working and the allocation arrangements shall be mutually agreed between the Management and the Shop Stewards.

(Section 8) Shift working

Rotating shifts or night shift working shall be the subject of mutual agreement. All hours worked on night shift or rotating shifts shall be paid at the rate set out in the attached schedule.

(Section 9) Wages

The minimum hourly basic rates of pay for each employee category are listed on the attached schedule to this agreement.

(Section 10) Improvement factor

During the period of the agreement, the value of the rates of pay may be re-assessed from time to time in relation to the cost of living and other factors.

(Section 11) Incentive bonus and payments by results schemes

In addition to the hourly rates referred to in Section 9 incentive bonus schemes or payments by results or other bonus schemes will operate *in each section*. These schemes will be mutually agreed between the Shop Stewards and Management and will conform with the agreement on incentive schemes between the Company and the Union.

(Section 12) Guaranteed minimum earnings

(*a*) Each employee shall be guaranteed a minimum earnings level of £ s. d. for a 40 hour week exclusive of any overtime or shift premium payments. (Applicable on a daily basis i.e. a minimum wage of .... for each normal day without overtime.)

(*b*) If work is not available to any employee for reasons beyond his or her control on any normal working day payment will be made at the rates listed in accordance with Section 9.

(*c*) Any employee who is temporarily placed on a job paying less than his normal rate shall not have his earnings reduced on account of such change. Permanent transfers will be by mutual agreement.

(Section 13) Holidays and holiday payments

Each employee will be allowed six public holidays and three weeks annual holiday in each calendar year. Payment will be at average earnings.

The days to be taken as public holidays and the period for holiday payment calculation shall be mutually agreed between Management and Senior Stewards.

(Section 14) Payment during sickness

Employees absent due to sickness or injury will be paid normal basic rates of pay if medical certificates are provided. Any allegations of abuse of the scheme shall be referred for consideration to a joint meeting of Management and Senior Stewards.

(Section 15) Union notices

The Company will provide a Notice Board within the plant for the posting of Union notices.

(Section 16) Modification or termination

This Agreement becomes effective .... and may be amended by mutual agreement between the Company and the Union or it may be terminated by either party giving three months written notice to the other party.

SIGNED .... Company

.... Union

Points for guidance

It will be found that in many instances much more favourable conditions can be obtained. The proposals put forward here are a foundation, however, on which a good comprehensive agreement can be built.

Negotiating rights (Section 1)

Where there is a clear field it is desirable to seek sole negotiating rights for the whole of the labour force. However, if another union is already established in certain departments it will, of course, be necessary to modify our approach. It will be noted that the wording is designed to cover both manual and clerical membership but separate agreements are often negotiated for clerical and supervisory membership.

Condition of employment (Section 1)

Many employers have accepted 100 per cent. trade union clauses in agreements, but in certain circumstances it may be necessary to agree a form of wording which leads to 100 per cent. membership without 'spelling it out', such as

'The Management will expect all employees to belong to the

TGWU and will provide adequate facilities for the recruitment and maintenance of trade union membership.'

Deduction (Section 1)
The number of companies deducting TU contributions has considerably increased in recent years. Make sure that the authorisation form signed by the member refers to 'union contributions' and not a specified sum. Contributions change from time to time.

Representation (Section 2)
Some employers prefer the term 'Union Representative' to 'Shop Steward'. Alternately, in some establishments we operate a Branch system of committee men acting as sectional representatives and Chairman and Secretary as senior representatives.

In multi-union establishments we should ensure facilities which allow our Union to progress matters through all stages of procedure without having to negotiate through the representative of another organisation.

Procedure (Section 3)
Procedure Agreements should be kept short and simple. The Union operates under the threat of legal enforcement; it is therefore essential that Procedure Agreements are easily understood by the membership and accepted as a speedy way to resolve grievances.

Under certain circumstances it may be necessary to seek the assistance of a National Officer or resort to Arbitration to resolve an issue, but it is not necessary to write this into an Agreement as an obligatory stage in negotiations—always keep it short and simple.

Employment security (Section 4)
In dealing with redundancy, severance payment schemes more favourable than, or supplementary to, the Redundancy Payment Act may be negotiated.

Seniority as a basis for redundancy selection has been substantially modified due to the operation of statutory and voluntary severance payment schemes. Voluntary redundancy is
now more common in some industries.

Working hours (Section 5)
Although this section specifies 40 hours there are strong cases in
some establishments for negotiating shorter working weeks. For
example, in the docks industry in order to combat the sharp
reduction in manpower due to technological change, agreements have been negotiated with some employers for a much
shorter working week without loss of earnings. It is increasingly
difficult for employers to justify a demand that manual workers
should work a longer normal week than their white collar
colleagues.

Wages (Section 9)
If wage categories are set out on a separate schedule it avoids
the need to re-write the Agreement each time an increase is
secured.

Incentives (Scheme 11)
Appendix 1 sets out the terms of an Agreement between the
Union and a well-known Brewery Company. This provides an
overall protection for the negotiation of incentive schemes at
departmental level.

Minimum earnings (Section 12)
In negotiating a minimum earnings level regard would be paid
to current Union policy on minimum earnings.

Holidays and holiday payments (Section 13)
The Agreement specifies three weeks annual and six public
holidays at average earnings.
    European countries generally have longer holidays than
Britain and bonus payments beyond average earnings are

frequently paid. The clause in the Agreement should be regarded as a minimum condition only.

Sick pay (Section 14)

Some sick pay schemes provide for normal wages to be paid less national insurance benefits, and others provide for 40 per cent. or 50 per cent. of wages without interference from state schemes. This latter approach seems to be gaining popularity.

In addition to the proposals suggested above there are many more items that could be properly included in a comprehensive plant Agreement; for example, pension schemes, recruitment of labour through Union offices, recall after lay-off, etc., etc. However, if Agreements like the suggested draft can be negotiated in the first place they can be added to later.

By having a model or standard draft Agreement of this kind it allows Union negotiators to take the initiative rather than work from an employer's draft.

Copies of all Agreements reached with employers should be sent to your Regional Secretary, and to the TGWU Research Department, Smith Square, Westminster, London, S.W.1.

Appendix 1
Agreed principles covering the negotiation of incentive bonus schemes

1　In all cases the employee's basic rate plus an agreed percentage shall be guaranteed, irrespective of earnings.

2　Overtime and night shift and Sunday and Holiday allowances etc., shall be paid in addition to bonus earnings.

3　The bonus time to be allowed either for a new job or for an altered job shall be fixed by mutual arrangement between the employer and the employee who is to perform the work, together with the Shop Steward. Where collective schemes operate agreement shall be reached with the Shop Steward.

4　No bonus or basic time once fixed may be altered unless the means or method of production is changed.

5   When the means or method of production is changed and
    the employer desires a modification in price or basis time,
    the modifications shall in no case be such as to effect a
    reduction in the earnings of the employees concerned.

6   In the event of an employee taking exception to any bonus
    time allowed, and being unable to arrive at a settlement,
    the matter shall be dealt with by the Shop Steward and
    Management who shall endeavour to settle the matter
    within seven days of the question being raised.

7   All settlements on a job shall be retrospective to the time
    when the question was raised.

8   No debit balance shall be carried forward beyond the
    weekly or other mutually recognised period of settlement.

9   The employers shall in all cases supply a card stating the
    nature of each job and the bonus or basis time allowed,
    such card to be available at any time for perusal by the
    employees covered by the Bonus Scheme.

10 Bonus or basic time shall be such as will enable employees
    to earn at least 33⅓rd over basic rates.

SOURCE: Urwin, Harry. *Plant and Productivity Bargaining*
(TGWU pamphlet, nd), 11–19

24 RAILWAY PAY AND EFFICIENCY AGREEMENT
FOOTPLATE STAFF, 1968

Agreement between British Railways Board, Associated Society
of Locomotive Engineers and Firemen and the National Union
of Railwaymen dated 29th August, 1968

1. General

Improved rates of pay will be introduced from 12th August,
1968. At the same time new measures will be introduced which
will improve the efficiency of footplate staff.

Progress will be reviewed at intervals after the implementation of this Agreement to assess the results of Stage 1 and to con-

sider any other changes which could be included in Stage 2. The parties will consider the method by which costs and savings can be objectively assessed.

The present Agreements will continue to operate subject to the amendments contained herein.

2. Night manning
Single manning will extend throughout the 24 hours subject to the provisions of the 1965 Manning Agreement (as amended herein).

3. Locomotives running light
The following to take the place of the existing clauses B(1) (b) and (c) of the 1965 Manning Agreement:

New (b):

Except as shown in Clause (a), locomotives running light will be manned by a Driver accompanied by a second man who may be a man in the line of promotion or a Guard according to availability:

  (i) at the beginning of a turn up to and including 15 miles;
  (ii) other than at the beginning of a turn without mileage restriction.

Where the distance is less than 5 miles the second man may be a man in the line of promotion, Guard or Senior/Leading Railman passed in protection rules.

4. Shunting turns of duty
Drivers on shunting turns away from their existing promotional point will book on and off at an approved booking on and off point as near as possible to the point where they commence duty.

Such turns to be limited to 8 hours inclusive of booking on and off times but exclusive of walking/travelling time to and from their promotional point, which will not count as part of the diagrammed turn but which will be paid for by an allowance representing 50% of the time so involved (at ordinary rate).

E

The existing arrangements for the reimbursement of fares is to be maintained.

The maximum walking/travelling time between the promotional point and the approved booking on and off point is to be limited to one hour each way.

5. On track machines

Mechanically propelled tamping machines, ballast-cleaning machines, lining machines and tamping and lining machines need not be accompanied by a man in the line of promotion to Driver provided the machine does not travel on main lines in excess of 15 miles from the point of commencement of the journey.

6. Three days' annual leave in winter

The three days' annual leave in excess of two weeks will be taken outside the customary staff holiday period, but not during seasonal peak periods at the depot concerned.

When desired and practicable, the additional leave can—by local agreement—be taken during the normal annual leave period.

7. Station pilots

Station pilots will be single-manned unless there are instances where the Management consider it is appropriate to double-man.

Where it is felt by the Staff Side of LDC No. 2 that in a particular case there is doubt regarding safety considerations involved with single manning station pilots, such a case may be referred to the Regional Manning Committee for decision (see Section C of Manning Agreement).

Pending a decision by the Regional Manning Committee, such a case will remain single-manned.

8. Locomotives running in multiple

Locomotives running in multiple (not more than two) to be manned as follows:

(*a*) When working trains the leading cab of the leading locomotive to be manned in accordance with the provisions of
Section A of the 1965 Manning Agreement (as amended
herein).

(*b*) When working light, the leading cab of the leading locomotive to be manned in accordance with the provisions of
Section B(1) of the 1965 Manning Agreement (as amended
herein).

9. **'Surplus staff'** (those who are protected against redundancy by the 1965 Manning Agreement).

It is understood that the primary objective in dealing with
staff who are 'surplus' or become 'surplus' in the future is that
they should be encouraged to volunteer to be effectively employed within the footplate line of promotion (it being noted
that provision for Engine Cleaners to transfer 'on loan' to
other vacancies is already made in the Amplified Redundancy
Arrangements).

To facilitate such movement the following arrangements
will be introduced.

(*a*) All Line Promotion

An all line Promotion Scheme will be devised with the
object of giving the maximum encouragement to men to
move between depots to fill vacancies wherever they
occur.

Every endeavour will be made to reach agreement on a
revised scheme to enable this to operate commencing with
the January 1969 posting of the footplate staff vacancy list.

(*b*) Transfer of Surplus Staff

(i) Facilities will be made available for 'surplus' footplate
staff to transfer to footplate posts at other depots where
there are essential vacancies.

(ii) To assist them to move they will be advanced a lump
sum of £320 on the understanding that the recipient
remains at his new depot for a period of not less than 12
months unless he is required to move away by reason of

promotion or redundancy. He will not again be eligible
to take up an 'M' vacancy.

(iii) If a man leaves the depot to which transferred (for
reasons other than subsequent promotion or redundancy) before the expiration of the 12 months period,
he will be required to pay back the lump sum on a
proportionate basis.

(iv) The foregoing arrangement is additional to any entitlement a redundant man may have under the provisions of RSJC Min. No. G.105—9.5.66, and for the
purpose of this exercise a 'surplus' man who moves will
be regarded as redundant and treated accordingly.

(c) Early retirement

Payment of resettlement in the event of early retirement
will be extended to men of 55 and over as necessary.

(The possibility of finding a basis for commuting the
continuing weekly payments into a lump sum to be
examined jointly.)

(d) 'M' Vacancies

At the end of the year, when the 'M' vacancy position is
due to be reviewed, the opportunity will also be taken of
reviewing the progress being made in reducing the 'surplus'
staff.

10. Further review of manning arrangements

Further savings from single manning at night—particularly in
relation to any excess in the anticipated savings arising from the
additional turns which will be re-diagrammed to conform to the
Manning Agreement; the elimination of steam heating; and the
elimination of single cab locomotives—will, as stated in Clause
1 of this Agreement, be taken into consideration together with
any other changes which would be included in Stage 2. The
parties will consider the method by which costs and savings can
be objectively assessed.

11. Rates of pay

The rates of pay set out in the Appendix will be introduced with effect from 12th August, 1968.

All bonus and mileage payments will continue to be calculated on the basis in operation prior to 8th July, 1968.

Talks will commence at an early date to examine existing schemes relating to mileage and bonus payment.

Appendix

Rates of pay—footplate staff

Grade	Rate
Driver	379/-
Senior Secondman*	
After 18 years' service in the grade or after 21 years' service in Line of Promotion	360/-
After prescribed number of driving turns have been worked representing one year, or after 10 years' service in the grade or after 15 years' service in Line of Promotion	340/-
Secondman	
2nd year	298/-
1st year	283/-
Traction Trainee and Cleaner	
After prescribed number of Secondmen's turns have been worked representing one year	283/-
Adults	260/-
Juniors—Age 19	208/-
18	182/-
17	143/-
16	130/-
15	117/-

London Allowance

Adults 6/- per week

Juniors in junior posts 3/- per week

*Senior Secondmen will be paid mileage on the basis of the

scale applicable to Drivers but at the rate applicable to
Senior Secondmen prior to 8th July, 1968.

25 RAILWAY PAY AND EFFICIENCY AGREEMENT FOOTPLATE STAFF, 1969

Agreement between British Railways Board, Associated Society
of Locomotive Engineers and Firemen and the National Union
of Railwaymen, dated 9th September 1969

Preamble

The Stage I Productivity Agreements reached in 1968 between
the British Railways Board and the two Railway Trade Unions
provided for a joint review of the Agreements and further discussions on pay and productivity.

These discussions have taken place over a lengthy period
during which many measures for further improving productivity
and efficiency in different areas have been jointly explored.

Agreement has now been reached on increased levels of pay,
improved conditions of service and additional measures for
improving productivity and efficiency in the industry.

Present Agreements will continue to operate subject to the
amendments herein.

Details are set out in the Terms of Agreement and the
Appendix which follow.

Terms of agreement

1 Programme for planned productivity improvement

It is an agreed objective to adopt a systematic approach to future
developments involving programmes for planned productivity
improvements and changes in terms and conditions of service.

2 Joint studies into labour motivation and participation

It is agreed that joint studies shall be initiated at National level to establish the scope for members of the staff to undertake a more positive role by participating to a greater extent than hitherto in the affairs of the Railway.

These studies will concern themselves with features relating to the satisfaction which people obtain from their jobs, the design of jobs, and the formation of working groups to ensure that objective and progressive policies are developed.

These features have an effect upon the level of labour turnover and it is anticipated that the findings from the studies will lead to an improvement in this respect.

3 Established status

It is the intention to give certain key hourly paid staff an opportunity to transfer to established status.

It is agreed as a first step that established status be granted to Drivers with thirty years' Railway service or more and that this will be extended to Drivers with twenty-five years' Railway service twelve months from the date of this Agreement. Further consideration to be given at that time to the extension of this arrangement in the light of the experience gained.

Staff who become 'Established' will be paid on an annual salaried basis including, where appropriate, London allowance.

They will continue to receive Wages Staff conditions with the exception that they will be regarded as Salaried Staff for the purposes of sick pay and superannuation.

For the purpose of determining entitlement to sick pay their appointment will be regarded as promotion from a Wages Grade.

Men appointed to 'Established' status, if under 55 years of age, will be given the opportunity of joining the Superannuation Fund subject to satisfactory medical examination.

For Superannuation Fund purposes subsequent appointments to 'Established' status shall be covered by the existing arrangements for staff promoted from a Wages Grade.

NOTE:

All such staff will have the option of taking up membership

of the Superannuation Fund or retaining their existing pension rights; only staff who are under 40 years of age on promotion to 'Established' status and who are not covered by an existing pension arrangement will be required to join the Superannuation Fund.

Every assistance will be provided for explaining the circumstances in individual cases.

In the event of redundancy, such a man will retain his existing rights but shall retain his 'Established' status on a personal basis.

4 Trade Union membership

The Board and the Trade Unions accept that membership of a Trade Union, party to the Machinery of Negotiation, is in the best interests of employer/employee relationship.

It is, therefore, agreed that membership of one of the Trade Unions party to the Machinery of Negotiation shall be a condition of employment effective from 1st January, 1970. The detailed changes to be agreed between the parties concerned to give effect to this to be included in a further document.

5 Arbitration

In the event of a dispute occurring between the parties to the Machinery of Negotiation and this dispute not being resolved by the RSNC it shall be open to the parties:

(a) to unilaterally proceed to the next stage in the Machinery, i.e., RSNT in which case the decision of the RSNT will not affect the freedom of the parties concerning their future action;

OR

(b) the parties may between themselves jointly agree that a reference to the RSNT shall be made, in which case the terms of reference will be also jointly agreed beforehand and the ensuing decision of the RSNT will be binding on the parties.

6 Extension of national agreements to cover local productivity bargaining

It is agreed that consideration will be given at National level to introducing arrangements for a form of local bargaining and the guidelines which could apply.

Local bargaining would not in any way supplant negotiations at the National level and any arrangements proposed would require to be submitted for ratification at National level.

7 Training for redeployment

It is agreed that when the effect of change upon staff makes continuation in their own grade and/or at their present location impossible, training will be provided to equip them for alternative employment in the Railway service.

8 Rationalisation of enhanced payments for overtime, night duty, etc

It is agreed that a joint study shall be undertaken at an early date to investigate the possibility of rationalising the various enhancements applicable under the National Agreements, including the question of devising a basis for the payment of shift allowances. Existing items in the Machinery will be cleared as early as possible.

9 Joint studies into productivity indices

It is agreed that the Board and the Trade Unions will undertake joint studies to devise the type of indicators for measuring productivity which could be used as one of the factors in determining future pay movements.

10 Annual leave

As from 1st January, 1970, Conciliation Staff on completing three years' service will be granted three weeks annual leave with pay. The third week to be taken at a mutually convenient time outside the seasonal peak period at the depot concerned.

As from 1st January, 1970, payment will be made during annual leave on the basis of the current weekly rate of basic pay plus 20% of the difference between average weekly basic pay and average weekly earnings during the fiscal year preceding the date of the leave.

11 Sick pay

Consideration was given to improving the sick pay scheme for Wages Staff and, as a first step, to reducing the present waiting period before payment is made under the scheme from the first *seven* days of sickness to the first *three* days of sickness.

It is agreed that this be introduced in 1970.

12 Outstanding claims

(*a*) It was agreed that the undermentioned outstanding claims should be regarded as having been overtaken by this Agreement:

Claim for leave in lieu for time worked on Saturdays prior to Bank Holidays.

Lieu days—Bank and Public Holidays (two turns in one day).

Abolition of Short Rest turns.

(*b*) Night Overtime Enhancement

It is agreed that overtime worked between 02 00 and 06 00 hours on weekday turns of duty should be paid at the rate of time and seven-twelfths.

(*c*) Rest Day Enhancements for Additional Turns

It is agreed that when staff who are normally rostered for a rest day are required to work an additional turn of duty, other than a rest turn, at the end of the week, payment should be made as for a rest day.

NOTE:

The following outstanding claims relating to enhancements were deferred for consideration in the Joint Study mentioned in paragraph 8 of the Agreement.

Overtime and Sunday/Monday turns—claim for revision of method of payment.

Improved payment for Sunday duty.

Application for shift allowance of 5/– per shift to all staff on shift working.

Improved payment for work performed on Bank and Public Holidays.

(d) Booking on and off Allowance—Claim for Increase

The claim for additional signing on and off allowance for all men is declined.

It is agreed that a Driver (including a Passed Secondman) who has been absent from duty continuously for four weeks or more due to sickness or paid leave will be allowed an additional 30 minutes, on the day he returns to duty, for the purpose of reading notices.

The 30 minutes will be in advance of and outside the man's normal rostered time and will be paid for at the appropriate ordinary rate.

(e) Cleaners with more than 15 years' service in the Line of Promotion to receive higher rates of pay

It is agreed that Cleaners*with 15 or more years' service in the Line of Promotion will be paid on the same basis as a Senior Secondman, i.e.:

after 21 years' service in the Line of Promotion (378/–)

after 15 years' service in the Line of Promotion (357/–)

*Cleaners in receipt of the same rates as Senior Second-men will, when on Secondmen's duties, be paid mileage on the scale applicable to Drivers but at the rate applicable to Senior Secondmen prior to 8th July, 1968. When not engaged on Secondmen's duties they will not qualify for the minimum mileage payment.

(f) Men engaged on Road Learning or attending medical examination to be paid in accordance with RSJC Min. L. 215—27.6.61

It is agreed that members of the staff attending for medical examination shall be paid in accordance with RSJC Min.

L.215—27.6.61. The claim in respect of men engaged on Road Learning to be reconsidered jointly.

(g) Seniority position of men in the service at 25th October, 1965 (Starred men) who have transferred to essential Secondmen's vacancies under the arrangements set out in Clause 9(b) of the August 1968 Pay & Efficiency Agreement, and who are not eligible to take up an 'M' vacancy

It was agreed that a starred man who has transferred to an essential vacancy and has accepted the £320 lump sum would continue to have the benefit of his seniority date in the event of redundancy occurring at the depot.

(h) Holding of Drivers' vacancies for Secondmen who are senior for appointment to Drivers' posts—Technical examination

It is agreed that in the case of a Secondman who has not passed the necessary technical examinations for driving duties and who is the senior eligible applicant (or who would be due for appointment at his own depot) to a driving position, the position will be held if necessary for a period of up to 10 months from the date originally scheduled for it to be filled. This is to enable the man to take up the position on his passing the technical examination.

13 Utilisation of surplus secondmen

It is agreed that LDCs should endeavour to introduce such link arrangements as will ensure the effective use of Secondmen at the depot so that essential work is covered to the greatest possible extent.

It is also agreed that the following should be issued for the guidance of the LDCs in formulating their rostering arrangement.

(a) The first priority for rostering of Secondmen at a Depot shall be the essential work, which includes the spare cover for this. All essential jobs may be placed in a link or links and the available Secondmen at the Depot allocated to these jobs.

(b) Any 'starred' Secondmen remaining surplus after this allocation should be booked on by local agreement at intervals of time, best suited to Depot requirements.

(c) All 'starred' Secondmen to be protected for earnings purposes against the Unstarred turn with which they are identified in their notional allocations.

14 Freight train bonus

Consideration was given to the extent to which schemes referred to in Clause (e) of the 1965 Manning Agreement had been introduced: also, to the current spread and levels of bonus earnings.

To rectify the situation where 23% of turns still had to be introduced and where a substantial percentage of staff were receiving unsatisfactory bonus earnings, it was agreed:

1. that the programme of introduction be accelerated. The target date for readiness to consult on all outstanding schemes shall be not later than the end of October, 1968, and the target date for implementation shall be not later than 31.12.1969.

2. in the event of implementation being delayed beyond 31.12.69 for any delay on the part of Management, that payments under the scheme, when introduced, shall be effective from 1.1.1970.

3. that consideration be given to a revised scheme (outlined by Management during the negotiations):

   (a) for introduction at depots where no freight train schemes have yet been introduced;

   (b) for introduction at depots where existing schemes are in operation.

Where schemes are in operation, choice will be given (by depots) whether the revised scheme or existing scheme shall operate.

Details of the 'amended' freight train bonus scheme shall be the subject of negotiations following immediately upon P & E II talks: the following conditions shall obtain, viz:

(a) that in return for a reasonable day's work, based on a standard performance, to be agreed between the parties, payment will be 80 minutes per day. (This in addition to 40 minutes per day minimum mileage payment.)

(b) every man participating in the amended freight train scheme will earn bonus: the basis of a minimum payment to be agreed at the freight train bonus negotiations to follow.

(c) it is acknowledged by the Board that certain additional costs will be involved in meeting commitments.

It is also the intention to accelerate the introduction of schemes affecting men in marshalling yards, stations and depots. In these cases, however, other factors have to be considered, e.g.,

(a) staff, other than footplate, where involved in the operation of schemes;

(b) unlike the freight train bonus schemes, Prices and Incomes clearance has to be obtained for each individual scheme where over 100 staff are involved.

These features tend to make progress slower. Additionally, more work has yet to be done to make introduction possible but, nevertheless, it is agreed that a target date of 1st July, 1970, be accepted for completing introduction. Retrospective payment to 1st July, 1970, will be made for schemes implemented later than this date.

The anticipated improvements in the freight train bonus arrangements will have certain repercussive effects on passenger men on low mileage: therefore, subsequent to reaching agreement on the freight train bonus amendments, consideration will also be given to a formula which will seek to meet this situation.

15 Operative date of agreement

Except where otherwise stated, the operative date of this Agreement shall be 4th August, 1969.

Rates of pay—footplate staff
Operative from 4 August 1969

Grade	*Rate*
Driver (Established status)	£1,040 p.a.
	(399/-)
Driver	399/-
Senior Secondman*	
After 18 years' service in the grade or after 21 years' service in Line of Promotion	378/-
After prescribed number of driving turns have been worked representing one year, or after 10 years' service in the grade or after 15 years' service in Line of Promotion	357/-
Secondman	
2nd year	313/-
1st year	297/-
Traction Trainee and Cleaner	
After prescribed number of Secondmen's turns have been worked representing one year	297/-
Adults	274/-
Juniors—Age 19	219/-
18	192/-
17	151/-
16	137/-
15	123/-

London Allowance—

Drivers on established status £70 p.a.

Other adults 18/- p.w.

Juniors in junior posts 9/- p.w.

*Senior Secondmen will be paid mileage on the basis of the scale applicable to Drivers but at the rate applicable to Senior Secondmen prior to 8 July, 1968.

26 BRITISH ACTORS' EQUITY ASSOCIATION
NUDITY AND SIMULATED SEX ACTS

Agreement with the Theatres National Committee

As from 1st January 1971 the following Regulations (agreed between Equity and the Theatres National Committee, representing the Living Theatre throughout Great Britain) shall supersede the Regulations agreed between the parties dated 24th September, 1969.

1. In respect of any production in which there is nudity and/or sex acts, all artists shall be informed in writing of this fact and of the general nature and extent of such nudity and/or acts, prior to the conclusion of the contracts of engagement.

2. Where nudity and/or acts of a sexual nature are required of a performer in the course of a production, the performer must be so advised in writing, clearly indicating the extent of the requirement including the degree of nudity and/or the nature and extent of any such acts required, in advance of his or her entering into a Contract and the script must be submitted to the performer if he or she so requests prior to his or her being contracted.

3. No performer may be required to disrobe in whole or in part until after he or she has been auditioned as an actor, singer or dancer, etc.

4. Nudity or semi-nudity at auditions may be permitted only if

(a) An official Equity observer or an observer agreeable to Equity is present.

(b) The direct professional and artistic interest of all persons present has been agreed between Equity and the Management.

5. No sex acts shall be required of any performer at any audition.

6. (a) Photographs depicting artists in the nude, partly nude and/or sex acts, shall not be used for purposes other than direct publicity for the production, other than by the express written consent of the artists.

(b) The Manager undertakes that the prints and negatives of
such photographs will be destroyed at the conclusion of the
production.

7. In the case of an artist arrested or charged with any offence
arising from his or her performance as directed, the Management will do all that is legally possible to assist the Artist.

8. For the purpose of these Regulations:

(a) 'Acts of a sexual nature' and 'sex acts' shall mean 'any act
which if performed in public would be regarded as an
indecent act'.

(b) 'Nudity', 'semi-nudity' and 'disrobe' shall mean 'to be in a
state of undress which if in public could be regarded as
indecent'.

9. All Contracts of Engagement shall henceforth include the
following Clause:

'The Regulations relating to nudity and simulated sex acts
agreed between Equity and the TNC on the 24th September
1969 (including any variation thereof for the time being in
force) shall be incorporated in, and the observance thereof
shall be a condition of, this Agreement.

Any dispute arising in relation to the said Regulations shall
be referred to the appropriate Theatre Council, which shall
meet within 72 hours of such reference, and whose decision
shall be binding on the parties. Failing such decision, the
dispute shall be referred for binding decision to the Independent Chairman or Vice-Chairman of the Theatre
Council or, should this be impracticable, to an independent
person appointed by the Theatre Council for the purpose.'

SOURCE: British Actors' Equity Association

**27 TUC 'TINA LEA' (This is not a legally
enforceable agreement)**

(155) Collective agreements
In March the General Council considering an Opinion from

Counsel on forms of wording and procedures for excluding legal enforceability in relation to collective agreements, and on April 1 a circular was sent to all affiliated unions advising them that if the Industrial Relations Bill became law, new agreements, or amendments to existing agreements, which were made in writing would be conclusively presumed to be legally binding unless a clause was inserted which stipulated to the contrary.

Unions were therefore advised that such exclusion clauses might take the following forms:

(a) The simplest formula would be: 'This agreement does not in any way constitute a legally enforceable agreement between the parties.'

(b) An equally effective formula but which included a reference to the obligations of the parties would be:

'Both parties accept that this agreement is binding in honour upon them, but both expressly agree that it is not intended to constitute a legally enforceable agreement between them.'

(c) As it was the practice for a small number of collective agreements to be drawn in legalistic language, unions were advised that in such cases a suitable exclusion clause (which should be the last clause in the agreement) should match the remainder of the agreement and could be along the following lines: 'Notwithstanding any other provision in this agreement, it is agreed between the parties that no part of this agreement shall create any binding legal obligation upon either of them or have any binding legal effect between them either as an enforceable contract or otherwise.'

Unions were informed that the presumption of legal enforceability would also apply to the 'decision' or 'award' of a negotiating body if 'duly recorded in writing' unless it contained an exclusion clause to the contrary. Unions were advised that the clauses in (a), (b) and (c) above might be adopted for this purpose by replacing each reference to an 'agreement' by reference to an 'award' or 'decision', but that they might find it more

convenient to adopt a simpler procedure along the following
lines:

(a) In the constitution or rules governing the operation or
procedure of the negotiating body, or in some other suitable
place such as the front page of a Minute Book, a clause
could be inserted reading:
'Wherever the words "Not Legally Enforceable" are inserted in the record of a decision (award, etc.) of this
(Council, etc.) they mean that the parties agree that the
decision (award, etc.) shall not be binding upon them as a
legally enforceable contract or otherwise enforceable between them in law.'

(b) Each minute or other written record should contain the
words 'Not Legally Binding'. This could be effected by
means of a rubber stamp.

It was stressed that such steps could only be taken by agreement and that the trade union representative on a joint body
would not be entitled to stamp the minute with an exclusion
provision unilaterally. Nor would a union be able to remove the
authority of a representative to make binding agreements.
Where agreement was obtained to the procedures outlined in
(a) and (b) above, it was stressed that the provision for exclusion
should be stamped or written into each recorded minute.

It was pointed out that in regard both to written collective
agreements and to written decisions of negotiating bodies the
exclusion clause must be inserted in each separate agreement or
decision. No advance 'umbrella' agreement between the parties
saying *future* agreements or decisions were not to be binding
would suffice. However, the parties could, for example, agree in
advance always to use a standard Collective Agreement form,
which would include a suitable exclusion clause, or a standard
Minute Book in which on every page there was printed in advance a formula such as 'Not Legally Binding'. Joint signature
of agreements or minutes on standard form documents would in
each case avoid legal enforceability.

On May 6, 1971, a further circular was sent to affiliated

unions stating that although a Government amendment to the clause dealing with legally binding agreements appeared to exclude from the provision, agreements made before the Act came into force, unions should include exclusion clauses in agreements signed before the Bill became law. This would avoid future doubts and give added force to union objections to the Bill. Unions were asked to let the General Council have information about agreements in which they were able to include a clause excluding legal enforceability. In June replies were received from unions reporting agreements that had been signed with more than 100 employers or employers' associations incorporating clauses excluding legal enforceability and covering all or part of the workers belonging to the organisation concerned. The agreements applied in a wide range of industries and operated at different levels, with individual employers or through industry-wide negotiationg bodies. Industry-wide groups included food, clothing, and cement manufacture. Individual companies reported included, in particular, major employers in the engineering industry (notably in motor manufacture), oil refining and distribution, road haulage, and car delivery. A list of the industries and companies concerned was published in the July issue of *Labour: the TUC Information Broadsheet*.

Source: TUC. Annual Report (1971), para 155, 102–4

PART FIVE

Trade Union Structure 1

(a) INTERNAL

There has always been a special fascination about the enormous variety of means by which different British trade unions have developed democratic structures and organisational devices to meet their changing needs. The most outstanding analysis of trade union activity ever produced, the Webbs' Industrial Democracy, *unravelled the main threads of development in the first hundred years or so. The close observer will know that the special kind of social contract called trade union government is in process of continuing development and upheaval.*

To understand why this should be so and how such changes are handled will give us a better grasp of the general pattern of modern trade union organisation—despite its bewildering variety.

Trade union government has to fulfil two basic requirements. It has to provide adequate channels of membership participation to meet the needs for representation on the part of specific groups of members, whether occupational or industrial. At the same time it must provide an organisational framework which will give effective servicing and shrewd judgement in times of trouble and dispute. Suppose the union constitution provides for election of full-time officers, such as has been characteristic particularly of trade unions of skilled manual workers. Very short periods in office, and barriers to re-election, might be advocated as democratic devices, but they would be likely to disrupt efficient and consistent operation. This tension is not easy to resolve.

As the structure of particular industries changes, and as firms (parti-

cularly large ones) regroup and merge, union organisation has to be adapted to meet new servicing needs. New demands for membership representation may go hand in hand with this. Workers in a particular part of a public service, or in different parts of the country employed by the same firm, may seek opportunities for joint discussion and a share in policy making. The union may find that the balance of its membership shifts, by region, occupation and industry, possibly as a result of conscious choice on its part or of a more 'open' definition of its appropriate membership area. Many unions find themselves organising and recruiting in ways that overlap with other unions; this also may serve to stimulate fresh thinking on the range of representation and services that the union offers.

In addition, unions have had to adapt their organisation to incorporate the great extension of trade union activity on the shop floor, with its key figure, the shop steward.

There are two main ways in which union structures are changed to respond to new needs and opportunities. The first can be called executive initiative. The union's national executive committee may develop new services, call ad hoc conferences of particular groups of members, and gradually develop a range of activity and membership participation that is not obvious from a perusal of the rule book. Secondly, periodic rules-revision conferences are held, where branch initiative may lead to changes of rule as well as proposals put before conference in the name of the executive.

In fact, delegate conferences of many kinds play an important part in the life of modern trade unions. Union government only goes so far in accepting the style of representative government; the emphasis on participation, on the direct voice of the members or their delegates, remains a strong one.

The documents in this section attempt to illustrate some of these facets of union government, beginning with a simple explanation, addressed to non-members, of a union's democratic structure. We show the complex mechanism of a trade union executive committee, reflecting pressures for a balance of regional and occupational representation, and with all its extensive functional responsibilities.

Conference activities are briefly illustrated, with extracts from agendas, and a debate at a rules-revision conference on whether the executive committee should consist of full-time officers. The issues associated with an extension of recruitment by a more 'open' definition of the union's scope are indicated from a union which has since regrouped as a section of a federal union of engineering workers and widened its recruitment area still more.

Diverse aspects of membership involvement are covered in further documents: firstly, the role of shop stewards; secondly, a speech by Jack Jones, general secretary of the largest union, stressing membership participation in the making of agreements; and thirdly, the existence of organised factions seeking to influence the outcome of elections and redirect union policy.

28 NATIONAL AND LOCAL GOVERNMENT OFFICERS ASSOCIATION: NALGO IS RUN BY ITS MEMBERS

NALGO'S members decide how NALGO shall be managed and what it shall do. The members run NALGO: NALGO doesn't run them.

Every member belongs to a branch, normally composed solely of fellow employees in his own service. Branches send delegates to the Association's annual conference, where policy is decided.

That policy is carried out by a National Executive Council (the 'NEC') which is elected each year by ballot of all the members.

In addition, branches send delegates to a district council—the main link between members, branches, and the NEC.

Each separate service covered by NALGO has its own branch, district, and national service conditions committees. Through these, the members in each service effectively control their own policies, subject only to the overriding direction of the annual conference.

To keep its members informed about what it is doing, NALGO sends a weekly circular to all its branches, and gives a copy of its monthly newspaper, *Public Service*, free to every member, while nearly 300 of its branches publish their own magazines or news-sheets.

There is no more democratic union in Britain than NALGO —nor any that tells its members so much about everything it does.

SOURCE: NALGO. *About NALGO* (nd), 10

29 POST OFFICE ENGINEERING UNION NATIONAL EXECUTIVE COUNCIL

1. The National Executive Council shall be appointed each year by the Annual Conference and shall consist of 23 members.

2. The President of the Union shall be appointed each year by the Annual Conference and shall be selected from the members of the National Executive Council appointed by and at the same Conference.

3. The members of the Executive shall be elected from fully paid-up members of the Union of at least three years' continuous standing at the date of nomination who have during that period:

(a) served upon the Executive and who at the date at which the voting strength of the Union is determined were effective members of the Union; or

(b) served upon the Committee of a Branch for a period amounting to two years and who at the date at which the voting strength of the Union is determined were effective members of the Union.

4. Nominations (if any) by the Branches of candidates for the Executive shall, subject to the provisions of paragraphs 3 and 5 hereof, be made by each Branch from fully paid-up members of the Union, and the Branch in selecting candidates for the Executive may at the same time, if it so desires, select alternative candidates to provide against the incapacity or withdrawal of the first subsequent candidates selected by it, but no alternative

candidate shall be put forward for election if a prior candidate remains eligible.

5. A Branch may nominate as a candidate for the Executive:

(a) Any fully paid-up member of any Branch in the Region in which the Branch is situated; and

(b) Any fully paid-up member of the Union whose occupation is appropriate to membership of the Branch or any Occupational Section thereof.

6. Subject to the provisions of the preceding paragraph hereof, a member eligible under the provisions of this rule who is nominated by a Branch as a candidate for the Executive on his Regional qualification may also be nominated as a candidate for the Executive on his Occupational qualification, or vice versa.

7. The Branch to which any member of the Executive belongs may, in the event of such member seeking re-election, petition the Executive against his being presented for re-election on the ground that he is an unsuitable candidate for the position, and any such petition, with the report (if any) of the Executive thereon, shall be placed before the Annual Conference in session for the purpose of being dealt with by it.

8. The members of the Executive shall assume office immediately after the conclusion of the Annual Conference, and on that event the retiring Executive shall cease to hold office. The member of the Executive appointed President of the Union shall assume office as President and Chairman of the Executive upon assuming office as a member of the Executive . . .

12. The general management and administration of the Union's business and, during all times other than actual sessions of an Annual Conference, the government of the Union shall be vested in the Executive, whose authority in that respect and to that extent shall be supreme, and power to appoint and remove any member or members of the Executive and of the Committees, and the Trustees and the Treasurer and other officers or one or other or any of them, and to appoint and remove such

other officers as they consider desirable, shall be vested in the Executive.

13. In the case of any finding being arrived at by the Executive on the interpretation of the rules, or on the conduct of course to be pursued or carried out with reference to any matter on which the rules are silent, such finding shall be conclusive as regards such case, but the Annual Conference may lay down other principles with reference to such conduct or course for the Executive's future guidance.

14. The Executive shall be the sole judge of all domestic matters concerning the Union and its affairs, and its decision shall be final.

15. The Executive shall meet in each quarter, and at other times on a demand of two-thirds of its members or on an instruction issued by the Emergency Committee or on a request issued by the General Secretary.

16. The Executive may, if it so desires, permit any member of the Union to be present at its sessions, but no such member shall take any part in the business of the Executive.

17. Every member of the Executive shall be entitled to be heard upon all matters coming before the Executive for deliberation, and every member present, including the Chairman, shall have one vote. Decisions shall be taken in accordance with the majority of the votes cast, and in the event of equal voting the Chairman shall have an additional casting vote.

18. The quorum for a meeting of the Executive shall be 15 . . .

21. The Executive shall, as and when required:

(i) Authorise and establish Regional and/or Occupational Councils relating to the Regions or Occupational Groups, comprising at least one delegate from each Branch within the respective Regions or Groups, and local co-ordinating committees on which committees each Branch within the appropriate area shall be represented;

(ii) Make regulations for the government and conduct of the aforesaid Councils and Committees and present them for ratification and/or amendment to the Annual Conference next ensuing; and such regulations shall include the following provisions.

Regional Councils shall be appointed in each Region annually and shall consist of a representative from each Branch in the Region. The Branch representative shall have not less than two years service as a Branch Officer and three years continuous membership of the Union. Councils will be appointed at a meeting called by Head Office and under the chairmanship of a member of the National Executive Council and a National Officer acting as Secretary of the meeting. The meeting will consist of two members from each Branch in the Region, the nominated member of the Council and one other Branch member. On the Council being appointed, the Council will elect a Chairman, Secretary and such other officers as is required for the Council's work. After the election of the officers, the meeting will then discuss with the National Executive Council member and the Union Officer the Union policy and matters of common interest to the members. The Councils will meet at least once a quarter throughout the year to conduct the Union Regional business as at present carried out by the Regional Council. The NEC subject to ratification by Conference shall have power to make and amend the regulations governing Union Regional Councils and such regulations shall have the same power as these rules.

(iii) Publish or cause to be published as appendices to the rules of the Union any such regulations ratified as aforesaid.

(iv) To make regulations for the Government and conduct of Branch Representatives and present them for ratification to the Annual Conference next ensuing. Such regulations shall include provision for the following:

(a) That whilst Branches shall remain the basic unit of the Union structure, there shall be a system of representatives at TECs, Depots, Offices, etc.

(*b*) That such representatives shall be nominees of the group of members involved and shall be elected by them through a system of ballot.

(*c*) Their duties shall include distribution of items of literature, meeting notices, etc., as approved by Head Office or Branches and they shall be given by regulation power to take up questions with first line management on behalf of the groups or individuals whom they represent.

(*d*) Questions unsettled should then be brought to the attention of the Branch Secretary or referred to a Branch or Committee meeting as appropriate.

(*e*) Such representatives will require recognition and this shall be obtained by the issue of a representatives card by Head Office of the Union.

(*f*) Representatives cards shall display the name of the representative, the limits of the representation, the rules relative to his powers and shall be endorsed by the Union's President and General Secretary. Such cards shall remain the property of the Union and shall be returned upon the holder relinquishing office.

(*g*) A system of remuneration shall be set up to cover the proper expenses of such representatives.

(*h*) A scheme of training for such representatives to be organised.

22. The Executive may appoint any member from any Branch:

(i) To visit, on behalf of the Union, Officials of the Post Office or other persons, or other institutions or organisations; and

(ii) To organise new Branches or otherwise conduct propaganda on behalf of the principles of the Union.

23. The Executive shall fill such vacancies as occur within itself during the year and such vacancies shall be filled by the highest loser in the appropriate electoral group from which the original member was elected.

24. The Executive may from time to time at its meeting consider and prepare proposals for submission to the Annual Conference.

25. In the administration of the Branches of the Union the Executive shall have power:

(i) To open, or authorise the opening of, new Branches.

(ii) To unite two or more Branches into one.

(iii) To divide one Branch into two or more.

(iv) To advise and instruct the Branches on all matters of organisation and propaganda.

26. Minutes of the proceedings of the Executive shall be taken by the General Secretary or a deputy appointed by him, and the Executive may direct reports of its proceedings, or such extracts therefrom as it indicates, to be published in *The Journal*.

27. The Executive may also frame such standing orders, by-laws or other regulations as it deems necessary for the conduct of its business and of the affairs of the Union generally.

28. Minutes of the Occupational Committees shall be subject to ratification by the Executive but shall not be subject to vote if the Occupational Committee is unanimously in support of the recorded decision.

Source: POEU. *Rules* (1969), rule 8

30 UNION OF SHOP, DISTRIBUTIVE AND ALLIED WORKERS: CONFERENCE AGENDA

. . . Negotiating machinery

5. By London Multiple Footwear

This ADM considers that lay members should participate in all future negotiations to which this Union is a party.

> Amendment by London Multiple Tailoring
>
> Add at end: 'especially when company agreements are taking the places of Wages Councils, JIC or agreements with Employers' Associations'.

Recruitment

6. By Liverpool Food Manufacturing

This ADM recognises that the recruitment and expansion of Union membership is of prime importance at this crucial time. To this end, it asks the Executive Council to give further and most serious consideration to making the image of the Union more attractive to greater numbers of workers in manufacturing industries, wholesaling and services and possibly technical and supervisory staffs. It believes that a change of title might assist in broadening the base of Union activities and involvement.

Amendment by Liverpool Wholesale Food Trades

Add at end: 'The altered title to be Amalgamated Distributive, Allied and Process Trade Union (ADAPT).'

Amendment by Liverpool Heavy Chemical No 1

Add at end: 'and that the title Allied Workers' Union (AWU) be considered as having a wider appeal'.

Amendment by Birmingham Co-operative

Delete all after 'workers' in line 4 and substitute 'by pursuing aggressive policies to advance wages and improve working conditions in the distributive industry and by using the full strength of the Union in enterprises where we have membership, including the Co-ops, to obtain levels of wages considerably in advance of legal minima. Only by such policies can the mass of the unorganised be attracted to see the value of trade union membership.' ...

... Milk

14. By Coatbridge SCWS

This ADM urges the Executive Council to negotiate for the wages of milk testers to be brought into line with pasteurisers.

15. By Whittington Dairy

This ADM requests payment at double-time rate for all work on Sundays and rest days.

16. By North Staffordshire Dairies
This ADM instructs the Executive Council to press immediately for double-time payment for work done on rest days not being a Sunday, and for treble-time payment for all work on a Sunday, being also a rest day . . .

. . . Working week
67. By Chilterns Co-operative
This ADM instructs the Executive Council to press for a 35-hour working week . . .

. . . Lords reform
94. By Gateshead
This ADM considers that the House of Lords is a useless luxury the country can ill afford, and asks the Executive Council to do all in its power to abolish it . . .

SOURCE: USDAW. Interim Agenda Paper for 23rd Annual Delegate Meeting (1969)

31 ELECTRICAL TRADES UNION: PROPOSAL FOR FULL-TIME EXECUTIVE

This Executive Council and previous ones have for a number of years been convinced that if this organisation is to expand and develop, as indeed we think it should, then it must have an Executive body that is occupied full-time in the process of that development. It should not be a body of frustrated Executive Council Members who are frustrated in determining the conflicting claims of Union responsibility, employment responsibility and domestic responsibility. I might say that domestic responsibility is not a small one. Therefore, the Amendments I wish to propose on behalf of Executive Council are all necessary to allow for a full-time Executive Council drawn from the rank and file of our organisation.

I would remind Conference—and particularly the Delegates who were present at the 1962 Rules Revision Conference—of the statement which I made at that Conference, the final paragraph of which says, and I quote: 'I must advise you that it is our intention to bring this proposal before the membership of the Electrical Trades Union at some future time.' This is the future time. Events since then have emphasised to a marked extent that the problems I related at that time have increased with the passage of time.

The first Amendment to Rule 9, Page 4, means that the Executive Council are proposing that in future the Union should have the benefit of a full-time Executive Council, elected for a five-year period of office. In the past, as far as our rules are concerned, we have always had a part-time Executive Council. In the early days of this Union, this was not an unreasonable system to adopt. The Union was small and composed very largely of contracting electricians. Everyone understood the conditions of that trade, and there was something to be said for putting the ultimate authority into the hands of the rank and file members who serve on the Executive Council in a part-time capacity. The situation today, however, is entirely different. The Union has nearly 300,000 members and has a greater potential rate of growth than any other Union in this country. At the same time, this growth is not taking place because of the expansion in the Contracting industry only. Our Union now contains members from a greater diversity of industries than any other Union in this country. Consequently, it is not so easy now for part-time Executive Council members to understand the working conditions of all our members in these diverse industries, primarily because in all probability they have no working experience in most of the industries from which our members are drawn. The number of industries with which the Union has agreements and negotiating rights has trebled since 1945, and this number is still continuing to grow. The Executive Council has the responsibility to examine and ratify every agreement negotiated by the Union at both national and local levels. For this reason alone, the part-time Executive Council member inevitably tends to become the servant of the officials who have had time and facilities at their disposal to master all and every detail of every section of every trade.

We agree with the early founders of our Union, that the Executive Council must have the final authority in the Union. We also believe that they have to a very large extent lost that authority because they have not had the time to master their job. This was the very point which emerged very clearly from the High Court Action Case which was, incidentally, acknowledged by both sides, and it prompted the Judge to observe that one reason for the mess the Union was in was that a part-time body of amateurs would always be dominated by a full-time body of professionals. Though the Court Case may now be disappearing into the realms of history, these points raised by the Judge then are still as relevant today. This Union could easily return to the conditions prior to 1961 for these very reasons.

We are proposing, therefore, to give this authority to the Executive Council by making it a full-time body. We believe that a full-time Executive Council would be more efficient in every way. Every Executive Council member will have the duty of understanding the issues in every section of the trade and, accordingly, the responsibility for decisions taken by the Union will fall entirely on his shoulders. Every Executive Meeting would take place at least every month, and, possibly, fortnightly instead of the present constitutional two-month period and, as a consequence, the business of each meeting would be much more manageable. In the past we have had the position of part-time provincial Executive Council members coming down to London for a two-day Executive Council Meeting, which very often extended into a three- or four-day meeting because of the amount of work in hand. They have been given a hundred pages of Minutes to digest, numerous strikes to discuss and take immediate action upon. It is not surprising, therefore, that under such conditions and circumstances the functions of the Executive Council were usurped. At the same time, this part-time

F

Executive Council lacks even the virtue of economy. I am sure
it is in this regard that the following figures will be very illu-
minating to you. A survey conducted by our Accounts Department by our new Chartered Accountant, Mr. Diamond, revealed that for the last quarter in 1964, the average cost per
member of the Executive Council was £542 3s. 0d. or £2,168
per year. For the first quarter of 1965, these figures were
£483 5s. 0d. average of £1,933 average per year. Also—and
this is more important—the average costs in terms of expenses
paid to Executive Council members in October to December,
1964 were £269 12s. 0d. per quarter or £1,078 per year. The
figures are worse in the January to March quarter, 1965. These
figures are £310 per quarter or £1,240 per year which, when
deciphered, mean that it is costing this Union on an average
£1,240 per Executive Council member per year for the Executive Council as it exists at present.

During the past ten years or so, the Executive Council
members—and this is usually well known—have been employed
for the whole of their time because of the very nature of the job
and the calls upon their time made by the Union, although they
have never been recognised as Full-time Officers by this or
previous constitutions for their services rendered.

In addition to the two Executive Council members, four or
five Executive Council members are working in effect full-time,
either outside or from Union Headquarters. These are not
necessarily always the same four or five people. It depends upon
their availability at the time. This availability is, of course, dictated by the employer or, perhaps, the type of industry in which
the member is engaged. You can well imagine, of course, what a
contracting employer would say to one of his employees being
an Executive Council member when he requests unlimited and
unspecified time off work. Attached to this difficulty is the question of the Executive Council member who has been allowed
time off work to assist the Union temporarily in a full-time
capacity losing his holiday entitlement or his superannuation
allowances. Some of the Executive Council members, both past

and present, have lost considerable superannuation entitlements, some as much as 30 to 40 years of benefit. All this because they were willing to assist in resolving our members' problems. Under our present rules there is no recompense whatsoever.

I made reference earlier to the availability of the Executive Council members to be engaged on a temporary full-time basis. I would draw your attention to these members of the Executive Council who were unable to obtain the necessary time off work to be so engaged. This is a problem which will continue in this unsatisfactory manner unless you accept this rule change.

I have further to remind you of the tremendous amount of time spent in travelling from the provinces to London and the various towns where their presence is required on Union business. When you realise that provincial members have to spend the day before and the day after meetings travelling, you will see that there is this added difficulty of obtaining not two or three days off work for Executive Council or Sub-Committee Meetings but four or five days off work, which brings me to the point: are we always as an Executive Council to be at the employers' mercy to obtain time off work to do our legitimate trade union business which the members have elected us to do?

To conclude, I ask you to support the Executive Council in this Amendment to Rule 9, Page 4, to make the Executive Council a full-time body for as long as our present constitution lasts. Let me say finally that we feel that a full-time Executive Council will be able to maintain a closer contact with the division the Executive Councillor represents and will cease to be the least-known representative in his division. By adopting greater responsibility for his division, he will give it more effective representation on the Executive Council itself. We are convinced as a body that we cannot proceed to function in this day and age on a part-time basis. Because of these lengthy reasons I have given you, I am asking you unanimously to support this Amendment and carry it to provide a full-time Executive body.

SOURCE: ETU. Abridged Report of the Second Biennial Delegate Conference (May 1965), 46–8. Motion proposed by E. Hadley, member of the Executive Council

32 J. E. MORTIMER: NEW CATEGORIES OF TECHNICIANS

The growth in drawing office employment in the years before and during the war, and the development of new industrial techniques resulted in the creation of a considerable number of new technicians whose work was allied to the drawing office but who were not draughtsmen. The largest such group were the planning engineers, whose function is to analyse a product drawing with a view to determining the method of manufacture, including the sequence of manufacturing operations. The work of planning engineers is closely related to that of jig and tool draughtsmen, and many planners receive their early training as tool draughtsmen. Some, however, graduate direct from the workshops and the toolroom without passing through the intermediary stage of the tool drawing office.

In 1942 the rules of the AESD were silent on the subject of planning engineers. It was generally held that planners who had joined the Association whilst employed as draughtsmen were eligible to retain their membership, but that planners who applied whilst employed as planning engineers were ineligible for membership.

The eligibility of planning engineers for membership was discussed on a number of resolutions at the 1942 conference. One of them, from Bristol No. 2, sought to amend the rules to make planning engineers eligible for membership equally with draughtsmen, estimators and calculators. The mover of the motion, Mr. D. J. Haddon, stated that his motion was intended to remove an anomaly in the rules. The job of the planning engineer, he contended, was generally recognised as being of a higher grade than that of the jig and tool draughtsman. The motion was seconded by Mr. H. Baker of Birmingham South who said that the ineligibility of planning engineers for membership was a serious matter in the aircraft and motor car industries where many of them were employed. The motion was carried.

Another motion was also carried instructing the Executive Committee to investigate the extent to which the division of labour was being applied to the function of draughtsmanship, and to report on the desirability of extending the rules to cover certain categories of workers who were ancillary to the drawing office.

The Executive Committee reported the findings of their investigations to the following year's conference. They examined the functions of a number of categories of workers—including estimators, plant engineers, material allocators, template draughtsmen, contract engineers and others—suggested to them by the branches. Except where it could be reasonably shown that the duties of a particular category of worker were a sub-division of the one-time function of draughtsmanship the EC recommended that they should not be admitted to membership. They stated, for example, that where a plant engineer was, in fact, a plant draughtsman he was already eligible for membership. Where he was not a plant draughtsman he was ineligible, and they did not feel that any alteration should be made.

The proposals of the EC were accepted, with the exception of their recommendation that template draughtsmen should not be admitted to membership. Template draughtsmen were described in the EC report as men 'engaged on completion of details between the layout drawings and actual production; in some cases taking site dimensions, preparing shop drawings, and development of plate work'. Mr. W. Gillan, Paisley, moved an amendment to the report urging that template draughtsmen should be recognised as eligible for membership under the existing rules. He referred, in particular, to a large firm in the area of his branch where more than fifty template draughtsmen were employed on work which would otherwise have been performed in the drawing office.

Mr. Young, on behalf of the Executive Committee, pointed out that there were special demarcation difficulties in the case of template draughtsmen. In some firms the kind of work on which they were engaged was done by members of the Boilermakers' Society. He suggested that each case should be dealt with on its merits having regard to local circumstances. Mr. Gillan's amendment was, nevertheless, carried.

There was a sequel to this debate some eleven years later in 1954 when AESD members employed in the template office of Messrs. Babcock & Wilcox, Renfrew, went on strike for trade union recognition. This was the office to which Mr. Gillan had referred in the 1943 conference debate. The strike was officially supported by the AESD and was successful.

SOURCE: Mortimer, J. E. *A History of The Association of Engineering and Shipbuilding Draughtsmen* (1960), 219–21

33 TECHNICAL AND SUPERVISORY SECTION OF THE AMALGAMATED UNION OF ENGINEERING WORKERS: RECRUITING NEW RANGES OF WORKER

The Executive Committee received a report from the Recruitment and Publicity Sub-Committee on the recruitment campaign launched with the June issue of *TASS Journal* . . .

The Executive Committee hopes that each member of our union will actively support the campaign by:

Consolidating existing areas of partial organisation.

Recruiting new ranges of allied technical worker.

Recruiting all support staff, where this increases the general strength of the union and does not conflict with the established organisation of other unions.

SOURCE: *TASS Journal* (July 1972), 2

34 TRANSPORT AND GENERAL WORKERS' UNION: THE SHOP STEWARD'S JOB

The shop steward is the key figure in carrying out the TGWU's policy for high wages and effective organisation. The two aspects of the policy advance together. Our plans for high wages based on the maximum extension of plant and local bargaining depend upon workshop representatives who are able to take the initiative and play a positive part in negotiations with management. For their part workers quickly appreciate the value of being union members when they see their shop stewards in the forefront of the struggle to keep up their wages and protect their working conditions.

As a shop steward there is no doubt that the eyes of the members in your shop are upon you. You are the Union as far as they are concerned.

You are the agency through which come any services our Union provides for them, and through which they normally hear about us. When the public at large think about us they often have in mind the general secretary. But to the members in your shop the image which the Union will conjure up will certainly be you. Make sure you are a good advertisement. The way to do this is to carry out efficiently your job as a shop steward. It is the only way.

Remember first of all that you are an official of the Union. Rule 11 lays down your status.

'Shop stewards shall be elected wherever possible by the membership in organised factories, garages, depots, wharves and on building jobs, etc., and shall receive the fullest support and protection from the Union, and immediate inquiry shall be undertaken by the appropriate trade group or district committee into every case of dismissal of a shop steward with a view to preventing victimisation, either open or concealed.'

You carry in trust a responsibility for an organisation which has taken generations of struggle and service to build up. Pledge yourself that your spell of office will keep up its high traditions. Remember that in the last resort the power of trade unionism depends upon workers acting in unity. Trade-union unity doesn't involve barrack-square discipline. We are a voluntary organisation: not an army. But unity in action does mean paying intelligent regard to the policy of the Union, and the wider movement.

If you do your work well as a shop steward the workers will see daily evidence of the value of their trade union membership. You need nevertheless to seize every opportunity of taking action to build up the strength of the Union—by recruiting new members, by keeping existing members up to scratch, and by turning 'cardholders' into trade unionists.

As a shop steward you represent on behalf of the Union its members in the workplace. You are responsible for ensuring that wages and working conditions are a credit to the Union. If any of your members has an individual grievance or a problem, you have the responsibility to see that you do your best to help him. In dealing with many of your problems the Union will expect you to be able to manage on your own. If you cannot, you know you have the power and resources of the TGWU behind you.

In doing your job as a shop steward you have to guard against two dangers. One is of relying so much on yourself that, in effect, you run your own union and proceed without any regard for the importance of working as a team. Sooner or later, however, even the strongest workshop group needs help from fellow workers outside. It is, therefore, a matter of self-interest not to undermine the unity of the working class which is expressed in the trade-union movement.

The other extreme to guard against is the shop steward who becomes a mere messenger. Every problem, even though it is clearly within his own competence to settle, is referred to his convenor, branch officer, or district official for advice.

SOURCE: TGWU. *Shop Stewards Handbook* (1969), 4–6

35 NATIONAL UNION OF PUBLIC EMPLOYEES FACILITIES FOR TRADE UNIONS

(Appendix to Advance Letter (ASC) 2/71
issued by the Department of Health and Social Security)

A. Union stewards

It is in the interests of both employing authorities and of staff that Union stewards should be suitably trained and competent in their duties, and that their rights and responsibilities should be clearly understood.

Recognition

1. A Union steward who has been appointed in accordance with the rules of a recognised Union represented on the Ancillary Staffs Council, has been duly accredited by the Union and has been in the employment of the authority for at least six working days shall, upon written notification by the Union to the authority of his appointment, be recognised as the representative of the members of that Union employed as Ancillary Staff in the hospital Group, hospital or other organisation, or particular section or Department thereof.

Functions

2. The functions of a Union steward, within the context of this agreement, shall be to represent the Union members concerned to investigate any complaint or difficulty raised by those members; to make representations on such matters to the management and to co-operate with management to ensure that the agreements of the Council are observed.

Facilities

3. The employing authority shall give recognised Union stewards facilities for exercising their functions, and stewards shall ensure the proper use of such facilities.

Other rights and duties

4. Stewards may, with permission from the management (which shall not be unreasonably withheld), leave their work to conduct such Union business as is necessary and relevant to that part of the hospital Group, hospital or organisation which they represent and to the functions referred to in paragraph 2 above.

5. In the event of a difficulty arising which cannot be resolved between the management and the Union steward, the steward shall immediately report the circumstances to his Union in order that the matter can be dealt with under the agreed procedure for settling differences.

6. Stewards shall be subject to all the provisions of the Council's agreements in the same way as any other employee, but no recognised steward shall be dismissed or otherwise penalised in any way whatsoever for carrying out his functions as a steward in accordance with the provisions of this agreement.

Training

7. While recognising that it is the responsibility of the Union to ensure that stewards are appropriately briefed on, and trained in, their duties, the rules and practice of the Union, the appropriate Whitley agreements and procedures, and the practice of Industrial Relations generally, the Council asks employing authorities to assist Unions to discharge this responsibility by exercising their discretion to allow adequate time off with pay (which should be calculated in the same manner as holiday pay) for stewards to take part in relevant training activities whether organised by Trade Unions or others. Responsibility for fees and expenses for such training rests with the Union.

8. It is to the advantage of both management and staff that stewards be included in official training schemes which are likely to assist them in the proper discharge of their duties: e.g.,

courses on work study and incentive schemes and on subjects such as communications, NHS organisation and consultation procedures. In such cases it is hoped that employing authorities will use their discretion to meet expenses and fees, such training being clearly to the benefit of the hospital service.

B. Other local representatives

9. The above provisions do not cover workers' representatives specially appointed for the purposes of interim or payment by results schemes, whose rights and responsibilities are those necessary to enable them to discharge their duties in connection with such schemes.

C. Full-time Trade Union officers

10. Full-time Union officers shall be permitted to visit the work-place in the performance of their trade union duties and for the purpose of seeing that the Council's agreements are observed, provided they make prior arrangements with the employing authorities' senior representative and inform him of their arrival at the work-place.

D. Meetings of employees

11. The prior permission of management must be received before any meeting of employees is held during working hours.
12. Wherever possible employing authorities should permit suitable accommodation to be used for Union branch meetings, provided that these are held at reasonable times.

E. Inspection of cards

13. The prior permission of management must be received before any inspection of Trade Union membership cards is held during working hours.

SOURCE: NUPE. *Your Job as a Union Steward* (1971), 36–9

36 JACK JONES: SUCCESSFUL DEMOCRACY

Publicity, necessary as it is, is not the key to the way forward for the trade union movement. The trade unions will be judged —rightly—by the results they get for their members and the impact they have upon the needs of the community. And this is to be established not by publicity; or any gimmicks, but by effective bargaining.

Many people, however, have talked as if all we had to do in the trade union movement was to streamline ourselves— modernize the structure—and become more commercial and 'businesslike'. More experts, more professionals, more computers. Well, we are getting those—including the computers— but that is only the fringe.

Our success—and indeed the success of industry itself is going to be determined by the extent to which we can decentralize— spread decision making amongst the workpeople, and above all get industrial agreements settled where they are going to be operated. *That* is the key.

For example, many people have taken up the point made by the Royal Commission that more trade union officers are needed. The Royal Commission was a body largely made up of professionals—and we now have a large body of experts involved in practically every aspect of policy in this country who have a vested interest in the idea that 'professionalism' is the answer.

Not authoritarian

I do not discount the professional but I believe we have to draw on the expert that is inside almost every worker—we have got to get our agreements down to the point where the workers themselves are involved in the negotiations—and want to keep the agreements because *they* have had a decisive hand in making them and therefore understand them. Such industrial agreements in my view will be 'efficient'—they will become increasingly comprehensive and professional—*but they won't be authoritarian*—and that I am afraid is what lies behind a great deal of the argument for professionalism.

There is an idea that the full-time official will be more amenable to management, more willing to bring the men into line. There is the similar view that behind any trade union there should be professionals running things even if the facade is democratic.

These have been the myths—but they are increasingly being exploded as work-people themselves are taking authority, rightly, into their own hands. The mood is changing and because of this we should not look for trade union reform that is based on small, permanent full-time decision-making bodies. This is not justified, and will not be accepted.

I look to see the trade union official as being very much the co-ordinator, the encourager, the man to call in when a problem cannot be resolved or when it gets a wider significance. He is the man, to be honest, who should be (increasingly) working where trades unionism is weak, where it needs to be built up. Where it is strong he should not be required so much.

This is the way forward for trades unionism in the '70s—not the authoritarian order giving machine that some of our 'friends' urge upon us. For that reason, if I might make a personal point to the press; I know the word 'boss' is a nice short word which will often fit into a column or a headline—but *please don't call me a trade union boss*—I am not a boss, and I don't want to be one. I am working for a system where not a few trade union officials control the situation but a dedicated, well-trained and intelligent body of trades union members is represented by hundreds of thousands of lay representatives—every one of whom is capable of helping to resolve industrial problems and assist in collective bargaining and the conclusion of agreements.

The results will be improved wages and wages systems and efficiency in output and services well beyond the stage reached at present. No one need fear this except the bad employer—

who relies upon low wages to mask inefficiency, or who seeks to assert a personal brand of authoritarianism that is more suited to the 1870s than the 1970s.

SOURCE: Jones, Jack (General Secretary, TGWU). *Trades Unionism in the Seventies* (TGWU pamphlet 1970), 5–6. From a speech to the Institute of Personnel Management in 1969

37 CIVIL AND PUBLIC SERVICES ASSOCIATION THE PROBLEM OF SECRET GROUP ACTIVITY

The next debate might well have been acrimonious. It wasn't. The subject was sufficiently contentious to have split Conference right down the middle. It didn't. As a debate it was chock full of good speeches and it is to the immense credit of all who spoke that the matter was given a very full airing in an extraordinary unemotional manner.

[895] In view of the spread of ever increasing unity of purpose amongst the membership, this Conference believes that the existence of a 'group' or 'groups' in an atmosphere of secrecy hinders such moves. The National Executive Committee is therefore instructed to investigate the constitutional changes necessary either to end such secret groupings, or, to establish all such groups within the framework of our constitution. The choice being governed by the best interests of the membership. [CARRIED]

The motion was moved by Brian Oldrey, who said we are now in a situation in which there is increasing unity in CPSA and that such unity needs to be nourished by openness and honesty. 'Secret groupings', he insisted, 'will destroy that unity by destroying the trust that is essential.'

He thought that there was nothing wrong with grouping together, provided it is done openly and that groups are prepared to explain openly the purpose of their activities.

He went on to say that the motion might be opposed on the grounds that it would be impossible to stop this kind of thing but he asserted that it was not the intention to stop anything, but to try 'to involve everybody in the organisation and unity of Association'.

There were loud cheers for Brian and more cheers for Clive Bush who seconded. Speaking very seriously Clive reminded Conference that almost without exception candidates in the group list were elected to the NEC and that smear tactics were used against other candidates. He went on to describe his own painful personal experience in this respect and asked Conference to support.

The first opposition came from Wally Walton, who asserted that this was not the first time such allegations were made, but certainly his Branch which had a sizeable vote had not been approached by anyone.

He concluded amid applause and was followed by Mrs. A. Rose, Kidbrooke, with a reminder that delegates are free to choose whom they vote for so 'what the blazes are you discussing this for'.

The next speaker was the GENERAL SECRETARY who had been given a free hand by the NEC to support the motion.

He pointed out that this issue touched on the health and future organisation of the Association.

Secret group activity did exist which effectively influenced all elections.

He did not object to canvassing but he believed the domination of Association affairs by one group was unhealthy. He felt the membership should be trusted to deal with any political force which attempted to subvert Association policy. The time has come, he concluded amid wide applause, for the voluntary dissolution of unofficial groups.

For the NEC, Mary Layton agreed it was time for the voluntary dissolution of unofficial groups but argued that the motion would not achieve that. She believed that whatever the fate of the motion, the membership were sensible enough to govern their own future.

Next to the rostrum was Charles Smith, MOD Chilwell to

support the motion, and Walter Stubbs from the same Branch
followed him to the rostrum to oppose.

Another NEC speaker, Ken Blinkhorn offered opposition.
His argument was that the proposal was misguided; more
likely to divide than unite the Association. He rejected the picture painted by the supporters of the motion of 'a sinister Ku-
Klux-Klan organisation' in CPSA. The discussion had centred
about one group but he suggested there was more than one. He
spoke of his experience before he was elected to the NEC of
attempts to influence delegates by a Communist group. He
believed that there 'is still a movement in this country from the
Communist Party to influence the labour and trade union
movement'. He concluded amid cheers that Conference should
reject the motion because it would only create the impression
of a divided Association.

There followed a short supporting intervention by Clarrie
Muston, DHSS, and then came Brian Oldrey's right of reply,
which clinched the matter. The motion was carried by a
considerable majority.

SOURCE: *Red Tape* (July/August 1970), 332

PART SIX

Trade Union Structure 2

(b) EXTERNAL RELATIONS

One way of considering the question of structural arrangements for handling inter-union relations is to use the analogy of large firms. At least in some areas of their activity large firms find themselves in competition with other firms. This may lead them to reconsider the kind of product or service they provide. At the same time, for all sorts of reasons, such as lobbying directed at the government, negotiations with trade unions, or the setting up of research and information services, firms operate jointly through a network of federations and agencies which represent varying degrees of co-operative action. In addition, instead of taking existing arrangements between firms—or competition—as given, there may be a pursuit of mergers.

So, it should be less of a surprise to find equivalent pressures and trends in relations between trade unions. Both in structure and function, unions are deeply influenced by the changing structure of industry. A succession of trade union amalgamations in recent years has reflected the need to re-think union organisation to match much more concentrated business power. The recent amalgamation of the National Union of Vehicle Builders with the Transport and General Workers' Union is clearly a response to the situation in the motor industry. Another example is the regrouping of engineering unions into the Amalgamated Union of Engineering Workers, with four federal sections covering engineering, foundries, constructional engineering, and technical and supervisory work.

Regrouping of this kind may follow more limited attempts at co-operation, such as special arrangements between particular unions for joint working, or industrial federations or joint trade union committees with collective bargaining responsibilities. There may also be agreements in spheres of influence. Many of these arrangements have a long history; some have been influenced more recently by the changed pattern produced by amalgamations, and by a development of TUC-based initiatives to strengthen co-ordination between unions, particularly within major industries or sectors.

The TUC has also been influential in preventing the competition and overlapping of trade union recruitment areas from leading to serious conflicts. The most important arrangements here are the rules, known as the Bridlington Principles, governing exchange of members and organisation by potentially competing unions. TUC affiliates are expected to operate these rules and, in the event of a disagreement that cannot be resolved, to submit to the arbitration of the TUC Disputes Committee. It is worth mentioning that this arrangement is seen as of such positive value in avoiding inter-union disagreements that a union such as the National and Local Government Officers Association accepted the authority of the Disputes Committee even before it decided in the mid-1960s to affiliate to the TUC.

The documents are designed to display these various facets of the structure of inter-union relations. The Bridlington Principles are followed by an example of a TUC Disputes Committee award. There is a rule from a trade union rule book which reveals the existence of traditional tension between particular unions. A long extract gives the key information about the most important industrial federation, the Confederation of Shipbuilding and Engineering Unions, and a short one notes a recent closer working arrangement between two non-manual unions. This arrangement is especially interesting, since it is designed to attract staff associations towards the trade unions concerned, thus drawing attention to yet another element in the competitive struggle for the representation of employees. Amalgamation is illustrated by the case presented to members of two unions to form the Association of Scientific, Technical and Managerial Staffs.

There is also a speech by Will Paynter, then General Secretary of the

National Union of Mineworkers, at the last Congress of the TUC he attended. He was advocating industrial unionism or, as he put it, 'adapting trade union structure to industry', an attempt to suggest a coherent and consistent approach to the question of change in union structure. This method has not been particularly popular within the TUC and was attacked in J. D. M. Bell's pamphlet, Industrial Unionism, *in 1949 (reprinted in McCarthy.* Trade Unions, *1972). However, the establishment of industrial committees within the TUC (see extracts 49 and 50) perhaps goes some way towards meeting the desire of those who want stronger union organisation along industrial lines.*

38 TUC: PRINCIPLES FOR THE AVOIDANCE OF DISPUTES

Adopted by the Bridlington Congress 1939

1. Each union shall consider the possibility of joint working agreements with unions with whom they are in frequent contact; such agreements should deal, where possible, with:

(a) Spheres of influence;

(b) Recognition of cards;

(c) Machinery for composing difficulties;

(d) Conditions for transfer of members.

Note: Agreements referred to may be bilateral, or arranged through existing joint machinery such as Federations. In all cases the machinery of the General Council is at the disposal of affiliated unions to promote harmony and smooth working.

2. No one who is or has recently been a member of any trade union should be accepted into membership in another without inquiry of his present or former union. The present or former union shall be under obligation to reply within 14 days of the inquiry, stating:

(a) Whether the applicant has tendered his resignation;

(b) Whether he is clear on the books;

(c) Whether he is under discipline or penalty;

(*d*) Whether there are any other reasons why the applicant should not be accepted.

Note: No member should be allowed to escape his financial obligations by leaving one union while in arrears and by joining another.

3.   Each union shall use an Inquiry Form as proposed by the General Council in the case of all inquiries under (2) above, and forward reasoned replies on any such form as they may receive from an inquiring union.

4.   No union shall accept a member of another union where inquiry shows that the member is:

(*a*) Under discipline;

(*b*) Engaged in a trade dispute;

(*c*) In arrears with contributions.

Notes: In regard to the question of arrears, the policy has been adopted that where no rule appears as to exclusion of members for arrears of contributions the period of 26 weeks shall be applied.

It should be a general understanding that both national and local officials of trade unions should refrain from speaking or acting adversely to the interests of any other union during any period in which the members of the latter union are participating in a trade dispute. Much trouble could be avoided if unions about to participate in a trade dispute would take care to inform other unions whose members would be likely to be affected thereby.

5.   No union shall commence organising activities at any establishment or undertaking in respect of any grade or grades of workers in which another union has the majority of workers employed and negotiates wages and conditions, unless by arrangement with that union.

Notes: On March 10, 1938, a circular was sent to affiliated organisations, headed 'Inter-Union Competition', which was approved at the 1938 Blackpool Congress. This circular asked that each union affiliated to Congress should agree not to initiate recruitment activities in any industrial concern where it had no membership if another affiliated union catering for the same grade or grades of workers had already succeeded in 'securing and maintaining membership'.

In formulating the 1939 Bridlington Congress Proposals, the General Council recommended the more precise form of wording contained in (5) above because they did not wish the impression to be given that the securing and maintaining of membership, no matter how small, should preclude another organisation from attempting to organise what might be a majority of the workpeople at the firm, as this would be placing a premium on non-unionism.

The TUC General Council and affiliated organisations know, however, of circumstances in which a union may not at a particular time have a majority of organised workpeople in an undertaking, although they may have had a majority at some time previously; or of cases where in face of exceptional difficulties a union may have been trying for some time to secure organisation. Under such circumstances, there should be consultation and agreement before another union commences organising activities.

6. Each union shall include in its membership form questions on the lines of the TUC Model Form, in regard to past or present membership of another union

The essential questions on the Model Form are as follows: Are you, or have you been, a member of any other Trade Union or Unions? Give the name of the Union or Unions of which you are or were formerly a member.

If you are a member of any other Trade Union and are not in benefit, please state what is the amount of your arrears.

Note: Failure by a union to include the necessary questions on its application form will make it impossible for a union to pursue the course of inquiry laid down, and will be regarded by the Disputes Committee as an important factor in determining any complaint brought against such union.

INQUIRY FORM

From ....
....
To ....
....

We have received an application:
Dated... from
Name ....
Address ....
Employed at ....
(Department) ....
to join our Union.

Before accepting the application we should be glad if you would, within 14 days, in accordance with the decision of the

Trades Union Congress, let us have your comments on the points raised overleaf.

Signed .... *Date* ....

Office held ....

Address ....

REPLY TO INQUIRY

The present or former Union (of a member making application to another Union) shall be under obligation to reply within 14 days of the inquiry.

FROM ....

....

To ....

....

In regard to the person named overleaf, I desire to reply as follows:

    1. Has the applicant tendered his resignation?

      Answer ....

    2. Was he clear on the books on the date he made application?

      Answer ....

    3. Was he under discipline or penalty on that date?

      Answer ....

    4. Any other reason why application should not be accepted?

      Answer ....

      ....

      ....

      ....

Signed .... *Date* ....

Office held ....

NOTE: *The Reply Form normally appears on the back of the Inquiry Form. Hence the use of the word* overleaf *in the above specimen.*

SOURCE: TUC. *Relations between Unions* (1952, revised 1964), 4–5, 8. The 1964 edition states: 'This is a revised edition of the pamphlet first published in 1952. It contains no new material but its contents are arranged in a manner which is considered will be more helpful. The four "Main Principles for the Avoidance of Disputes", first approved by the 1924 Congress and re-affirmed and revised by the 1939 Bridlington Congress, have been merged (without alteration) with six "Recommendations Adopted" by the Bridlington Congress. It has become customary to refer to these six points as the "Bridlington Principles" . . .'

39 TUC DISPUTES COMMITTEE
REPORT OF A DISPUTE AND AWARD

(36) Civil Service Union and National Union of Agricultural & Allied Workers: Meat and Livestock Commission

A Disputes Committee composed of Mr. D. H. Davies, Chairman, Mr. E. Moore (President, Amalgamated Society of Leather Workers) and Mr. W. Lewis (Assistant General Secretary, Amalgamated Union of Building Trade Workers), with Mr. K. Graham as Secretary, met in Congress House on Tuesday, June 23, 1970 to consider a dispute between the Civil Service Union and the National Union of Agricultural & Allied Workers relating to which union should be regarded as appropriate for the purpose of organising and negotiating on behalf of stockmen employed by the Meat and Livestock Commission. The CSU were represented by Mr. P. J. Gresham and Mr. B. J. Francis and the NUAAW by Mr. F. Coffin and Mr. R. Pierson.

Award

After consideration the following Award was made by the Disputes Committee:

The issue before the Disputes Committee concerns a difference between the Civil Service Union and the National Union of Agricultural & Allied Workers as to which union should be regarded as appropriate for the purpose of organising and negotiating on behalf of stockmen employed by the Meat and Livestock Commission.

The CSU claimed that it had membership within the Meat and Livestock Commission since its formation in 1968, and prior to that in its predecessor the Pig Industry Development Board, and that they had a current membership of 25 of the 44 stockmen employed by the Commission. They stated that they had commenced negotiations with the Commission on behalf of stockmen on February 13, 1969 and that these negotiations were interrupted in December 1969 when the NUAAW also claimed the right to negotiate on behalf of stockmen. The CSU claimed that they had been the first to organise the men concerned and were the more appropriate union as the stockmen were basically civil servants. The CSU had a great deal of experience organising and negotiating in this field.

The NUAAW claimed that the stockmen were basically agricultural workers and on that basis they were the more appropriate union to organise and negotiate on their behalf. They stated that they had experience of organising and negotiating on the behalf of agricultural employees of the Ministry of Agriculture and the Milk Marketing Board and similar bodies. They had had members among stockmen from the inception of the Commission and claimed a current membership of 30. The NUAAW had approached the Commission in December 1969, in an effort to gain negotiating rights and claimed that had it not been for the opposition of the CSU these rights would have been granted.

Both unions agreed that in view of the small number of workers involved it would not be practicable or desirable for the two unions to be recognised and they undertook to facilitate transfers of members in conformity with the terms of the Disputes Committee's Award.

The Disputes Committee accept that the CSU had established organisation and had begun negotiations with the Meat and Livestock Commission prior to the NUAAW taking an active interest in these matters. The Committee have formed the view that the NUAAW had only taken an active interest in organising and representing the Commission's stockmen when their attention had been drawn to the position by a CSU circular dated August 1969 and an application for transfer received from the CSU in October 1969 in respect of a member of the NUAAW. The Committee have therefore reached the conclusion, having regard to the above paragraph, that the CSU is the appropriate union for the purposes of organising and negotiating on behalf of stockmen employed by the Meat and Livestock Commission and they award accordingly.

The Committee wish to make it clear that this decision applies only to stockmen employed by the Meat and Livestock Commission.

SOURCE: TUC. Annual Report (1971), 32-3

40 ASSOCIATED SOCIETY OF LOCOMOTIVE ENGINEERS AND FIREMEN: A UNION DISCIPLINE CLAUSE

Any member who is disloyal to the Society's interest by opposing official candidates in Sectional Council or Local Departmental Committee elections or holding official positions in another railway trade union will render himself liable to expulsion from the Society or such disciplinary action as the Executive Committee may think fit.

SOURCE: ASLEF. Rules (revised 1967), rule 13

41 CONFEDERATION OF SHIPBUILDING AND ENGINEERING UNIONS: STRUCTURE AND FUNCTIONS

Organisation

14. On paper, the organisation of the Confederation appears formidable, providing direct representation for over 2 million

trade union members. There are 31 unions affiliated (June, 1965) but owing to the composition of two of the unions the affiliation list shows 35 affiliated organisations. The two unions concerned are (1) the Amalgamated Society of Boilermakers, Shipwrights, Blacksmiths and Structural Workers which affiliates its Boilermakers' section, its Blacksmiths' section and its Shipwrights' section separately, and (2) the Transport and General Workers' Union which has its main affiliation in the name of the Union and is in fact the affiliation of its members in General Engineering: and also affiliates two of its sub groups:—The National Union of Enginemen, Firemen, Mechanics and Electrical Workers, and the National Association of Clerical and Supervisory Staffs as separate organisations. In addition, of course, the Confederation-negotiated agreements determine the wages and conditions of all the non-trade union members, and influence the wages and conditions of members of non-Confederated Unions working in the industry. It is estimated, therefore, that the number affected by Confederation National Agreements is around 3 million workers.

15.   There is a comprehensive arrangement of meetings at Central District and Works level.

Annual conference

16.   The Confederation holds its policy-making conference annually in June. In attendance are from 2 to 9 representatives (depending upon affiliation) from each of the 35 affiliates, and one representative from each of the 49 Confederation District Committees. The purpose of the Annual Conference is to receive reports of the past year, to declare common policy in matters relating to wages, hours and general working conditions, and to elect the Executive Council which will serve until the next Annual Meeting.

Voting procedure

17.   Voting on resolutions at the annual conference is usually taken on a show of hands and thus a majority of the delegates

present will have determined a particular policy. However, any union may call for a card vote to be taken and should a card vote be demanded by the delegates of any union, it must be taken at once; each union is then entitled to cast one vote for each member for whom affiliation fees have been paid. (Rule III, Clause 4).

General council

18. The General Council meets three times a year in January, April and October, and is responsible for the general administration of the Confederation business. Representation is on the basis of one representative per 10,000 members or part thereof, with a maximum of 9 representatives from any one affiliated society.

Executive council

19. An Executive Council of 30 is elected at the Annual Conference, and serves for a term of office of one year, retiring members being eligible for re-election. Election is by card vote and unions are restricted to a maximum of one EC member from unions with up to 50,000 affiliated membership, two EC members from unions with 50,000 to 200,000 affiliated membership, and nine EC members from unions of over 200,000 affiliated membership.

20. The EC is given wide powers to deal with questions arising in the industries, and has authority to conclude agreements on behalf of the Confederation in all negotiations which were entered into by authority of the General Council.

21. Meetings of the EC are held each month at York, and coincide with the Central Conference, which discusses matters arising through the 'Procedure Agreement'.

22. At the first meeting of the EC each year Sub-Committees and representatives to outside bodies are appointed. The normal pattern is:

Main Standing Committees

Engineering Committee
President, and Full EC.

Shipyard Committee
President and Full EC.

General Purposes Sub-Committee
President, and five EC members plus three substitute members (also from the EC).

Railway Sub-Committee
At its first meeting, the Executive Council appoints ten members to serve on the Railway Shopmen's National Council. These ten representatives then become the Confederation's Railway Sub-Committee. They need not necessarily be members of the Confederation Executive Council, but they must be Executive Council members of their own union, or national officers carrying executive authority. Unions are restricted as to the number of their members they can have appointed to the Railway Shopmen's National Council. Unions with up to 200,000 affiliated membership may have one member appointed, and unions with over 200,000 affiliated membership, a maximum of three members. (Rule II, Clause 9.)

Sub-Committees
Aircraft Committee; and Craftsmen's Negotiating Committees for Gas, Water, Hospitals and Local Authorities' Services.

The Founding Unions Committee is a committee of Unions with members working in Foundries. It meets quarterly under the Chairmanship of a Confederation EC member, and a record of its meetings is kept and submitted to the General Council for information.

The Confederation General Secretary (or Assistant General Secretary acting as his deputy) acts, without voting power, as secretary to all Committees.

23. The Confederation EC nominates to many outside industrial and government-appointed bodies, including Engineering and Shipbuilding Advisory Councils, National Joint Body on

Recruitment and Training of Apprentices (Engineering), National Advisory Council for the Motor Industry, Industrial Relations in the Motor Industry, Ministry of Aviation and War Department Industrial Councils, Railway Workshops National Council, as well as representatives on Boards for Industrial Training and Economic Development Committees.

District committees

24. All unions affiliated to the Confederation and having branches in an area where a Confederation District Committee is formed must become affiliated locally. Representation is on the basis of affiliated membership ranging from one representative from unions with up to 250 members to eight representatives from unions with over 4,000 affiliated members in a District. The function of the District Committees is to provide forums at District Level and to facilitate the transmission of information. They can organise joint action in the Districts only if (a) such action is in conformity with Confederation policy and (b) does not violate rules or policy of any member union. The District Secretary is the only means of communication between the General Council and local bodies in his District. The Confederation does not have any full-time officials as such in the Districts, but the District Secretaries in almost every case are elected from the ranks of full-time Trade Union officials of affiliated Unions.

Works committees

25. The Shop Stewards of Confederation Unions in an establishment elect the Joint Shop Stewards Works Committee; two appointed members of which are issued with credentials as Confederation Chairman and Secretary, and act as such on behalf of their Confederation District Committee. Here again their function is merely one of co-ordinating the activities of member unions, and they are in the first instance responsible as Shop Stewards to the Union to which they belong.

Staff unions

26. In the case of Staff Unions, there are separate recognition agreements with the Employers' federations governing the wages and conditions of staff members. These agreements have been negotiated outside of the normal Confederation procedures and so the Confederation rules expressly exclude non-manual working unions from the obligations to:— 'support other societies on wages and hours'; 'identify themselves with a movement which has received Confederation approval'; and 'to use the Procedure Agreement as laid down for manual workers'.

27. However, there is a co-ordinating procedure for Confederation staff unions which acts on an ad hoc basis to enable joint claims to be presented. This is the 'Joint Consultative Committee of Staff Unions'; it is convened by the General Secretary of one of the Staff Unions (at present DATA) and he informs the Confederation General Secretary of all meetings which are called.

Confederation powers

28. The power of the Confederation is—similar to that of the TUC with its affiliates—more moral than constitutional. It is more realistic to refer to influence rather than power. The constitution provides for the expulsion of an affiliated society which 'declines to identify itself with a movement which has received the approval of the Confederation' (Rule VII, Clause 6), but in practice great pains are taken to achieve unanimity wherever possible. It says much for the spirit of democracy and loyalty displayed by affiliated Unions when it is shown that even where completely unanimous decisions have proved impossible, the majority decisions have been accepted and pursued as a common Trade Union Front by all the unions concerned.

29. This influence, which the Confederation is able to exert has been built up by virtue of the trust which successive Officers of the Confederation have earned from the unions, and by the realisation of each that 'Unity' is indeed 'Strength'.

Working of the confederation

30. The administrative work of the Confederation is very limited in relation to the size of its affiliated membership and can be seen in perspective if viewed in the light of its annual financial turnover. Total income for the year 1964/5 was £50,000 (£37,000 from affiliation fees and £13,000 from sales to affiliated unions of publications, etc.). Expenditure also totalled £50,000 of which the major items accounted for:

Printing and Stationery	£15,000
Delegations and Meetings	£11,000
Staff Salaries	£7,800
Head Office Expenses	£4,400
Annual Conference	£3,800
District Committee Expenses	£3,400

This is a very small turnover indeed when compared to that of most of the affiliated Unions, in some cases running into millions of pounds per annum; but such comparisons are deceptive, for the Confederation performs a different function to that of a Union with all its Friendly Society Benefits, etc.

31. Despite the financial and staffing limitations, the Confederation provides a service, particularly in the field of co-ordination of industrial activities and dissemination of information, which makes a valuable contribution to industrial peace.

32. Many of the smaller Unions can, by virtue of their affiliation, receive a regular supply of circulars giving them information concerning negotiations, agreements, meetings with Ministers of the Crown and the work of Government Departments and committees, which might otherwise never percolate through to them.

Negotiations

33. National negotiations with Employers and Employers' Associations are conducted on behalf of the Confederation by the Executive Committees, e.g., in engineering by the Engineering Committee, in shipbuilding and shiprepair by the Shipyard

Committee, the spokesman being the Chairman of the committee concerned. This arrangement means that the part taken by individual unions is the same as if they came together to present a common claim under the leadership of the major union in that section of industry. It is not exactly the same though; the fact that there is a permanent central secretariat who—though members themselves of one of the unions—are not aligned to any particular Union's part in negotiations, gives rise to a greater feeling of solidarity than would be the case if there was no such secretariat. It becomes much easier for TU leaders to overlook the fact that they are being led by the President of a Union other than their own when he is wearing his other hat, i.e., as the democratically elected chairman of a Confederation Committee.

34. But there are many aspects upon which the CSEU has no mandate nor authority to conduct negotiations. For example all matters relating to individual crafts designation, differentials and demarcation issues are the sole prerogative of the Unions organising such craftsmen. These prerogatives are jealously guarded by the Unions, and there is no delegation of authority to enter into agreements on these issues.

Procedure agreement (engineering)

35. The procedure for dealing with questions arising and the procedure for the avoidance of disputes in the engineering industry is laid down in an agreement of 1922 (the famous 'York Memorandum') which, though subsequently modified and amended, is unchanged in principle from the 1922 format. The original agreement was made at a meeting between the Engineering Employers' Federation and the FESTUK, but each of the unions in attendance signed the agreement individually. The most important amendment to the Agreement was that of February, 1943, which recognised the Confederation as the co-ordinating authority (locally and centrally) under the Provisions for Avoiding Disputes.

36. This amendment makes provisions for the Confederation

to submit references to both local and central conferences, subject to the acquiescence of individual unions concerned in the reference.

37. Thus there are four ways in which the Procedure Agreement can be invoked: by Employers' reference; by a single Union reference; by a joint Unions' reference, submitted jointly by two, three or even more unions; or by Confederation reference. In the case of a Confederation reference all unions which are affected, are entitled to be represented.

38. The only Confederation representative entitled to attend is the District Secretary (local conference) or the General Secretary (central conference). In practice these officers seldom attend, and Confederation references are usually conducted at central conference by the Engineering Committee Chairman who also represents his own union.

Central conference

39. Central Conference is a standing conference which takes place on the second Friday every month at York. Different courts sit and deal with references from different unions. For example all Confederation references and AEU references go to one court, all ETU references go to another court, and so on, depending upon how many references there are to be dealt with; although some courts may deal with several unions' references taken in rotation.

40. The Procedure Agreement does not guarantee that a positive result will emerge from local or central conference deliberations. Indeed, there is a high rate of failures to agree when issues are dealt with at central conference. Nearly half result in no mutually agreed recommendations being made. Of the rest, some result in agreed recommendations, some are referred back to the works for settlement at that level, and some are retained for subsequent central conference discussions. Eventually, however, some 54 per cent. of all cases referred to central conference result in a settlement being achieved. This figure looks much better when we note that in an average year only about

45 per cent. of local conference issues are remitted to central conference; so it is only the more difficult or irreconcilable problems which eventually proceed to the York central conference stage.

41. Nevertheless, it is the constant aim of the unions to improve upon this figure of 54 per cent. settlements, and in addition to minimise the effects of the inevitable time lag which is inherent in the procedure. To this end the 1965 CSEU Annual Conference decided that attempts should be made to secure certain amendments which will bring the Procedure Agreement more into line with contemporary industrial circumstances.

Procedure agreement (shipbuilding)

42. There is a Procedure Agreement similar to that in Engineering, which was negotiated in 1924 for the Shipbuilding and Shiprepair Industries. At Yard and Local Conference level, the procedure appears to be operating fairly satisfactorily, but, unlike the engineering side, the 'statutory' Central Conference procedure is not operated. The agreement states that: 'Central Conferences shall be held fortnightly (on fixed dates) . . .' and provides for a 'General Conference' in the event of a failure to agree at Central Conference. In practice, Central Conferences are held on an ad hoc basis, and the procedure for General Conference has not been invoked since the war.

43. This agreement also is considered by several unions to have its shortcomings relative to modern industrial conditions, and they would like a new procedure to be adopted which was more in keeping with modern industrial circumstances.

Minute No 741

44. One of the major problems facing the industries is the snowball effect of a strike which starts off in a key section or sector of a firm or industry. Great difficulties arise in reconciling the widely differing rules or procedure governing the authorisation of strikes and stoppages in individual unions. Here again, use can be made of the Confederation Secretariat.

45. In December, 1946, a letter from the Electrical Trades Union suggested that 'the Confederation should act as the co-ordinating body for Unions involved in unofficial stoppages of work, so that such issues could be dealt with jointly'. The matter was referred to a sub-committee of the Executive, and as a result of the sub-committee's report, minute 741 was adopted as follows:

'In the event of a dispute arising involving a stoppage of work of more than one Union, the machinery of the Confederation should be used either locally or nationally to call the Unions together so that consideration can be given to the matter from all aspects.'

46. This minute has been misinterpreted by some people who have thought that it gives the Confederation power to take the initiative in settling disputes. Such is not the case. It is the Unions which take the initiative, it is they who 'use the machinery of the Confederation'. In practice it works as follows. An affiliated Union having its members involved in a dispute, either directly or indirectly, which also affects the members of other affiliated Unions will write to the Confederation Secretary (locally) or General Secretary (Nationally) requesting that a '741' meeting be called. The Confederation will then circulate the information to all affiliated Unions, naming a time and place for the meeting. The function of the Confederation has been fulfilled when the meeting has elected its Chairman and he takes over from the Confederation Secretary.

The functional role

47. Thus it can be seen from the foregoing that the Confederation is not the monolithic structure that some people might have thought it to be. It neither dictates to, nor leads, its affiliated members. Its powers are those of persuasion only, and do not usurp the powers, rules or constitution of any member union. Action of any kind is only taken after the authority of the General Council (Quarterly Meeting) has been sought and obtained.

48. On the occasions when major contentious decisions have to be taken, it is normal for the Confederation to call an ad hoc meeting of the Executive Councils of all affiliated unions to determine policy. Such a meeting was held in December, 1964, to deliberate upon the question of the Engineering Three Year 'Package Deal'.

49. The main function of the Confederation at all levels, is one of providing the co-ordinating machinery which can achieve common objectives for workers in the industries with a minimum of sectarian strife; it has usually fulfilled this purpose quite effectively.

SOURCE: *An Introduction to the Confederation of Shipbuilding and Engineering Unions* (January 1966)

42 DRAUGHTSMEN'S & ALLIED TECHNICIANS ASSOCIATION: CLOSER WORKING

Discussions have taken place between our union and the Clerical and Administrative Workers' Union on closer working in the engineering industry. One result of the discussions is that we will combine as a single unit for the purpose of offering overall services to staff associations which, although originally set up by the management as house unions, have decided to become genuine independent trade union organisations. When this happens the separation of one part of the association, the technical side, from the clerical side is often unacceptable to employees accustomed to working together. Therefore the two unions agreed to provide a single service with a single representative committee, with powers to take industrial action and to authorise strike pay.

The national officers elected by the national council would have access to the joint union executive committee on vital issues.

This revolutionary suggestion will do a great deal to help

staff associations, who when dissatisfied with their present status, move towards genuine unionisation.

SOURCE: *DATA Journal* (February 1971)

43 ASSOCIATION OF SCIENTIFIC WORKERS AND ASSOCIATION OF SUPERVISORY STAFFS, EXECUTIVES AND TECHNICIANS: THE CASE FOR AMALGAMATION TO FORM THE ASSOCIATION OF SCIENTIFIC, TECHNICAL AND MANAGERIAL STAFFS

1. The National Executive Councils of both the AScW and ASSET have been giving consideration to the possibility of amalgamation. Both Unions have received mandates from their Annual Conferences urging that the possibilities should be fully explored and it is manifest that there is considerable support for amalgamation among members of both bodies.

2. There are obvious advantages in the merging of the two organisations. The pattern of industry, commerce, social services and education is changing remarkably as a result of technological innovation: new types of employment and prospects are being created in new ways. Each union covers in its membership a wide spectrum of scientific and technical employment with basically similar training, with work stemming from the application of science and technology to industry and to the public services and with work that looks forward to new discovery and new techniques of application. If ASSET and the AScW merged, a new organisation would be created able to cover the complete spectrum—from the technically based white-collar worker in industry to the scientist in research—and able to speak for those carrying responsibility in a wide range of social activity.

3. In discussing the concept, both Executives have had in mind both the need to provide more expert officer-hours in the field to service the growing needs of the memberships and the

desirability of creating a large, well-funded, influential policy-
making organisation resting not only upon the existing qualities
of the two memberships—but with a persuasiveness of numbers.

4. *We assert that both our memberships are under-valued in terms of
salary—and under-regarded in terms of status. Any amalgamation
moves are squarely aimed at changing this state of affairs.*

5. Together, the AScW and ASSET could accomplish much
that has hitherto been just beyond the powers of the two
organisations acting as separate entities. Both unions have concentrated their energies on collective bargaining and ASSET
has concentrated especially on improving its expertise in big-
company negotiations. The AScW as well as fulfilling its basic
union functions has also paid attention to science policy and has
sponsored significant public work on matters falling within this
field. A new organisation would be able to combine both types
of activity and to make marked advances in each. *It would be
dedicated to raising the status of the scientist, technician and managerial
staff member.*

6. At present the AScW has 22,000 members, while ASSET
has 53,000. Both Unions have substantial membership in the
engineering industry where each has a Procedure Agreement
with the Engineering Employers' Federation. Both have
membership in the chemical and allied industries. ASSET has
membership in transport with representation on the negotiating
machinery in British Rail, London Transport and Civil Air
Transport. The AScW has membership amongst the technical
and scientific staff of the Health Service and the Universities.
Both have groupings within other important industries but,
equally, both are substantially under-organised and could be
much larger.

7. Each union has a staff of fulltime officials at the respective
Head Offices and in provincial offices. If the two unions were
to join forces it would be possible to provide officer coverage
from a network of district offices as follows: Glasgow, Durham,
Leeds, Sheffield, Liverpool, Manchester, Birmingham, Not-

tingham, Gloucester, Bristol, Belfast, West London, South London, East London.

This would give additional officer coverage to all members, relieve the strain of present fulltime staff in certain areas and provide a much more flexible and comprehensively backed service. Where both unions have organisation at the same establishment, duplication of effort by fulltime Officers would be avoided: there would be a great accretion of strength and membership from the beginning. Where the two unions have organisation at different places, a merger would have the effect of opening up new possibilities of recruitment.

8. It would be the policy of the new union to strengthen and develop the existing advisory committees and national councils for existing occupations and industries in order that their needs and expertise are appreciated and their problems are fully dealt with.

9. The estimated combined income of the two Unions, projected for 1967, amounts to £330,000. In 1968, without allowing for more than the existing growth rate, the estimated joint income would be £355,000. It is obvious that with an income at this level steps could be taken to strengthen existing staffing arrangements and to improve membership service still further.

10. With a combined membership at the beginning of at least 75,000 (May 1967 figure), taking into account present membership trends, the new organisation should attain a membership of 100,000 within three years. This would put it among the largest unions in the country and it would be the biggest technicians' union in the world. It would be a union capable of wielding immense influence, both inside the TUC where presure could quite legitimately then be exerted to secure more adequate representation, and with employing organisations, Ministries and other policy-forming institutions. Neither of the merging Associations see this as a final exercise in the rationalisation of the technical unions. They would, in fact, consider a successful and integrated amalgamated Union to be only a prelude to further advances.

11. Amalgamations are often rather complicated exercises. The Executives of both unions have sought the advice of the Chief Registrar of Friendly Societies and the method hereafter proposed seems to be the most effective and the simplest. Both Executives desire to merge on the basis of *complete equality* without paying any regard to differing size. It is proposed that there should be Joint General Secretaries and that the existing staff, both Officer and clerical, should not be disadvantaged in any way by the merger, but could rather look forward to more fulfilment within the ambit of a powerful new body.

12. The method of amalgamation proposed is that set out in the draft Rules and Instrument. A new body—the Association of Scientific, Technical and Managerial Staffs—would be established. The Executive Council of the ASTMS would consist of six members each from the Executives of the present Unions. It would be charged with the responsibility for effecting a complete merger. Initially, there would be a three-part rule book. The first part of the Rules—Part I—sets out briefly the title and objectives of the new body and would be administered by the Executive Council of the ASTMS.

The second two parts represent the present rules of the merging organisations. Eventually, at a time to be decided by the organisations themselves, the two separate sets of rules would cease to exist and the appropriate provisions merged into the rules of the new body.

13. The Executive Council of the ASTMS would be the employing authority for all the staff of the merging organisations. It would also be responsible for the administration of the joint property and funds of the new body. But the present Executives would continue to exist and be responsible for the administration of the policies of their own sections of membership, ie, the two present unions. Fulltime Officers would be expected to work for either sector of membership as convenient. But obviously they would need some time to become familiar with the specific problems of the membership of the other union if required to undertake this activity.

14. It is hoped that in this way the two previous organisations may be merged together over a transitional period with as little difficulty as possible. It is expected that within a time span of three years, a new rule book for ASTMS would have been drafted by the Executive Council for approval by the membership and the two previous organisations would then cease to exist.

15. Each Union would have to follow the procedures set out in its own rules for effecting amalgamation. Under the Trade Union (Amalgamation) Act of 1964 a ballot of the memberships of both Unions must be conducted. Further information in this regard will be issued as soon as the joint body which has already been established by both Union Executives has completed the necessary arrangements.

16. The object of this document is to advise the membership of both organisations, at a very early stage in the proceedings, precisely what the two Executives have in mind, both with regard to the actual mechanics of amalgamation and in relation to future long-term objectives. The Executives have worked on the assumption that amalgamation is desired by the memberships of both Unions and that this should be accomplished as smoothly and as quickly as possible.

It is appreciated, however, that the memberships of both unions may wish to put questions which have not been effectively covered in this paper: it is therefore proposed that a series of meetings should be held for the membership of both Unions. These will take place in all the main centres of membership when members of the Executives together with the two General Secretaries or Assistant General Secretaries of both organisations will be present to answer questions. Details of these meetings will be circulated at an early date.

SOURCES: AScW and ASSET. *The Case for Amalgamation to form the Association of Scientific, Technical and Managerial Staffs* (1967), 1–4

44 WILL PAYNTER: A GUIDING PRINCIPLE FOR UNION STRUCTURE?

I come to the rostrum to question whether the policy now being pursued by Congress affecting trade union structure is really relevant to the situation with which the trade union Movement in Britain is confronted. It does not necessarily follow that reducing the multiplicity of unions by mergers, changes the basic structure. Indeed, the logical end-product of the developments reported in this section of the Report could result, in effect, in what would be two or three gigantic general workers' unions, spread horizontally over Britain's industries and services.

In previous debates the general secretary has contended that structure should be a reflection of our purpose. Our purpose remains constant, but the environment in which we pursue our purpose undergoes fundamental change. It is against an assessment of change in environment that I consider the present trend towards change in trade union structure to be inadequate and slow. There is the direct role of central Government in industrial affairs generally and in industrial relations in particular. This is not a temporary innovation brought about by financial and economic crises, but a permanent and universal development in capitalist society. It is now an inescapable obligation of central Government brought about by the interdependence of national economies and the technological revolution, necessitating simple Government legislation and policy action to meet the financial, economic and social problems thrown up.

Secondly, there are the changes taking place in the structure of the national economy. The publicly-owned sector is valued at £12,000 million and its annual investment is more than that of private manufacturing industry. Central Government income is now one-third of the national income and its expenditure has increased to over £10,000 million annually. Mergers and takeovers are being encouraged, leading to huge capital concentrations dominating the main sectors of the economy. Trade unions now face this powerful combination of central Government and big employers in the prosecution of any major reforms.

It is against this combination that the effectiveness of our present trade union structure has to be measured. While it is true that great advances have been made and our trade union Movement is an established institution that has to be consulted by both employers and Government on all matters of importance, the extension of industrial democracy now being demanded requires the streamlining of union structure. The issue as to whether agreements and collective bargaining procedures ought to be reorientated to apply to a firm basis is, I suggest, a subsidiary consideration. Collective bargaining and agreements, whatever their basis, will depend upon the overall economic and financial policies pursued by Government and by the dominant employers in sectors of the economy. Thus the prosecution of trade union purpose in our present environment necessitates shifting the weight of trade union activity to influencing national policy and policies within the various sectors of the economy.

It seems to me that to be most effective in this situation we need to examine again the question of adapting trade union structure to industry, although this should entail a much less rigid conception and definition of what we mean by industry than hitherto, and a strengthening of the authority and power of the Trades Union Congress. I would suggest the setting up of a small committee by the General Council, comprised of people who have no vested interest in the present structure, to prepare a blueprint and revision both of the structure and the power and functions of Congress and the General Council. I consider that this is necessary as a part of trade union development towards socialism in Britain and as the application of socialist planning to our own Movement that we demand from the Government for the national economy.

Source: Speech by Will Paynter, then General Secretary of the National Union of Mineworkers, TUC Annual Report (1968), 429

PART SEVEN

Trade Union Structure 3

(c) THE TRADES UNION CONGRESS

No account of British trade unionism can avoid emphasising the growing role played by the TUC. The 1960s were important to the TUC in two senses. Firstly, most of the major unions still outside its ranks, including the National and Local Government Officers Association and the National Union of Teachers, joined during this period, bringing its affiliated membership to ten million. Secondly, increased state intervention, not only in incomes policy but in many other aspects of trade union conduct, enhanced the importance of the General Council and its main committees, since it was only in so far as the trade union movement could co-ordinate its response that it could exert counter-pressure on successive governments.

The best way of obtaining an overall view of the TUC's modern role is to examine its annual reports, which are more meticulous and detailed than those of any other equivalent organisation. For example, its 1969 report contains a revealing account (unfortunately too long to include here) of the successive meetings of General Council representatives with the Labour Government in the negotiations which forced the withdrawal of the government's proposals, In Place of Strife.

The influence of the TUC and the services it provides are developing continually. One important structural innovation has been the development of Industrial Committees of TUC unions, which are strengthening the co-ordination of unions within particular sectors, and also directly linking such federal activities with TUC servicing and initiatives.

The following documents set out some of the more important rules of the TUC, including those that extended its authority over disputes between affiliated organisations. This increased authority arose out of the negotiations with the Labour Government in 1969, mentioned above. The announcement and subsequent TUC circular, which terminated these discussions, are also included. Earlier and later examples of TUC agreements: in 1964 on productivity, prices and incomes; in 1972 (with the CBI) on conciliation and arbitration, show the attempts to establish a consensus with other interested groups. A long extract from the TUC's interim report on Structure and Development *sets the scene for the further development of TUC activities in the 1970s and shows the TUC attempting a self-assessment at a critical time. An extract of 1972 describes progress made in one of the areas: Industrial Committees. Finally, a debate among women trade unionists, held under the auspices of the TUC, illustrates another feature—by no means a new one—of the TUC's work.*

45 TUC: RULES OF THE TUC

Rule 8: Duties of general council

(*a*) The General Council shall transact the business in the periods between each Annual Congress, shall keep a watch on all industrial movements, and shall, where possible, co-ordinate industrial action.

(*b*) They shall watch all legislation affecting labour, and shall initiate such legislation as Congress may direct.

(*c*) They shall endeavour to adjust disputes and differences between affiliated organisations.

(*d*) They shall promote common action by the Trade Union Movement on general questions, such as wages and hours of labour, and any matter of general concern that may arise between trade unions and trade unions, or between employers and trade unions, or between the Trade Union Movement and the Government, and shall have power to assist any union which is attacked on any vital question of trade union principle.

(*e*) They shall assist trade unions in the work of organisation, and shall carry on propaganda with a view to strengthening the Trade Union Movement, and for the attainment of any or all of the above objects.

(*f*) They shall also enter into relations with the Trade Union and Labour Movements in other countries with a view to securing united action.

(*g*) They shall have authority to invest and administer the funds of the Congress and to make grants to any organisation or person, whether in Great Britain or abroad, for such purpose as it seems desirable, but in so doing they shall have regard to the directions, if any, from time to time given by Congress. They shall also have authority to raise funds for any special purpose and to invest and administer such funds and to make grants therefrom.

(*h*) For the purpose of carrying out the objects of the Congress, of conducting its affairs and in relation to the matters specifically referred to in this Rule the General Council shall have power to utilise the funds and property of the Congress, to enter into any transaction and by any one or more of their members to execute in the name and on behalf of the Congress any deeds or documents that may be necessary.

(*i*) The General Council shall have power whenever they deem necessary to convene a Special Congress or Conference to deal with any contingency that may arise, and to arrange the agenda and procedure whereby the business of such meetings shall be conducted.

(*j*) In the event of a legal point arising which in the opinion of the General Council (after consultation with Counsel) should be tested in the House of Lords in the general interests of trade unionism, the Council shall be empowered to levy the affiliated societies *pro rata* to provide the necessary expenses. Any society failing to pay the levy shall be reported to Congress.

(*k*) In order that the Trade Union Movement may do everything which lies in its power to prevent future wars, the General Council shall, in the event of there being a danger of an outbreak of war, call a Special Congress to decide on industrial action, such Congress to be called, if possible, before war is declared.

(*l*) The General Council shall prepare a Report of their work for submission to the Annual Meeting of Congress. The Report shall contain a list of the General Council meetings with dates, and also names of those members who were present at such meetings. The Standing Orders of Congress, and the General Council shall be published with each Annual Report of the proceedings of Congress.

. . .

Rule 11: Industrial disputes

(*a*) It shall be an obligation upon the affiliated organisations to keep the General Council informed with regard to matters arising as between them and employers, and/or between one organisation and another, including unauthorised and unconstitutional stoppages of work, in particular where such matters may involve directly or indirectly large bodies of workers. The General Council shall, if they deem necessary, disseminate the information as soon as possible to all organisations which are affiliated to the Congress, and which may be either directly or indirectly affected.

(*b*) The general policy of the General Council shall be that unless requested to do so by the affiliated organisation or organisations concerned, the Council shall not intervene so long as there is a prospect of whatever difference may exist on the matters in question being amicably settled by means of the machinery of negotiation existing in the trades affected.

(*c*) If, however, a situation has arisen, or is likely to arise, in which other bodies of workpeople affiliated to Congress might be involved in a stoppage of work or their wages, hours and conditions of employment imperilled the General Council may take the initiative by calling representatives of the organisation into consultation, and use their influence to effect a just settlement of the difference. In this connection the Council, having ascertained all the facts relating to the difference, may tender their considered opinion and advice thereon to the organisation or organisations concerned. Should the organisation or organisations refuse the assistance or advice of the Council, the General Council shall duly report to Congress or deal with the organisation under Clauses (*b*), (*c*), (*d*) and (*h*) of Rule 13.

(*d*) Where the Council intervenes, as herein provided, and the organisation or organisations concerned accept the assistance and advice of the Council, and where despite the efforts of the Council, the policy of the employers enforces a stoppage of work by strike or lock-out, the Council shall forthwith take steps to organise on behalf of the organisation or organisations concerned all such moral and material support as the circumstances of the dispute may appear to justify.

Rule 12: Disputes between affiliated organisations

(*a*) Where disputes arise, or threaten to arise, between affiliated organisations, the General Council shall use their influence to promote a settlement.

(*b*) It shall be an obligation on the affiliated organisation or organisations concerned to notify the General Council when an official stoppage of work is contemplated in any dispute between affiliated organisations whether relating to trade union recognition, trade union membership, demarcation of work, or any other difficulty.

(*c*) No affiliated organisation shall authorise such a stoppage of work until the dispute has been considered by the General Council, as provided by Clause (*f*) of this Rule.

(*d*) Where a dispute between unions has led to an unauthorised stoppage of work, it shall be an obligation on the affiliated organisation or organisations concerned to take immediate and energetic steps to obtain a resumption of work.

(*e*) The affiliated organisation or organisations concerned shall notify the General Council as soon as possible of any stoppage of work which involves directly or indirectly large bodies of workers, or which if protracted may have serious consequences. In addition to such notification, the affiliated organisation or organisations concerned shall inform the General Council of the causes and circumstances of the dispute and of the steps they have taken, or are taking, to secure a resumption of work.

(*f*) Upon notification from an affiliated organisation, as required by clauses (*b*) and (*e*) of this Rule, or upon the application of an affiliated organisation, or when they deem necessary, the General Council shall have the power to investigate cases of dispute or disagreement between affiliated organisations and to refer such cases to the Disputes Committee.

(*g*) If the parties to a dispute fail to submit the case to the Disputes Committee of the General Council as provided by this Rule, it shall not be permissible for such dispute to be raised at any Annual Congress.

(*h*) The General Council shall have power to summon the contending affiliated organisations to appear before the Disputes Committee of the General Council, and to require such organisations to submit all evidence and information that the Disputes Committee may deem essential to enable it to adjudicate upon the case.

(*i*) If the result of such an inquiry be that the complaining organisation fails to prove the charge, it shall bear the whole cost of the investigation including the expenses incurred by the defending organisation.

(*j*) Should any affiliated organisation not carry into effect any decision of the General Council in connection with cases under this Rule the General Council may at once issue a report to all affiliated organisations. If the decision of the General Council is still not carried out, the General Council may, at their discretion, adopt either of the following methods of procedure:

The General Council may report the matter to the next Annual Congress to deal with as may be decided upon; or

Deal with the organisation under Clauses (*b*), (*c*), (*d*) and (*h*) of Rule 13.

Rule 13: Conduct of affiliated organisations

(*a*) If at any time there appears to the General Council to be justification for an investigation into the conduct of any affiliated organisation on the ground that the activities of such organisation are detrimental to the interests of the Trade Union Movement or contrary to the declared principles and policy of the Congress the General Council shall summon such organisation to appear before them or their appropriate Committee by duly appointed representatives of such organisation in order that such activities may be investigated. In the event of the organisation failing to attend, the investigation shall proceed in its absence.

(*b*) If after such investigation the General Council decide that the activities of the organisation concerned are detrimental to the interests of the Trade Union Movement or contrary to the declared principles of Congress, the General Council shall direct the organisation to discontinue such activities forthwith and undertake not to engage therein in the future.

(*c*) Should the organisation disobey such direction, or fail to give such undertaking, the General Council are hereby empowered in their discretion to order that the organisation be forthwith suspended from membership of the Congress until the next Annual Congress.

(*d*) The General Council shall submit a report upon the matter to the next Annual Congress.

(*e*) No affiliated organisation shall circularise, either in writing or by general oral communication, other affiliated organisations upon any matter concerning the business of the Congress, without first securing the General Council's authorisation for such circularisation.

(*f*) Should any such unauthorised circularisation take place concerning a motion for the Agenda of the Annual Congress or any Special Congress or Conferences, and the General Council after investigation decide that those responsible for such

motion connived at, or were party to, or concerned with
such circularisation, the motion shall not be included in the
Agenda.

(g) The General Council may investigate any violation of the
provisions of Clauses (e) and (f), and if after such investigation
they decide that any organisation has acted deliberately in such
violation they may deal with the organisation by investigation,
suspension and report under the terms of Clauses (b), (c) and
(d) of this Rule.

(h) Any affiliated organisation dealt with under this Rule
shall have the right to appeal to the next Annual Congress and
may appoint delegates in accordance with Rules 17 and 18 to
represent the organisation upon the appeal and at the Annual
Congress if the appeal is allowed. Congress shall upon such
appeal have final authority to deal with the matter by way of
re-admission, further suspension or exclusion from membership
of the Congress.

46 TUC: THE 1969 AGREEMENT WITH THE LABOUR GOVERNMENT

On June 18, 1969, at the end of a meeting between the Prime
Minister and the Secretary of State for Employment and Productivity and the TUC General Council at 10 Downing Street
the following announcement was made:

The Prime Minister and the First Secretary of State have
today had further discussions with the TUC General Council
on the TUC's proposals set out in *Programme for Action* approved
by the Special Congress at Croydon on June 5.

The General Council have agreed unanimously to a solemn
and binding undertaking the text of which is set out in the
annex to this statement. The General Council have further
agreed that this undertaking will forthwith govern the operation
by the General Council of Congress Rule 11 as recommended
by the General Council to the Special Congress on June 5. This
undertaking unanimously given by the General Council will

have the same binding force as the TUC Bridlington Principles and Regulations.

The text of the annex was as follows:

The General Council have unanimously agreed that in operating Congress Rule 11, as recommended by the General Council and approved by the Special Congress on June 5:

(*a*) where a dispute has led or is likely to lead to an unconstitutional stoppage of work which involves directly or indirectly large bodies of workers or which, if protracted, may have serious consequences, the General Council shall ascertain and assess all the facts, having regard to paragraphs 20 to 27 of *Programme for Action*.

(*b*) In cases where they consider it unreasonable to order an unconditional return to work, they will tender the organisation or organisations concerned their considered opinion and advice with a view to promoting a settlement.

(*c*) Where, however, they find there should be no stoppage of work before procedure is exhausted, they will place an obligation on the organisation or organisations concerned to take energetic steps to obtain an immediate resumption of work, including action within their rules if necessary, so that negotiations can proceed.

(*d*) Should an affiliated organisation not comply with an obligation placed on it under (*c*) above, the General Council shall duly report to Congress or deal with the organisation under Clauses (*b*), (*c*), (*d*) and (*h*) of Rule 13.

On June 25, 1969, the TUC General Council agreed that the following circular should be sent to all affiliated organisations:

The General Council informed the Special Congress held at Croydon on June 5 that, if the Congress endorsed the Report *Programme for Action*, and provided also that the Government agreed not to proceed with their proposed penal clauses, they would forthwith give effect to the proposals made in the Report. The General Council also indicated that they would subsequently submit to the September Congress formal proposals for amending Rules 11 and 12 along the lines which were set out in Appendices 2 and 3 of the Report.

Since the Croydon Congress the General Council have had lengthy and detailed discussions with the Government. In the course of these discussions the General Council not only emphasised the unalterable opposition of the trade union movement to any such penal sanctions but also, in response to requests by the Prime Minister and his colleagues, clarified certain aspects of the Report and in particular the way in which they proposed to operate Congress Rule 11 in relation to industrial disputes.

As a result of these discussions the Government have given an assurance that, provided that the General Council gave a satisfactory undertaking about the operation of Rule 11, they would not propose to proceed with the interim legislation on industrial relations; and that they would not include the so-called penal sanctions in the legislation to be introduced next session or in any legislation introduced during the life-time of the present Parliament. The Government stipulated that this must be subject to review if the TUC Congress in September fails satisfactorily to endorse the General Council's undertaking.

The General Council have throughout, as has Congress itself, been in no doubt that those proposals in the Report which relate to action by the General Council to promote the speedy settlement of disputes will be effective. They have emphasised to the Government that the authority of the General Council is to be judged not only, and not even mainly, by the form of the TUC's Rules, but by the willingness that unions have demonstrated to co-operate readily in the constructive reform of industrial relations set out in *Programme for Action*.

However, in order to remove any doubt that might remain in the minds of the Government about the intentions of the General Council and of affiliated unions, they have given the Government an explicit undertaking in relation to the action that will be taken when the General Council are, under Rule 11, investigating industrial disputes. This undertaking is reproduced in the statement attached to this Circular. The General Council are sure that affiliated unions will agree that it was right for them to seek to resolve the Government's uncertainty, and will welcome the fact that in consequence the Government decided not to proceed with its proposals relating to penal clauses.

Now that the situation has been resolved in a way which is satisfactory to the Government and to the General Council, the General Council have decided to put into effect forthwith the proposals endorsed by the Special Congress. The General Council are preparing for the guidance of unions a detailed memorandum setting out the procedures to be followed for notifying and dealing with industrial disputes and with disputes between unions. However, pending receipt of that memorandum, the General Council will expect unions from now on to act, and will themselves operate, in accordance with the procedures outlined in paras 38 to 42 (in relation to disputes with employers) and in paras 51 to 60 (in relation to disputes between unions). I will in the near future be sending you sufficient copies of *Programme for Action* (which will additionally reproduce the undertaking given by the General Council to the Government) for circulation to your union's Executive and will be making available extra copies for circulation to all your branches.

June 26, 1969.

SOURCE: TUC. *Industrial Relations; Programme for Action*. Report of Special Trades Union Congress (1969), 96–8

47 JOINT STATEMENT OF INTENT ON PRODUCTIVITY, PRICES AND INCOMES

The objectives

(a) The Government's economic objective is to achieve and maintain a rapid increase in output and real incomes combined with full employment. Their social objective is to ensure that the benefits of faster growth are distributed in a way that satisfies the claims of social need and justice. In this way general confidence will be created in the purpose of the national plan and individuals will be willing to make their utmost contribution towards its implementation.

(b) Essential conditions for the achievement of these objectives are a strong currency and a healthy balance of payments.

The economic situation

(c) The economic situation, while potentially strong, is at present extremely unsatisfactory. Drastic temporary measures have been taken to meet a situation in which the balance of payments was in serious deficit, with exports falling behind imports. But these measures can provide only a breathing space.

(d) To achieve a more permanent solution, we must improve the balance of payments, encourage exports and sharpen our competitive ability. Our longer-term interests lie in reducing the barriers to international trade. We must take urgent and vigorous action to raise productivity throughout industry and commerce, to keep increases in total money incomes in line with increases in real national output and to maintain a stable general price level. Unless we do this we shall have a slower rate of growth and a lower level of employment.

(e) We—Government, management and unions—are resolved to take the following action in our respective spheres of responsibility.

The Government

(f) The Government will prepare and implement a general plan for economic development, in consultation with both sides of industry through the National Economic Development Council. This will provide for higher investment; for improving our industrial skills; for modernisation of industry; for balanced regional development; for higher exports; and for the largest possible sustained expansion of production and real incomes.

(g) Much greater emphasis will be given to increasing productivity. The Government will encourage and develop policies designed to promote technological advance in industry, and to get rid of restrictive practices and prevent the abuse of monopoly power, and so improve efficiency, cut out waste, and reduce excessive prices. More vigorous policies will be pursued designed to facilitate mobility of labour and generally to make more effective use of scarce manpower resources, and to give workers a greater sense of security in the face of economic change. The Government also intend to introduce essential social improvements such as a system of earnings-related benefits, in addition to the improvements in national insurance benefits already announced.

(h) The Government will set up machinery to keep a continuous watch on the general movement of prices and of money incomes of all kinds and to carry out the other functions described in paragraph (j) below. They will also use their fiscal powers or other appropriate means to correct any excessive growth in aggregate profits as compared with the growth of total wages and salaries, after allowing for short-term fluctuations.

Management and unions

(i) We, the representatives of the Trades Union Congress, the Federation of British Industries, the British Employers' Confederation, the National Association of British Manufacturers, and the Association of British Chambers of Commerce accept that major objectives of national policy must be:

to ensure that British industry is dynamic and that its prices are competitive;

to raise productivity and efficiency so that real national output can increase, and to keep increases in wages, salaries and other forms of incomes in line with this increase;

to keep the general level of prices stable.

(j) We therefore undertake, on behalf of our members:

to encourage and lead a sustained attack on the obstacles to efficiency, whether on the part of management or of workers, and to strive for the adoption of more rigorous standards of performance at all levels;

to co-operate with the Government in endeavouring, in the face of practical problems, to give effective shape to the machinery that the Government intend to establish for the following purposes:

 (i) to keep under review the general movement of prices and of money incomes of all kinds;

 (ii) to examine particular cases in order to advise whether or not the behaviour of prices or of wages, salaries or other money incomes is in the national interest as defined by the Government after consultation with management and unions.

(*k*) We stress that close attention must be paid to easing the difficulties of those affected by changed circumstances in their employment. We therefore support, in principle, the Government's proposals for earnings-related benefits and will examine sympathetically proposals for severance payments.

(*l*) We—Government, management and unions—are confident that by co-operating in a spirit of mutual confidence to give effect to the principles and policies described above, we and those whom we represent will be able to achieve a faster growth of real incomes and generally to promote the economic and social well-being of the country.   (16 December 1964)

SOURCE: TUC. *Productivity, Prices and Incomes*. Report of a conference of Executive Committees of Affiliated Organisations held on 30 April 1965, 9–11

48 CBI/TUC JOINT STATEMENT: CONCILIATION AND ARBITRATION SERVICE

The Confederation of British Industry and the Trades Union Congress have agreed the details of a non-Governmental Conciliation and Arbitration Service, to be initiated on Friday, September 1, 1972. The joint statement of the two bodies is given below.

Preamble

1. The TUC and the CBI are agreed that collective bargaining is best brought to a satisfactory conclusion by voluntary means. Both recognise the need to improve the voluntary system of industrial relations.

2. The TUC and CBI believe that widespread availability of conciliation and arbitration can make an important contribution to the promotion and maintenance of industrial peace. When trade unions and employers have failed to reach agreement through the processes of negotiation, a third party acting either as a conciliator or arbitrator may provide a means of reaching a settlement without either side taking action which would lead to interruptions in the output of goods or services, the consequent material losses this entails to both employers and workers, and in some cases serious damage to the economy.

3. The conflict between Government's role as manager of the economy on the one hand, and as agent for the promotion of industrial peace on the other has undoubtedly weakened the confidence of unions in the impartiality of Government-provided conciliation and arbitration, particularly in pay disputes. Both CBI and the TUC believe that an independent service created by the will of employers and trade unions acting together would offer the best hope of acceptance by the parties to disputes and would have the best chance of lasting credibility.

4. We have considered the question of public interest. CBI and the TUC believe that an independent service would operate with due regard for the interest of others. In particular, independent conciliation would best serve that interest by ensuring that all the issues and implications in disputes were thoroughly understood by both sides.

Objective

5. The purpose of this agreement between CBI and the TUC is to initiate and plan the development of an independent ser-

vice from which could be drawn conciliators and arbitrators whose authority and impartiality would be respected and whose credibility would be lasting.

Definitions
6. Conciliation is defined as a means whereby parties to a dispute may be offered the opportunity of exploring ways of coming closer together so that they may themselves resolve their differences voluntarily by agreement. It normally involves a single conciliator who may be accompanied by assessors.

Arbitration means the handing down of a judgment; thus arbitrators are charged with making a decision based on the information they obtain, and on their experience, which will settle a dispute. Arbitrators may act singly or a small number may be grouped to act as a tribunal.

Implementation
7. CBI and the TUC have as their aim the creation of a body of conciliators and arbitrators capable of dealing with all situations and available both nationally and regionally. There are, however, practical difficulties about creating such a comprehensive service quickly. It should in the first instance be well founded, and it should grow on the basis of its proven effectiveness and on the demonstration of its ability to bring about fair and responsible solutions. It is, therefore, proposed that it should be introduced by stages as set out below.
8. The independent service, whether for conciliation or arbitration, would be made available only with the agreement of both parties to a dispute. It would not seek to take the place of established and existing procedures. It would be available to the public and the private sectors of industry.

Stage 1
9. At the commencement the service would concentrate on disputes of major importance in which a stoppage of work had

occurred or was apprehended. A dispute would be regarded as having major importance if it involved, directly or indirectly, large numbers of workers. Conciliators and arbitrators would be drawn from a panel of people, nominated with the unanimous approval of a joint CBI/TUC committee, and available on a part-time basis; not all of them would necessarily have been involved in the function of management or of employee representation. Parties to a dispute would address their request for assistance to the General Secretary of the TUC and to the Director-General of CBI. Staff assistance to support the conciliator or arbitrator/s would be provided by the TUC and CBI. At this stage, the costs of the service would be met by these bodies.

Stage 2

10.   The joint CBI/TUC committee would appoint a full-time Director to whom requests for assistance would be addressed and under whom there would be set up a staff large enough to fulfil the support role. The funds necessary to finance a full-time staff would initially be made available jointly by employers and unions, by direct contributions or by charging fees for services. As soon as was practicable the independent service would extend its activities and there would be greater regional activity. The number of part-time conciliators/arbitrators would be increased.

Stage 3

11.   The service would be further extended to cover disputes of all kinds nationally and regionally. Regional offices would be established and a staff of full-time conciliators/arbitrators would be built up to supplement those whose services had been provided on a part-time basis. The TUC and CBI would look to Government for support from public funds for what would essentially be a public, though independent, service.

The joint CBI/TUC Committee, set up on Monday, July 31 [1972] consists of the following:

For the CBI:

Joint Chairman:
    President (Mr Michael Clapham)
    Director General (Mr Campbell
    Adamson)
Mr Richard O'Brien
Mr T. Carlile
Mr Alex Jarratt
Sir John Partridge
Mr Alan Swinden
Lord Watkinson

For the TUC:

Joint Chairman:
    Chairman of the General
    Council (Mr George
    Smith)
General Secretary
    (Mr Victor Feather)
Mr Alfred Allen
Mr Walter Anderson
Lord Cooper
Sir Sidney Greene
Mr Jack Jones
Mr Hugh Scanlon

SOURCE: TUC. Press Release (2 August 1972)

49 TUC: STRUCTURE AND DEVELOPMENT

The role of the TUC

4. Congress itself is responsible for laying down broad lines of policy, and for exercising such authority over the constituent unions as they have delegated to it. The General Council, guided by their functional Committees and advisory bodies and Conferences, apply and interpret that policy between Congresses. Congress is and must always be the ultimate policy-making body, but as the formulation and administration of policy have become more closely interwoven the ability of Congress to initiate and to innovate has declined. This has been accompanied by a corresponding growth in the responsibility of the General Council. Even so the General Council must command the confidence of Congress: the policies they propose and pursue must be seen clearly by Congress to be well-conceived and thus to be worthy of endorsement and support.

5. The TUC is primarily concerned with developing policy rather than with acting as an executive body. It provides a means through which unions can collectively achieve objectives which they cannot achieve, or which it would be difficult for

them to achieve, separately. It identifies things which unions should be doing, but which for one reason or another they are not doing, and stimulates them to take the necessary action. It reminds individual unions or groups of unions of their duty to take into account the interests of other unions, and the broader interests of trade unionists as a whole. It thus establishes standards of good trade union practice. These are its internal functions. Externally it represents the movement to the Government and other outside organisations, asserting the independence of the trade union movement and the right of trade unionists to a share in decisions which affect them, accepting the corresponding obligations and reminding unions of those obligations, and when necessary defending particular unions against external bodies.

6.   The basic fact that the Executive Committees of unions are accountable to their members means that for most practical purposes unions must be autonomous. This is however compatible with leadership of their members by Executives and with leadership of the movement by the TUC, and it is consistent with unions taking a broader view of the interests of working people than might be dictated by unqualified concern with the immediate interests of their own membership. But it means that the authority of the TUC must, with clearly specified and justified exceptions, be defined in terms of influence, not of power. The TUC's authority derives from a willingness by unions, and by their members, to abide by decisions to which they are parties. The role of the TUC is to facilitate the reaching of agreed decisions by democratic processes. Where it has the right to compel unions to adhere to decisions it is because unions themselves have collectively given it that right.

7.   The TUC is inevitably distant from the branch room and from the shop and office. That can be a weakness but it can also be a strength. It is a weakness if it leads to an inadequate understanding of the reality of the industrial situation as it appears to the men and women in the factory and the office. It is a strength insofar as the TUC—and especially the General

Council—can take a more objective view based on a wide range of considerations and can make a longer-term assessment of prospective developments. The TUC has the perennial problem of reconciling the special interests of particular unions, or groups of members, with the general interests of the trade union movement, and of deciding when which set of interests should prevail. This has on occasion led the TUC to make general statements which, because they are capable of different interpretations, offend none and are minimally acceptable to all. A propensity not to offend and not to appear to be interfering with union autonomy has historically often led the TUC to eschew taking initiatives.

8. Recent years however have seen marked changes in all these respects. More emphasis has been put on the TUC's job of drawing conclusions for action from the experiences of unions (e.g. in *Programme for Action*); on becoming involved in particular industrial and union situations (e.g. in relation to the steel industry and the industries with Economic Development Committees, and in wages developments); and on stimulating action by unions (e.g. in amalgamations, trade union training, and spheres of influence). The TUC has been extending the range of its services to unions, has been establishing standards of good trade union practice over a wide area, has been intervening in more specific ways for defined purposes, and has been exercising more initiative in the field of industrial relations. It is in these directions that progress can best be made. This report examines how the TUC can help unions to become more representative, to improve their effectiveness in collective bargaining, and to use their resources more efficiently; and what changes this would require in the structure and functions of the TUC itself.

Increasing the representative capacity of unions

9. Becoming more representative involves unions both in recruiting and holding more members and also in ensuring that their policies reflect the needs and the views of their members.

10. For the purpose of identifying target areas for recruitment

it would be helpful if unions knew more accurately than at present the proportions of their members who are working in different industries, and the proportion of the organisable workers that they have in membership in each industry. Unions should examine the pattern of distribution of their membership in order, as a minimum, to identify situations where with relatively little effort a high existing degree of membership can be built up to and held at one hundred per cent.

11.   More unions are now adopting the check-off as a means of ensuring maintenance of membership. The General Council intend to examine the extent and the nature of existing check-off systems and to make the information available to unions. Unions might also study the cost to them of recruiting new members, and also the cost of short-term membership, particularly in the light of the fact that more frequent changing of occupations has implications for the turnover of trade union membership.

12.   The 1969 Congress resolution called for co-ordination through the TUC of trade union activity in extending membership recruitment in unorganised areas.

13.   The General Council have already initiated through their Organisation Committee a study of what help the TUC might give in this field. As the next step they have decided to conduct a pilot scheme with the unions involved in a particular area of weak organisation. The scheme will entail a detailed examination of the potential membership in the area in question; the resources of the union; and possible methods of conducting a recruitment campaign. The unions in conjunction with the TUC will draw up the physical plans for the campaign. If the proposed experiment is successful similar exercises can be carried out elsewhere, but in any case much should be learned which can be of value in pointing the way ahead.

Recognition

14.   Establishment of an adequate degree of organisation is itself the best guarantee of securing recognition. Even so, in

H

some situations evidence that the union has recognition or will
be able to win it if it can secure enough members may well be a
necessary basis for organising. The power of the Commission on
Industrial Relations to examine complaints by unions that they
are unreasonably being refused recognition should be of
assistance to unions both in specific cases and in changing the
attitudes of other employers. Nevertheless, this will not give an
open sesame to recognition, and unions will still need to combat
the reactionary attitude of some employers. In doing so they
have the right to look to the TUC for assistance. The TUC
might be able to help by approaching the Confederation of
British Industry to put pressure on a firm if it is in membership
of the CBI. Where the CBI is unwilling or unable to help, the
TUC may, if it is satisfied that the union has established its
claim and that recognition would not lead to inter-union
difficulties, consider giving assistance more directly to the
union. This might take the form of a direct approach to the
employer, or of asking other unions concerned for their assistance. As a last resort the TUC has the right in exceptional
circumstances of sponsoring an appeal by a union for financial
assistance from other unions. Obviously assistance cannot be
given unconditionally by the TUC. Intervention by the TUC
is only warranted if in its judgement an important principle is
at stake, and that it is not possible for the union to secure
recognition by other means.

Inter-union relations and closer working between unions
15. In their replies to the TUC circular, unions laid emphasis
on the need to avoid the haphazard growth of multi-unionism
and 'catch-as-catch-can' organising. It is unlikely that inter-
union rivalry is a serious impediment to recruitment—indeed it
can stimulate recruitment—though it may have an effect on
some trade unions' finances by holding down the level of contributions. Although inter-union rivalry is sometimes advanced by employers as an excuse for refusing recognition it is
doubtful whether it has much significance in this connection. It

is, however, desirable to eliminate such competition in order to
avoid the waste of trade union organising resources and to
prevent friction between unions.

16. The Bridlington Principles already provide a code of conduct for unions, and in approving the changes to Rule 12 the
special and ordinary Congresses held in 1969 endorsed the
General Council's view that failure by unions to reconcile their
disputes peacefully was a matter of concern to the movement
as a whole. The General Council intend to examine, in the
light of their experience whether the Bridlington Principles or
the powers or practices of Disputes Committees, need to be
changed.

17. However useful these arrangements may be as methods of
settling disputes between unions, they are at best ways of solving
problems that should never have arisen. One proposal that has
been made for avoiding conflicts between unions is that where
a new opportunity for organisation appears, the TUC should be
empowered to determine, after consulting unions which have a
prima facie interest, which unions should have the right to recruit. The General Council do not doubt that in the vast
majority of cases agreement could be reached between unions,
and their role would consist of bringing unions together and
providing such services as might be needed, as they have recently done in connection with the organisation of university
non-academic staffs and of staffs of training boards. There may
be cases in future where it is impossible to achieve a mutually
agreed settlement, but the General Council believe that, rather
than propose a change of rule forthwith to empower them to
make a determination in such instances, it would be better to
proceed on the assumption that this will not be necessary, and
to report to Congress if they consider that the need for such a
change has arisen.

18. A growing number of unions have set up bilateral or in
some cases multilateral machinery for resolving disputes between themselves. This is a wholly desirable development in
which the General Council are taking an active interest and,

following a survey of existing inter-union procedures and spheres of influence agreements, they have written to affiliated unions recommending them to review their arrangements with other unions with whom they are in frequent contact. The circular reminded unions of the advantages of developing procedures for resolving particular issues and also specific arrangements concerning spheres of influence, transfers of members and benefit rights, recognition of cards, and demarcation of work. The General Council will be reviewing the progress made by unions in reaching agreements, particularly in areas of special difficulty.

19. The main stimulus to closer working is the need to agree on bargaining objectives in forthcoming wage negotiations. This is discussed in more detail in the following section, but a related aspect is the desirability of unions meeting regularly to determine, in the light of prospective changes in their industries, longer-term strategy for recruitment, organisational development and the provision of services to members. In some industries, Federations and the trade union sides of National Joint Councils provide basic machinery which could be developed more systematically in this direction, but it is clear from the replies of many unions that they consider that the functions and activities of these bodies need to be reviewed. In some cases these reviews might extend to examining whether there is unnecessary duplication in cognate NJCs and whether they might be combined to provide more effective bargaining units.

20. One subject which was broached in Resolution 22 of the 1969 Congress is whether unions should adopt standard practices in relation to benefits and protection of membership rights on the transfer of members. This issue is not confined to transfers of members within the same industry, and it can be argued that the need for such protection is more likely to arise in the case of trade unionists who move from one industry to another, but broadly the same considerations apply in both situations. Two proposals for achieving this have been put to the General Council. The first is that the transferring union should continue to treat the member as a full member until the receiving union

can accept him into full benefit, and the second is that the receiving union should accept as a full member an applicant who has been in membership of another affiliated union for a reasonable period. There is a prima facie case for saying that, if a member who has to transfer through no fault of his own is to have accelerated entry into full membership, whatever special obligations are involved should lie on the receiving rather than on the transferring union, as he represents an addition to the strength of the receiving union. The member should however have been in compliance for a stipulated period, and the transfer should of course, be in accordance with the Bridlington Principles. As was mentioned earlier the General Council have recommended unions to develop arrangements for the transfer of members and benefit rights and they have asked their Organisation Committee to examine the implications of these specific proposals.

21. Apart from the possibility of establishing Industrial Committees, examined later in this report, the General Council are, through the medium of the Collective Bargaining Committee, in the process of defining cognate groupings of unions which might be brought together to discuss common problems in the negotiating field. It might be possible to use the same machinery to promote discussion of closer working generally.

22. Proposals for actual amalgamations are more likely to emerge from discussions of this sort than from any endeavour by the General Council to establish theoretical criteria, whether on the basis of industrial unionism or general unionism or on any other principle of combination. There are however two ways in which the General Council might help to speed up the process. The first is by helping groups of unions to take a collective, longer-term view of the economic and other factors that are likely to affect their industries, and in particular their effects on manpower and on the structure of the industry. This would involve the study of selected industries, in the light of information on major trends and significant developments, and information of how close working arrangements, extending where appro-

priate to amalgamation, would help to meet prospective problems and opportunities. Second, the General Council intend to examine the types of obstacle that unions encounter in amalgamation discussions, in order to ascertain whether there is any advice that the General Council can offer to unions who are contemplating or are preparing plans for amalgamation.

Collective bargaining

23. Although the most conspicuous collective bargaining objective is the improvement of wages and basic working conditions, this is only a special—though obviously a very important —aspect of the general trade union objective of ensuring that employers are not free to determine unilaterally the conditions in which their employees spend their working lives. The definition of bargaining objectives thus goes beyond the size of the pay-packet to questions embracing manpower planning and job security, the duration and pattern of working life, safety requirements and access to promotion. Initiatives in such areas, which are becoming a more important constituent of the total pattern of working conditions, cannot be left to particular employers, and in order to use local precedents for the purpose of extending such benefits by trade union action it is desirable to collect this information systematically.

24. A further area of trade union activity where more systematic study is needed is the use of the strike for the purpose of securing improvements. It is essential that strikes should be properly thought out in tactical terms, and also that their use should have regard to the effects on other trade unionists—in the union concerned as well as more generally. More attention should be given to the circumstances which justify the use of the strike, to the techniques of the strike, and to the tactical use of the strike in the context of the overall strategy of the union or unions concerned. Unions might also examine whether the deliberate accumulation of substantial strike funds would itself help to achieve results without having to resort to strikes, whether existing strike benefits are adequate, what effects pros-

perity, the readier availability of social security benefits, hire purchase commitments and home ownership have on militancy, and how public relations services can best be used to explain why strike action has to be taken in particular cases. This is not to argue for or against the use of the strike, but to argue for its most effective use when a resort to strike action is unavoidable. It is also essential that groups of members should have regard to the consequences of their actions for other trade unionists, and should accept that membership imposes limitations on their right to take unilateral action. The movement as a whole, while insisting on protection of the right to strike, has made clear its distaste for use of the strike weapon against other groups of trade unionists.

25. One suggestion that has been made is that the benefits of collective bargaining should be restricted to union members. It is very understandable that trade unionists should resent 'free riders' but with very few exceptions unions have been neither willing nor able to insist on restrictions of this nature. On the one hand has been the consideration that they could result in a class of cheap labour, which could adversely affect trade unionists in times of redundancy or lay-offs: on the other, the practical possibility of enforcing them is strongest in the situations where they are least likely to be necessary. There is much to be said for denying non-unionists the benefits of access to procedures to which trade unions are parties, but on balance the restriction of substantive improvements to members is unlikely to offer much scope as a method of attracting workpeople into unions.

26. In defining their bargaining objectives unions must primarily be guided by the expressed demands of their members, but they also need information about the circumstances and prospects of the firm or industry concerned. In addition, particularly in industry-wide negotiations, they need to take account of developments in the overall economic situation. In the light of that information, they have to choose the appropriate objectives and the priority to be given to each.

27. The primary source of information about firms and industries must be unions' own resources. Some unions already
co-operate in compiling information about developments in
their industries. The TUC might encourage the systematic development of this by promoting discussions between groups of
research officers with a view to exchanging information and
possibly specialising, subject to the agreement of Executives to
any such arrangements. The unions concerned in a particular
industry, or a particular major firm, might examine the possibility of pooling all the information that each obtains on matters
of common interest, for instance on production, location, employment, financial results, wage structures, procedures and
conditions of work. The information would be stored and
analysed and provided on request or for the purposes of joint
negotiations. The TUC would supply such information as it
possessed and would also have access to the stored information:
it might also develop a standard form of classifying and analys-
ing such information, so as to facilitate cross-referencing and
inter-industry comparisons.

28. The TUC keeps under review major changes in the economic and industrial situation: so to varying extents do at least
the bigger unions. The TUC annual *Economic Reviews* provide a
valuable account of current trends each year, but it might be
helpful, if resources permitted, for the TUC to issue a more frequent bulletin, providing a summary of information on important general economic indicators, together possibly with
items of major significance about particular industries.

29. Unions might also find it useful to receive regularly, information about improvements secured in negotiations, particularly in the field of non-wage benefits. For this, unions will
need to supply the TUC regularly with copies of new agreements, drawing attention to improvements that they have
secured, and to new areas in which they have established negotiated standards. The TUC also intends to keep under review
major bargaining developments in other countries, particularly
in North America and Europe, and to promote the regular ex-

change of such information: on some specialised aspects unions can well supplement this through the International Trade Secretariats. The General Council's decision to establish the Collective Bargaining Committee envisages a more active role for the TUC in encouraging unions to pursue common objectives simultaneously when the situation appears to be ripe for a common advance in an area which is of sufficiently general interest.

30. The advice that the TUC can give about the level at which particular improvements are most likely to be won—plant or office, company or industry—is bound to be limited, since much will depend on the structure and the economic position of the industry or service. What the TUC can do in cooperation with unions—and what it is anticipated that the Collective Bargaining Committee will undertake over a period of time—is the comparative examination of procedures and negotiating systems. The method by which it will do this job is essentially by promoting discussions with groups of unions, which should throw light on the question of bargaining levels. It should also help the TUC to provide unions with information about minimum standards that should be set in such areas as the establishment of the status quo, and about the use of arbitration.

31. The provision of services for collective bargaining purposes is closely linked to services in support of other objectives (e.g. the rationalisation of structure, the need for which frequently arises from the need to unify resources for bargaining). This applies clearly to the provision by the TUC of training facilities for trade union officers, full-time and part-time, an area in which the TUC has in recent years been actively developing its services to unions and their members.

32. The TUC's Production Department is already responsible for keeping under review, and for providing information on and training in, production and management subjects, particularly work study and allied techniques and payment systems. It also provides, to a very limited extent, direct advice to unions on

I

specific problems that they meet in particular workplaces. The development of local bargaining, particularly insofar as it involves one of the variants of productivity and efficiency bargaining, will require the expansion of advisory and support services by union officials. This will in turn require the extension of the TUC's training facilities. The General Council have also considered whether the TUC should, after consultation with all the unions concerned, make available on request on-the-spot advice and if so on what terms. They would welcome union views on this.

33. There are some necessary conditions that unions have not been able to secure by bargaining with employers, and to achieve which they have demanded action by the State: current examples are equal pay, safety provisions, and the right to belong to trade unions. There are dangers in relying on State action, as was pointed out in the TUC discussion document on low pay, but situations will continue to arise where unions will want to examine the options of collective bargaining or legislation. The controversy about the proposals in *In Place of Strife*, some of which the TUC actively supported, and to some of which they were vigorously opposed, and the outcome of those discussions illustrated the fact that the relationship between the Government and the trade union movement can best be seen in terms of bargaining; and it also emphasised that the TUC's ability to prevail on the Government depends on its capacity to speak collectively on behalf of a united trade union movement. For the General Council to be able to commit the movement to a course of action means that they must keep unions informed about current developments and secure the agreement of unions to their proposed line of action.

The TUC and closer working with unions

34. The demand for increased participation by unions in decisions that affect them emerged clearly from the Congress debates and the response to the General Council's circular. In principle the place where such decisions should be made is

Congress itself, but in modern conditions Congress cannot in practice play the part that was envisaged when it was established in 1868 or reformed in 1921. Unions are increasingly looking for opportunities to contribute to the formulation of detailed policy proposals by the General Council for the endorsement of Congress, particularly so as to reflect the interests of their members.

35. The General Council have already responded to this need, most obviously in convening conferences of executives (e.g. to discuss the *Economic Review*), in establishing machinery for consulting unions about incomes policy (now transformed into consultations about collective bargaining) and in laying the foundations of a new form of Industrial Committee. This response has been largely ad hoc, but it now needs to be developed systematically.

36. The steps in identifying a policy issue and endorsing a policy statement will depend upon the nature of the issue and the urgency with which action on it is required. Unions will expect not only to be consulted but to have the help and guidance of the TUC in assisting their members to examine the implications of proposed policy developments. This stage of providing information to trade unionists as a means of widening the understanding of issues confronting the movement has not been ignored by the TUC: *Action on Donovan* was widely used by unions as a forerunner to the General Council's formal consultation with them about the Donovan Commission's Report. The TUC's publicity and information services, and particularly the Education Service, need to be more geared to helping active trade union members to contribute to the movement's policy-making through their own unions.

Industrial committees

37. One of the TUC's basic functions is to provide a forum in which unions can meet to discuss common problems and agree on common action. The TUC has regularly convened meetings of unions for these purposes, and, while these have often been

confined to dealing with specific issues, it has also established
some specialised committees on a permanent basis for particular
industries, such as the Local Government Advisory Committee,
or for more general horizontal groupings, such as the Non-
Manual Workers' Advisory Committee. There were also at one
time nominally in existence committees composed of representatives of Trade Groups of Congress, but they have long since
ceased to meet.

38. Two more recent innovations have led some unions to
propose that the TUC should develop a new type of industry-
based Committee. First, when the National Economic Development Council set up the Economic Development Committees the General Council and the unions concerned agreed that
the TUC should service the trade union members. Subsequently the research officers of some unions began to share this
work, so that now the latter service some EDCs and share with
TUC staff the servicing of others. The trade union members
have gained from having access to the TUC's resources, and
when necessary the General Council's support, and by seeing
the problems of their industries in a broader context. The TUC
has gained more knowledge of the industries concerned and of
the practical problems faced by unions in their industries, and
has thus developed its general policies on a firmer foundation
of industrial experience. Joint servicing has also led to closer
working relationships between the TUC and union staffs concerned. The General Council have decided to convene (in
October) a conference of representatives of unions associated
with Industrial Training Boards to discuss matters of common
interest: one of the matters to be discussed will be what servicing facilities are needed by the trade union members on these
Boards and how they might be provided.

39. Second, when the steel industry was being nationalised,
the General Council set up the TUC Steel Industry Trade
Union Consultative Committee for the purpose of co-ordinating
union views. This Committee initially reported to the General
Council through the Economic Committee: it has developed

along its own lines and no longer reports to the General Council although some account of its work is given to Congress. It has continued to be serviced by TUC staff. Some affiliated unions have criticised what they regarded as the unduly restricted membership of the SICC, but as a method of promoting closer working between the unions concerned there is general agreement that this has been a useful innovation which has helped to secure more co-ordination of the views of unions than has ever existed before.

40. Earlier this year, arising in part from the discussion at the post-Donovan Conference on the Construction Industry, and in the light of the advantages that have been derived from the existence and activities of the SICC, the General Council and the unions concerned agreed to set up a Committee for the Construction Industry.

41. The General Council have given very careful consideration to the views expressed in the Congress debate and by unions in response to the General Council's circular that the TUC should further develop its activities on an industrial basis and should be linked much more directly with the industrial interests of affiliated unions, and to the suggestion that, to this end, they should establish a number of Industrial Committees. These, it has been argued, would act as a channel through which unions and the General Council could co-operate in identifying and solving major problems affecting particular sectors, and as a channel for TUC initiatives in relation to groups of unions, particularly in relation to collective bargaining developments.

42. In the General Council's view this would be a natural and desirable development of what has already begun to happen. Such Committees would give the unions in the industry concerned a way of expressing their collective views to the TUC, and of ensuring that the General Council took their interests fully into account in formulating policy on that industry and more generally. On the other hand the General Council could through such Committees impress on the unions concerned the

wider interests of the movement and the ways in which other trade unionists would be affected by their decisions.

43. Such a Committee would thus perform a dual function. It would advise the General Council on matters affecting the industry; and if the unions represented on the Committee agreed it would have the right to take executive action on matters of common concern to those unions. It would be necessary to distinguish those functions, and in particular not to give the appearance that, when the unions concerned were collectively acting on their own initiative and not on behalf of the TUC, they were committing the General Council to support such action. It might therefore be best to designate such a Committee as the Committee of TUC (name of the industry) Unions, which would also make it clear that other TUC Committees, dealing with particular subjects (e.g. education, economic issues, employment policies), would have the right to examine matters affecting the industry concerned insofar as they fell within their purview.

44. It appears to the General Council that the structure and method of working of these Committees should be as follows. The TUC would be represented on each Committee by General Council members drawn from the industry concerned, one of whom would be chairman. The unions concerned would appoint the other members of the Committee on an agreed basis. The Committee would report on its activities to the General Council, but only those recommendations for which the Committee requested the General Council's support would be subject to endorsement by the General Council. Other recommendations would be addressed by the Committee to the unions concerned: the General Council would have the right to comment on such recommendations, but would not have the power to veto them. The General Council would account in their Report to Congress for action they had taken on the first type of recommendation; but would only briefly refer to the latter type for the purpose of informing Congress.

45. The subjects to be dealt with by each Committee would be

a matter for consultation and agreement between the unions concerned and the General Council, but among issues which such Committees might wish to consider are recruitment, inter-union relations, the activities of relevant Economic Development Committees and Industrial Training Boards, the structure of collective bargaining arrangements, industrial and trade union training, wages structure, the pattern of non-wage conditions, and safety and health. It is unlikely that a Committee would at least in the early stages wish to take the initiative in formulating and pursuing claims for improvements in wages and conditions. It could however provide a forum in which unions could, if they wished, discuss collective bargaining strategy, and if they further took the view that the Committee should take on a wage-bargaining function in the course of time this would be allowed to develop. The unions concerned would in any event need to consider the implications that the establishment of such a Committee would have for existing Joint Industrial Councils or Federations.

46. The TUC would accept responsibility for providing the secretariat and servicing the Committees, where appropriate in conjunction with the staffs of participating unions, and the specialist services of the TUC Departments would be available to these as to other Committees of the General Council.

47. The General Council do not under-estimate, nor should unions, the strain that the establishment of such Committees would put on the resources of the TUC and of unions, and it would be unwise to take on in the early stages more than could effectively be handled. There should be a gain from avoiding duplication of activities and from the co-ordination of servicing, but the result—and indeed the justification—of having such Committees would be a net increase in the activity of unions, as of the TUC. It would be necessary for the TUC to expand its resources, and in particular to find and train staff.

SOURCE: TUC. *Structure and Development*. Interim Report of

TUC General Council adopted at the 102nd Annual Trades
Union Congress (1970)

50 TUC: INDUSTRIAL COMMITTEES

25. At the TUC, seven industrial committees have been
formed to provide a structure for the development of common
policies between unions covering all grades of workers within
one sector.

26. The most important aspect of the Steel Committee's work
has been in negotiating collective agreements on 'non-wage
benefits' with the British Steel Corporation. In this respect the
Committee has already acquired many of the characteristics of a
Trade Union Side of a National Joint Industrial Council. Agreements already concluded or in process of negotiation include
employment and income security for both manual workers and
staff; a holidays agreement for manual workers; a recognition
and procedure agreement concerning staff; and a comprehensive
agreement concerning staff salary structures, holidays, sick pay
and other aspects of non-manual workers' employment. A pension scheme and a sick pay scheme for manual workers have
been agreed in principle, and it is expected that the former at
least will be in operation by 1973.

27. In addition, the Committee have been in close discussions
with the Corporation about job evaluation and have given high
priority to developing effective means to ensure that workers'
interests are taken into account in plans for the future development of the Corporation. As a result of the Committee's pressure, the BSC gives a minimum of six months notice of plant
closures, but because of the general rise in unemployment the
Committee decided in 1971 to oppose all future closures.

28. The Construction Industry Committee first met in August
1970 and covers local government construction and engineering
construction as well as the main areas of building, civil engineering and ancillary trades. The Committee has urged the

establishment of a Public Procurement Corporation for Construction, has made substantial progress towards establishing a programme for decasualisation, and has made a detailed examination of the structure of the industry. The Committee has also maintained liaison with the members of the Building & Civil Engineering EDC's and the Construction Industry Training Board.

29. The Local Government Committee first met in June 1971 and was established out of the former National Advisory Committee for Local Government Service. The Committee has been concerned about the proposed reorganisations of local government and water supply, and particularly about their possible effects on staff. It has negotiated improvements to the local government superannuation scheme with the local government employers, and has decided that for an experimental period there should be a regular item on the Committee's agenda concerning all claims submitted to employers, all significant replies received, and all settlements concluded. The Committee has also been concerned about facilities for workplace representatives in the sector, and about the future of the Local Government Training Board.

30. The Transport Industries Committee first met in October 1971 and has prepared memoranda on bus licensing, civil aviation and airports policy. It is examining integrated transport policy in all its facets. In addition the Committee has kept abreast of developments in transport policy within the EEC, and has maintained liaison with trade union members of the Road Transport Industrial Training Board and the Air Transport and Travel ITB. The Committee will keep under review wages and conditions prevailing in the various sectors of transport.

31. The Fuel and Power Industries Committee was set up at the beginning of the Congress year and decided to review each of the coal, gas, electricity, nuclear power and oil industries. This process has been taking place as a preliminary to a major review of TUC fuel and power policy. In addition the Com-

mittee have given attention to the Electricity Bill and to the
Gas Bill. They held discussions, leading to amendments being
made to the Gas Bill with the responsible Government Minister.
The fuel and power industries all have well established industrial relations and collective bargaining arrangements but the
unions have agreed to keep the Committee informed about
wage and salary movements within their industries. They have
agreed also to co-operate in a review of various non-wage questions such as holidays, sick pay and pensions.

32.   The Textiles and Clothing Industries Committee first met
in March 1972. Unions with more than 2,000 members in the
industry were asked to nominate approximately in proportion
to their total members in the industry. Smaller unions in cotton
and wool textiles are represented through the National Association of Unions in the Textile Trade and the United Textile
Factory Workers' Association. In addition, the Northern Carpet
Trade Union, although below 2,000, has a seat because of its
special position. The Committee has sought safeguards for the
home industry in face of increasing competition from abroad
including country of origin markings, greater control over the
activities of multinational companies; and has considered textile
policy in the EEC. The Committee will maintain close liaison
with trade union members in the Clothing and Wool Textiles
EDCs, the Joint Textile Committee covering the NEDO
Medium Term Review, and the new British Textiles Confederation.

33.   The Health Services Committee, which was established
in September 1971, has already made representations to the
Secretary of State for Social Services on the care of the health of
staff employed in hospitals and for the establishment of an
industrial training board for the NHS. The Committee is also
considering problems which may arise for workers and unions
from the reorganisation of the NHS and, at the same time,
attention is being given to ways of improving trade union
organisation, particularly in the nursing field.

34.   The purpose of establishing the TUC industrial commit-

tees is to establish a close link between the unions concerned and the General Council, which enables the unions to express a collective view to the General Council, and the General Council to be fully aware of the specific problems facing the unions and the industries concerned. This has been done by appointing—to each of the Committees—General Council members drawn from the industry concerned, providing each Committee with research and administrative assistance from the TUC Departments which also service the General Council and putting the minutes of the Committees before the General Council at their meetings each month.

SOURCE: TUC. Report of the General Council (1972), Appendix A, paras 25–34

51 TUC: WOMEN TRADE UNIONISTS IN CONFERENCE

Mrs C. Helyer (Amalgamated Union of Engineering Workers: Engineering Section) moved the following Motion:

This Conference calls upon the trade union Movement to take vigorous measures to increase the recruitment of women workers into unions. Lack of trade union organisation among women greatly hinders the fight for equality.

She said: The recent defeat of the Anti-Discrimination Bill by Parliamentary play-acting is one of the examples of prejudice which women have to overcome in their fight for equal opportunity as well as equal pay. Women now form more than one-third of the labour force, yet unfortunately they have a very poor record of union membership—only 25 per cent as compared with 50 per cent for men workers. It did increase by 10 per cent in 1970 but it must increase far more if equality for women at work is to be achieved.

Before the implementation of the Equal Pay Act and other legislation can be effective, women's involvement in union affairs must be improved. So must the almost negligible numbers of women trade union officials and shop stewards, otherwise, how can the interests of women workers be adequately represented?

Discrimination against women means that they earn only about 60 per cent of men's rates on average. Moreover, the differentials are widening as was revealed in the 1971 Earnings Survey. Women are concentrated in less-skilled occupations, as manual workers in industries such as the food, clothing, textile and electrical engineering, and in junior non-manual jobs or clerical jobs. It is estimated that cheap labour by women saves employers many millions of pounds each year.

The Equal Pay Act, despite its inadequacies, should help to remedy discrimination through pay packets. But equality of opportunity is equally urgent. Legislation and effective trade union organisation are necessary in the fight against absurd archaic prejudices. ILO Convention III, among other things, prohibits discrimination on grounds of sex. Britain refuses to honour this Convention, and pays only lip service to it. It is up to the women workers in the trade unions and the trade unions themselves to free women from second-class status, as the exploited sector of the labour force. It is only through union organisation that this can be achieved. The law must be changed and discrimination overcome through the trade union Movement and its women members.

The Motion was formally seconded.

Miss J. C. Riddiough (Union of Shop, Distributive and Allied Workers) moved the following Motion:

This Conference believes the time is now opportune for a national campaign to be mounted by the Trades Union Congress using all aspects of the mass media to secure the extension of trade union organisation among all women workers.

She said: During the last few months we have heard more about women's rights than at any time in the past. We have had an Anti-Discrimination Bill; the National Joint Committee of

Working Women's Organisations campaign on women's and girls' career and employment opportunities; many articles in the national Press on equal rights for women, 'liberating women', etc.; and also 52 questions have been tabled in the House. On March 14 the Government announced the setting up of an Inquiry into discriminatory practices.

It is all very well to talk about equal rights, but surely the most effective way to gain equal rights is through the democratically instituted trade unions. It took over 80 years to get the Equal Pay Act on the Statute Book, and women in the trade union Movement do not want to wait another 80 years for our ideals and aspirations to be realised.

But having said that, however, I must stress that women at work need to appreciate that the only way in which they can achieve their aims is by acting collectively, or in trade union jargon 'by being organised'. Many inequalities in industry exist simply because of attitudes; exist because of the attitudes of profit-activated managements; exist because of the attitudes of this lame duck Government; exist because of the attitudes of women themselves and, moreover, they exist because of the attitudes of their menfolk.

Traditionally, women have been discouraged from joining, or where they have joined, from taking an active part in the trade union Movement because their fathers, their brothers, their husbands, and even their sons say, 'There is no need for you to bother your pretty little head about matters which, as women, you will never really understand anyway.' In fact, last night a member of our delegation, whose husband is a convenor —so you can tell how interested in the trade union Movement he is—told us that when she was selected at a late date to come on the delegation her husband turned to her and said, 'Well, you won't be able to go, will you? You have got a husband and child to look after'—the child being a son of 17 years of age! The point I am trying to make is that it is often the menfolk who do not want the women taking too active a part. Could it possibly be that our male members and colleagues are afraid

that if women do become well organised and active members of
the union there may be a takeover bid!

It is these traditional attitudes that we need to break down.
Women have been emancipated for many years and it is time
for them to assert themselves in their own right by joining a
trade union and by making their voices heard within the Movement. If we can accomplish a 50 per cent increase in the female
membership within the trade unions, then the possibilities of
job satisfaction, and the opportunities for promotion to more responsible positions within industry, will in my opinion become
limitless. We therefore believe that the time is now opportune
for a national campaign to be mounted by the Trades Union
Congress, using all aspects of the mass media to secure the
extension of trade union organisation amongst all women
workers.

The motion was formally seconded.

Mrs M. Morrison (Civil Service Union) moved the following
Amendment:

   Add at end: 'Special importance should be attached to industries with large numbers of low-paid women workers
   who are in some cases without even national negotiating
   machinery.

   She said: It might interest delegates to have some background information on what happens when women are not
organised. Delegates will no doubt have heard of the problems
we have with the employers of contract cleaners and must be
aware of the low wages which they are paid. Last year the
National Board for Prices and Incomes issued a report entitled
'Pay and Conditions in the Contract Cleaning Trade' which
pointed out the need to establish collective bargaining machinery
in contract cleaning. An ad hoc Committee of Trade Unions was
set up which gave evidence to the National Board for Prices and
Incomes. The contract cleaning employers refused to meet the
ad hoc Committee. Is it not an indictment of this present society
that so many thousands of women are outside recognised trade

union membership and that the employers are so confident that there will always be some women willing to work for a pittance, that they can ignore the unions?

What is to be done? Are men afraid that we will take over trade unions if we do get organised? The answer is, in two words, recruit and organise. Women trade union members should each recruit another woman member. Let the membership snowball in unity and strength, strength to fight the monopolies and strength to demand and get for every working woman a decent wage for her labours.

We say categorically it is now time for the women members in the TUC to receive some attention from the General Council. It is up to the General Council to make efforts now to get all women workers into the trade union Movement. The need is urgent. Spend money on posters and exhibit them on the Underground, in stations, in carriages, on the buses and the bus terminals. Take time on TV at peak hours to explain to women what they can gain by union membership, and what they can lose by not being trade union members. Let the secretaries and the members of the executive councils of the better-known unions go out and about in the country and explain the policies of their unions. And what about all the exhibitions which are organised by the daily papers and the local councils? Look at the thousands upon thousands of women who pass through the turnstiles of the Ideal Home Exhibition. Just think of the result of a stand there in the hands of good organisers. Loosen the purse strings of the General Council, and show the women of this country that they have nothing to be afraid of if they will only organise themselves within the trade unions.

The Industrial Relations Act is now law. It is now an offence for an employer to refuse a worker the right to belong to a trade union. Let us enforce it, now, this year. Never again let us have to face the fact that employers can refuse to meet the representatives of the trade unions who want to bargain for better conditions.

The amendment was formally seconded.

Mrs M. Lyons (Preston Trades Council): The Chairman has said that the way in which we can make progress is by fighting for ourselves. Unfortunately, there are several factors which hamper women in fighting for themselves because when they would like to attend trade union meetings and make themselves felt they have to consider their homes and children. The largest body of women within the trade union Movement consists of women who are between the ages of 40 and 49 whose children have grown up, women who could really and truly get inside and fight this battle. However, I would like to say to each trade union, 'Put your house in order.' We talk about the democratic process but, because women cannot attend meetings, the democratic process very often falls flat on its face.

I am a very ardent trade unionist. I am Vice-Chairman of the Trades Council. Unfortunately, on very many occasions I am the only female who attends the branch because although we have 500 members most of whom are younger women with children. I am in the fortunate position of having a grown-up family so I can attend meetings and try to represent the women's point of view. What I would like to see is the trade union Movement looking at the possibility of including women on a proportionate basis in delegations.

So far as paid officials are concerned, the Transport and General Workers' Union has 600 male full-time officers and only one woman. The General and Municipal Workers' Union has four. This does not sound awfully democratic to me. I know that people will turn round and say that the opportunities are available but there again you have got to get there and I would like to see women at all levels of structure in the trade union by right and not being forced to manipulate as a lot of us have to do to get anywhere.

Mrs O. White (Association of Teachers in Technical Institutions): We have got somewhere between 40,000 and 50,000 members all told. To my great astonishment, when I enquired how many of those were women, I was told 4,000. That is a total of 4,000 women teachers in technical institutions of any kind, from the ordinary follow-on further education college to the top polytechnics and we do represent most of the women that there are because we find that women will readily join the union. What they do not do is come along to the meetings.

I would say in passing that the fact that there are only 4,000 women in the technical teachers' union shows you what poor job opportunities there are for women even in a profession which on paper has got equal pay. It is not really equal pay, of course, because women are not promoted to the same extent as men. The same is true within the union. A few women attend Divisional Meetings, there are about four women at the National Council, but none on the Executive. When my colleague and I were briefed to come to this meeting today, we were briefed by two men—the Chairman of each of the sub-committees of the Executive. But it does not have to be that way. By now I have been in a total of five different trade unions and in each of them I have played an active part. It is determination that does it and that is a message that you should go back and tell the women in your branches.

Miss G. Jones (National Union of Tailors and Garment Workers) : I am an official of our union which gives very great encouragement to women to become officers. I was a shop steward for years and our union has quite a few women officers —about nine or ten.

On the question of recruitment, as an official I have often got entry into factories and recruited quite well on the floor. However, the main trouble is to get people to come forward as shop stewards or even collectors. I am appealing to every woman here who is a member of a union to take an active part in its work.

I can only speak from my experience and say that the main thing in recruiting is to get in the offices, the workshops and on the factory floor. Communication between people is my theme wherever I go.

Miss J. M. McKinlay (Union of Post Office Workers): I
think it is about time that we started looking at the motion
which is in front of us. At Conference we hear about womens'
problems and we have discussed them exhaustively. I think it is
about time we got down to deciding what positive action we
are going to take. The resolution says that we believe that the
time is now opportune for a national campaign to be mounted
by the Trades Union Congress.

I come from the public sector and from a trade union which
has always had a democratic approach to women. We have
been fortunate because our organisational problems are much
less serious than those of other unions. However, there was a
time when, despite the fact that our union had over 15,000
women members there was only one woman on the Executive
Council. I am happy to report that there are now five women
and one national woman officer but she is not a 'national
women's' officer. She is an official who deals with men's and
women's problems. I do not think that we who come from the
more privileged section of the women's working population
ought to overlook the problems which face trade unions like the
Transport and General Workers' Union, the AUEW and
USDAW. The thing which is absolutely appalling to my trade
union—because we have a very high percentage of female
membership—is the very low women's membership which
exists generally.

I would now like to come to what we ought to do in order to
publicise this. A membership campaign has been run by one
trade union in the public newspapers and I understand that it
was very successful. Surely, the Trades Union Congress and the
Women's Advisory Committee could get down to working out
that kind of public campaign and money must be made available for it. I am positive that, if the TUC is short of money for
this kind of campaign, the trade unions organising women or
even the trade unions who do not organise women—if they are
to be believed—would contribute funds. We have not yet solved

the problems of women's organisation and, if this Conference has a function at all—and I believe it could have—it is to spearhead the attack on the unorganised masses of women in employment in this country. Let us get out in the Press; let us get on the television and let us get the message home to women who are unorganised to show them just how bitterly they are being exploited. We know about the mother with young children, that she has to go to a job, but our function, in my view, is to deal with the organisational problems.

Mrs M. Fenwick (Union of Jute, Flax and Kindred Textile Operatives): I have never listened to so many reasons why women should not have equality because you are defeating every argument that has gone on before by your very attitudes. You have given every reason why women do not join the trade union Movement and why they do not take positions in the trade union Movement or in any other sphere of industry. Every employer in the country is terrified to give a woman a job with more responsibility. They claim that, because of their domestic duties, they cannot be sure that a woman will always be present at work as a man would be. The women who have just come to the rostrum have given exactly the same argument and it makes me wonder where we are going.

If a woman has the ability, she will get the position. I do not believe that a woman should specially have a position made available to her, any more than a man should. I do not really believe that any woman would want a position under those circumstances.

Seventy per cent of my union's members are men and 30 per cent are women. Last December they elected me their General Secretary and I say to any woman who wants to go anywhere, you will make the effort to attend meetings if this is what you want. I say this advisedly because I had four young children in only five-and-a-half years and I took them to my trade union meetings with me. I took them to the Labour Party meetings and I am now taking my grandchildren. There is nothing to

debar a woman from doing this if she is interested. Just make
them behave themselves. In fact, quite frankly, very often you
will find that this is the best way of controlling them because
they know that they have to be quiet and listen. I never had any
trouble with mine. For Heaven's sake, if you want equality,
have it on an equal basis. Have it on your own capabilities and
do not ask for concessions.

Miss M. A. Roberts (National Union of Insurance Workers):
I belong to one of those categories we have been hearing about
which is to some extent privileged in that in the majority of
cases it has been just a question on the clerical side of persuading
Management to give us equal pay. To a great extent we have
got equality of opportunity.

We have been making an awful lot of excuses here this morning and I am heartily fed-up with hearing women say that women
cannot go to trade union meetings. In saying that I realise that
I happen to be following a very able speaker who has put the
same opinion forward. I am a single woman but, you know,
single women have their problems too. In fact, sometimes I
think we have rather more than our married contemporaries. I
have not got any other life at the moment than trade unionism
but that is what I have chosen and I accept it. I enjoy it. It
has probably aged me a little but I am getting somewhere.

I belong to a union which is part of the National Union of
Insurance Workers and I am glad to tell you that this year, for
the first time in history, this particular union—the Liverpool
Victoria Workers' Union—has a woman President. For a
number of years I have been on the General Executive, not
because the members think I am absolutely brilliant, although
I may have tried to kid them I am. The reason they put me on
the General Executive is because I make a nuisance of myself. If
I have something to say, I say it. In the end they said, 'If you
think you can do any better, get on the General Executive and
do it' and for the last ten years that I have been on the Executive representing my clerical grade—elected not as a woman

but as a clerk—we have managed to get three years towards equal pay, Saturdays off and various other odds and ends. You can do it if you want to. Married women can get out in the evenings. I refuse to believe that every woman, when she puts a ring on her left hand, stays in the house for the rest of her life. If you want to go to the theatre, you arrange to get a baby-sitter. You can go to union meetings. When I say, 'You can,' I know that I am preaching to the converted here but this is a national issue which we must get over to every woman in the country. You only get what you fight for.

Mrs G. Taylor (Amalgamated Union of Engineering Workers: Technical and Supervisory Section): Firstly, I would like to touch on something the speaker before last said when she referred to the problems and the excuses we make for married women, particularly those who have families. Children are not just a product of the woman. They also are the children of the men but you do not very often find men saying that they cannot go to meetings because they have to stay and mind the children. Unfortunately, it is traditional in our Society that women have the responsibility of looking after the children. In my view, due to this fact, whoever has the responsibility of looking after them, Society should play some part in providing nurseries and after-school facilities to enable women to go out to work and take a full part in the trade union Movement without having to worry about the children. There would then not be the problem of deciding who was going to go out to their trade union meetings but, unfortunately, with the traditions we have, again it would generally be the men.

We believe that the recruitment of women into trade union membership is of paramount importance at the moment as the numbers of women employees increase. Many married women now, far more than in the past, stay on at work and a number of married women return to work after bringing up their children. It is important that all workers, both male and female, unite and organise to improve the standards of living and working conditions of all workers in this country. By so doing we would work towards changing and improving our Society to the benefit of all people. It is of paramount importance therefore that this section of Society should be recruited into trade union membership so that they are not exploited.

SOURCE: TUC. *Women Workers 1972*. Report of the 42nd annual conference of representatives of trade unions catering for women workers (16 and 17 March 1972), 47–53

Select Guide to Further Reading

In this brief select guide, we suggest ways in which the interested reader can pursue and keep up to date with various topics affecting trade unions. The most obvious method is to read the publications of the trade union movement. The first source is the Trades Union Congress, whose Annual Report, published towards the end of the year, contains the Report of the General Council to the annual congress and includes much statistical material, reprints of important TUC statements made during the year, and a verbatim report of the proceedings of the congress itself. The TUC also publishes many pamphlets on a variety of subjects, including the annual *Economic Review*. The most recent discussion of the TUC is by John Hughes, *The TUC—a Plan for the 1970s* (Fabian tract 397, 1969).

The General Federation of Trade Unions, catering mainly for the smaller unions, publishes a quarterly journal, *Federation News*, on matters relevant to the unions. For a recent discussion of the GFTU, see A. I. Marsh and M. D. Speirs, 'The General Federation of Trade Unions 1945–70', *Industrial Relations Journal*, 2 no 3 (Autumn 1971), 22–34.

Individual unions publish a considerable quantity of material for their members, including annual reports, newspapers and journals. Among those of interest presented as serious-minded journalism are the TGWU's *Record* and NALGO's *Public Service*. Pamphlets, such as shop stewards' handbooks, are also issued by the unions.

Much of the literature published by unofficial sources is ephemeral, relating to a particular topic or dispute. Regular publications include the monthly *Voice of the Unions*, of Voice Newspapers which also publish many pamphlets, and the numerous publications of the Institute for Workers' Control. Articles and documents are included in the annual *Trade Union Register* (from 1969).

Of the numerous historical studies of individual unions and unions in general, few are more than descriptively commemorative. See E. J. Hobsbawm, 'Trade Union Historiography', *Bulletin of the Society for the Study of Labour History*, 8 (Spring 1964). There is a select bibliography by R. and E. Frow and Michael Katanka. *The History of British Trade Unions* (Historical Association pamphlet H76 1969), and an annual bibliography in the *Bulletin of the Society for the Study of Labour History*. Among the general histories, the pioneering work by S. and B. Webb, *The History of Trade Unionism* (1894, last ed 1920), is still valuable, although many of their interpretations have been criticised; see, for example, the article in V. L. Allen. *The Sociology of Industrial Relations* (1971) and A. E. Musson. *British Trade Unions 1800–1875* (1972). The study by H. A. Clegg, A. Fox and A. F. Thompson, *A History of British Trade Unions since 1889, vol 1 1889–1910* (1964), while covering only part of the period, does explain rather more than most histories why the unions behaved as they did. The standard general history is by H. Pelling, *A History of British Trade Unionism* (2nd ed 1971). Richard Hyman. *The Workers' Union* (1970) usefully combines description with analysis; so also does H. A. Turner. *Trade Union Growth, Structure and Policy* (1963), which is perhaps the most satisfying discussion of trade unionism to appear since the war.

Among collections of documents referring to the past, including the recent past, are W. Milne-Bailey. *Trade Union Documents* (1929); K. Coates and T. Topham. *Workers' Control* (1970), and N. Robertson and K. I. Sams. *British Trade Unionism* (1972).

While these histories demonstrate that unions can and do change, the Webbs' analytical work, *Industrial Democracy*, retains important insights into trade union functions and methods. Apart from the output of a few writers, notably G. D. H. Cole, little of value appeared between the 1890s and the 1950s, but during the last decade or so there has been a flood of publications, stemming from two main sources. Firstly there is the work of the academics, who have undertaken more extensive research than ever before into trade unions and industrial relations. On the role of the trade unions generally, there is A. Flanders *Management and Unions* (1970), to which can be added the collection of readings which he edited, *Collective Bargaining* (1969). H. A. Clegg has produced a number of works, including two studies of the General and Municipal Workers Union, *General Union* (1954) and *General Union in a Changing Society* (1964). His work on *Trade Union Officers* (1959), with A. J. Killick and Rex Adams, is still valuable as is his *The System of Industrial Relations in Great Britain* (new ed 1972). The earlier book of the same title, edited by Clegg and Flanders, is dated but useful. George S. Bain. *The Growth of White Collar Trade Unions* (1970) is important beyond the study of this particular group: it has stimulating ideas on trade union growth and development. Shirley Lerner's excellent collection of essays, *Breakaway Unions and the Small Trade Union* (1961) includes an important one on the work of the TUC in resolving disputes between unions. *The Closed Shop in Britain* (1964) by W. E. J. McCarthy is the standard work on the subject. Of the many legal textbooks on industrial and labour law, perhaps the most readable analysis is by K. W. Wedderburn, *The Worker and the Law* (2nd ed 1971). On the relationship between trade unions and politics, there are the various historical writings of Henry Pelling, eg *The Origins of the Labour Party* (1965); and work by R. M. Martin, *Communism and the British Trade Unions* (1970), mainly on the 1920s, and M. Harrison, *Trade Unions and the Labour Party* (1960).

A great deal has been written on trade union structure and government: V. L. Allen. *Power in Trade Unions* (1954); several articles by J. D. Edelstein: 'Democracy in a National Union: the British AEU', *Industrial Relations* (California 1965); 'An Organisational Theory of Union Democracy', *American Sociological Review* (February 1967); and (with others) 'Patterns of Opposition in British and American Unions', *Sociology* (1970). See also, on the question of opposition within unions: G. Wootton, 'Parties in Union Government', *Political Studies* (1961); R. Bean, 'Policy Formation and Membership Opposition in the ETU', *Political Quarterly* (1965). More generally, see J. D. Hughes. *Trade Union Structure and Government* (Royal Commission on Trade Unions and Employers' Associations, Research Paper no 5 parts 1 and 2).

The student can keep up to date with events and relevant articles in *The British Journal of Industrial Relations* and *Industrial Relations Journal*.

The second source of the spate of publications in recent years has resulted from the government's role in economic management and attempts to intervene in industrial relations and trade union affairs. The many reports of the National Board for Prices and Incomes produced during the 1960s contain useful information on wages as well as other aspects of trade unionism. The Donovan Commission's *Report* (1968), together with the various Research Papers which it instigated, are a major source of information. There was also a mass of oral and written evidence, of varying quality, to the Commission. Inevitably some of this material is critical of union practices; for example, parts of the *Report* itself and the CBI's evidence to the Commission. Other critical approaches can be found in Michael Shanks. *The Stagnant Society* (1961, revised 1972) and in Inns of Court Conservative Association. *A Giant's Strength* (1958). The Conservative Political Centre's *Fair Deal at Work* (1968) provided the inspiration for the Industrial Relations Act, 1971.

On the relations between trade unions and coloured immigrants, there have been two recent studies, M. Rimmer. *Race and Industrial Conflict* (1972) and M. Meth. *Brothers to All Men?* (1972).

Comparisons with trade unions in other countries may help towards an understanding, providing the very different backgrounds are firmly noted. Among the mass of publications, the following are of particular interest: EUROPE—W. L. Kendall and E. Marx. *Unions in Europe* (1972); J. Gretton. *Workers and Students* (1971). The news-sheet *Trade Union News from the European Community* provides factual material on unions in the Common Market countries; USA—H. Pelling. *American Labor* (1960); J. Barbash. *American Unions: Structure, Government and Policies* (1967); AFRICA—I. Davies. *African Trade Unions* (1966); USSR—E. C. Brown. *Soviet Trade Unions and Labor Relations* (1966); M. McAuley. *Labour Disputes in Soviet Russia 1957–65* (1969).

The International Labour Organisation has published a series entitled *The Trade Union Situation in (name of country)*, which has some uses. Studies which are more specifically comparative are A. Sturmthal (ed). *White-Collar Trade Unions* (1966) and O. Kahn-Freund and Bob Hepple. *Laws against Strikes* (Fabian Research series 305, 1972).

Finally, general bibliographical assistance can be obtained from G. S. Bain and G. B. Woolven. 'The Literature of Labour Economics and Industrial Relations: a Guide to its Sources', *Industrial Relations Journal* (Summer 1970); V. L. Allen. *International Bibliography of Trade Unionism* (1970); A. W. Gottschalk, T. G. Whittingham, with N. Williams. *British Industrial Relations. An Annotated Bibliography* (1970).

Acknowledgements

The editors and publishers wish to thank the following for permission to reproduce material included in this book. The Trades Union Congress; Association of Scientific, Technical and Managerial Staffs; Association of University Teachers; Associated Society of Locomotive Engineers and Firemen; Amalgamated Union of Engineering Workers (Engineering Section); Amalgamated Union of Engineering Workers (Technical and Supervisory Section); British Actors' Equity Association; Civil and Public Services Association; Confederation of Shipbuilding and Engineering Unions; Electrical Electronic Telecommunication and Plumbing Union; National and Local Government Officers Association; National Union of Journalists; National Union of Mineworkers; National Union of Public Employees; National Union of Railwaymen; Post Office Engineering Union; Transport and General Workers' Union; Union of Shop, Distributive and Allied Workers; Mr J. E. Mortimer; Dr W. E. J. McCarthy and Messrs Basil Blackwell & Mott Ltd; and British Leyland Motor Corporation.

Index

Note: Names of trade unions are given as they were at the date of the document. For list of abbreviations, see pp 9–10.

About NALGO, 152
Action on Donovan, 235
AEU Journal, 95
Agency shop, 57, 58–60: *see also* Closed shop
Agreements, collective, 109–48
Amalgamated Engineering Union, 92–5
Amalgamated Society of Boilermakers, Shipwrights, Blacksmiths and Structural Workers, 113, 186
Amalgamated Union of Engineering and Foundry Workers, 65–74
Amalgamated Union of Engineering Workers: Constructional Section, 113, 177; Engineering Section, 113, 177, 243; Foundry Section, 113, 177; Technical and Supervisory Section, 166, 177, 253
Amalgamations of unions, 177–8, 197–201
Andrews, C. D., 11 n
Ashton, J., 95
Associated Metal Workers' Society, 113
Associated Society of Locomotive Engineers and Firemen, 128, 134, 185
Association of Engineering and Shipbuilding Draughtsmen, 164–6
Association of Patternmakers and Allied Craftsmen, 113
Association of Scientific, Technical and Managerial Staffs, 178, 197–201
Association of Scientific Workers, 197–201
Association of Supervisory Staffs, Executives and Technicians, 197–201

Association of Teachers in Technical Institutions, 248
Association of University Teachers, 31–3
AUT Bulletin, 25, 33

Bargaining, collective, 20–1, 23–4, 28–30, 109–48, 203, 229, 230–4, 240–3
Bell, J. D. M., 27, 179
Berry, H., 93
Birmingham and Midland Sheet Metal Workers' Society, 113
Bishop, Ted, 95
Blinkhorn, K., 176
Booth, A., 95
Bridlington Principles, 82, 107, 178, 179–83, 227, 229
British Actors' Equity Association, 110, 144–5
British Leyland Motor Corporation, 110, 111–13
Burger, G. C., 11 n
Bush, C., 175

Case for Amalgamation to form the Association of Scientific, Technical and Managerial Staffs, The, 201
Chamberlain, N. W., 26, 26 n
Civil and Public Services Association, 174–6
Civil Service Union, 183–5, 246
Clegg, H. A., 27 n
Closed shop, 57, 60–5; *see also* Agency shop
Closed Shop in Britain, The, 65

261

Coal Industry, 15, 52
Collective Bargaining, 57 n
Commission for Industry and Manpower, 101, 102
Commission on Industrial Relations, 106, 107, 110
Conciliation, 111, 218–22
Confederation of British Industry, 58, 98, 110–11, 218–22, 226
Confederation of Shipbuilding and Engineering Unions, 178, 185–96
Co-operate not Legislate, 105

DATA Journal, 96, 197
Demarcation problems, 57, 65–74; see also Inter-union relations
Democracy in unions, 149–76
Department of Health and Social Security, 169
Disputes Committee, TUC, 65–74, 178, 179–85, 227
Dockers imprisoned for contempt of court, 13, 111
Donovan Commission see Royal Commission on Trade Unions and Employers' Associations
Draughtsmen's and Allied Technicians Association, 95–6

Education, 58, 74–81, 82–5, 233–4
Electrical, Electronic, Telecommunication and Plumbing Trades Union, 113
Electrical Trades Union, 159–64, 195
Engineering Employers' Federation, 113–19
Equal Pay Act, 243–54 passim
Equity, see British Actors' Equity Association
Executive Committees (and Councils), 152–7, 159–64

Fenwick, Mrs M., 251
Flanders, A., 27 n, 57 n, 78
Forman, J., 93
Fox, A., 256
Furniture, Timber and Allied Trades Union, 113

Gardner, B., 93
General and Municipal Workers' Union, 113
Government relations with unions, 18–

20, 30, 39–40, 43–5, 234; see also Incomes policy; Industrial Relations Act
Grand National Consolidated Trades Union, 12

Hadley, E., 159–64
Helyer, Mrs C., 243
History, influence on union attitudes, 12, 13
History of the Association of Engineering and Shipbuilding Draughtsmen, A, 166
History of Trade Unionism, 34, 34 n
Hobson, C., 93
Hogarth, W., 65, 73
Hughes, J., 35 n

Incomes policy, 18, 20–1, 86, 98–102, 206, 215–18; see also National Board for Prices and Incomes
Industrial Committees, 205, 206, 235, 237–9, 240–3
Industrial democracy, 26, 42–3
Industrial Democracy, 35, 149
Industrial disputes, 208–9; see also pluralistic frame of reference; strikes
Industrial Relations Act (1971), 11–12, 13, 22, 57, 58–60, 82–5, 86–7, 90, 102–6, 106–8, 110, 111, 145–8, 247
Industrial Relations: Programme for Action, 212–15
Industrial Society, The, 111
Industrial unionism, 178–9, 202–4
Industrial Unionism, 179
Industry, changes in, 16–17, 202–3
In Place of Strife, 205, 234
Institute of Personnel Management, 174
International Labour Organisation, 244
Inter-union relations, 177–204, 234–5; see also Amalgamations of unions; Bridlington principles
Introduction to the Confederation of Shipbuilding and Engineering Unions, An, 196

Job regulation, 26, 56, 60, 62; see also Bargaining, collective
Jones, Miss G., 249
Jones, Jack, 151, 172–4

Kahn-Freund, O., 61

Kirkwood, D., 92
Kuhn, J. W., 26, 26 n

Labour force, changes in, 13–16
Labour Party, 19, 80, 81, 85, 86, 90–2, 205, 206, 212–15
Layton, Mary, 175
Lee, Fred, 86, 92–5
Liverpool Victoria Workers' Union, 252
Local conference (engineering), 116
Local Department Committees, 130, 140, 185
London County Council Staff Association, 11, 11 n
Lyons, Mrs M., 248

McCarthy, W. E. J., 57, 60–5, 179
McKinley, Miss J. M., 250
Medland, Bert, 93
Minute no 741, 194–5
Monopolies Commission, 16, 101
Morrison, Mrs M., 246
Mortimer, J. E., 164–6
Muston, C., 176
My Apprenticeship, 34 n

National and Local Government Officers Association, 18, 151–2, 178, 205
National Association of Clerical and Supervisory Staffs, 186
National Board for Prices and Incomes, 98–102, 246, 248; *see also* Incomes policy
National Coal Board, 109
National Industrial Relations Court, 82, 106–7
National Society of Metal Mechanics, 113
National Union of Agricultural and Allied Workers, 183–5
National Union of Enginemen, Firemen, Mechanics and Electrical Workers, 186
National Union of Insurance Workers, 253
National Union of Journalists, 36, 52–5
National Union of Mineworkers, 36, 52, 204
National Union of Public Employees, 169–71

National Union of Railwaymen, 128, 134
National Union of Sheet Metal Workers, Coppersmiths, Heating and Domestic Engineers, 65–74, 113
National Union of Tailors and Garment Workers, 249
National Union of Teachers, 18, 205
National Union of Vehicle Builders, 113, 177
Non-members, 31–3, 58–60, 231, 243–54 *passim*

Oldrey, B., 174–5, 176

Pargiter, G., 93
Parry, T., 65
Paynter, W., 178–9, 202–4
Plant and Productivity Bargaining, 128
Plant bargaining, 110, 111–13, 119–28
Pluralistic frame of reference, 25–6
Post Office Engineering Union, 58, 74–81, 152–7
Pressed Steel Fisher Ltd, 65–74
Preston Trades Council, 248
Productivity, Prices and Incomes, 218
Programme for Action, 212–15
Progress Report 1909–1959: The First Fifty Years in the History of the LCC Staff Association, 11 n

Railway Staff Joint Council, 132, 139
Railway Staff National Council, 136
Railway Staff National Tribunal, 136
Red Tape, 176
Redundancy, 125–6, 131–2
Relations between Unions, 182–3
Riddiough, Miss J. C., 244
Roberts, Miss M. A., 252
Robinson, S. A., 65
Roper, J. I., 27 n
Rose, Mrs A., 175
Royal Commission on Trade Unions and Employers' Associations, 14, 16, 17, 18, 23 n, 31, 34, 35, 35 n, 45, 81, 110, 119, 172, 235
Ruskin College, 78, 80

Shop stewards, 17, 22–3, 23 n, 116–19, 150, 151, 167–72
Shop Stewards Handbook, 168
Smith, C., 175

Smith, C. H., 80
Strikes, 12–13, 21, 111, 230–1; *see also*
  Industrial disputes
Structure and Development, 206, 239
Sunday trading, 86, 96–8
*System of Industrial Relations in Great
  Britain, The*, 27 n

Taff Vale case, 12
Tanner, J., 93
TASS Journal, 166
Taylor, Mrs G., 253
Theatres National Committee, 144–5
Time to Think Again, 105
Times, The, 87, 111
'TINA LEA', 145–8
Tolpuddle Martyrs, 12, 13
Trade Union Act (1913), 86, 87–90
Trade Unionism, 31, 45
Trade union membership, 14, 17; *see
  also* Non-members
Trade union purposes, 25–33
Trade Unions, 179
Trade Unions and the New Society, 27 n
Trade union structure, 21, 27–31, 149–
  254 *passim*; *see also* Democracy in
  unions
Trade Union Structure and Government, 35 n
Trades Councils, 92, 97, 105, 248
Trades Union Congress, 11, 13, 18, 19,
  20, 25, 27–31, 36–45, 46–7, 58, 82–4,
  85–6, 98–108, 110–11, 145–8, 178,
  205–54
Trades Unionism in the Seventies, 174
Transport and General Workers'

Union, 36, 47–51, 65–74, 113, 119–
  28, 167–8, 172–4, 177, 186
Tribune, 105

Union government, 82–4, 149–76; *see
  also* Democracy in unions; Executive
  Committees (and Councils)
Union of Construction, Allied Trades
  and Technicians, 113
Union of Jute, Flax, and Kindred
  Textile Operatives, 251
Union of Post Office Workers, 250
Union of Shop, Distributive and Allied
  Workers, 86, 96–8, 157–9, 244
Urwin, H., 128

Voluntary collective bargaining, case
  for, 28–30

Walton, W., 175
Webb, S. and B., 34, 34 n, 35, 57, 149
Wedderburn, K. W., 104
White collar workers, 15, 178, 190
White, Mrs O., 248
Wilson, Harold, 104
Women trade unionists, 14, 206, 243–54
Women Workers 1972, 254
Workers' Educational Association, 76,
  77, 78
Workplace Industrial Relations, 23 n
Works Committees, 116–17

Young, Sir Robert, 92
Your Job as a Union Steward, 171